T0329972

NEW PERSPECTIVES ON BUSINESS CYCLES

To my parents

'Dogmatism is a deadly sin in science.'
Luc Montagnier,
Discoverer of the AIDS virus,
TIME Magazine, 3 August 1992

New Perspectives on Business Cycles

An Analysis of Inequality and Heterogeneity

Satya P. Das

Professor of Economics
Indiana University
Bloomington, Indiana
USA

Edward Elgar

Published by
Edward Elgar Publishing Limited
Gower House
Croft Road
Aldershot
Hants GU11 3HR
England

Edward Elgar Publishing Company
Old Post Road
Brookfield
Vermont 05036
USA

A CIP catalogue record for this book is available from the British Library

Library of Congress Cataloging-in-Publication Data
Das, Satya P.
    New perspectives on business cycles: an analysis of inequality and heterogeneity/Satya P. Das.
    256p.   23cm.
    Includes bibliographical references and index.
    1. Business cycles.   I. Title.
HB3711.D27   1993
338.5'42—dc20   92–36096
                                                            CIP

ISBN 1 85278 800 3
Printed on FSC approved paper
Printed and bound by CPI Group (UK) Ltd, Croydon, CR0 4YY

Contents

Figures

Tables

Preface

This project began in 1987, when I was attracted by some of the ideas in a best-selling book, *The Great Depression of 1990* by Ravi Batra. It may be recalled that it contained an implicit prediction of a stock market crash and an explicit prediction of a severe downturn for the American economy during the 1990s. It was not these predictions which attracted me most. I was intrigued by the intellectual speculation in it as to a probable cause of depressions in general – namely, the build-up of massive wealth inequities – in a capitalist economy. Most economists seem to shrug off Batra's work on the grounds that there is no well-developed theory in it. However, it did contain, in my view, the precursor of a theory. While this book remains controversial and generally unaccepted among professional economists, I found quite fascinating those parts of the book directly relating economic inequities across households to business cycles. I was tenured at the time it was published and had established myself as a scholar in the field of international trade. I then decided to redirect the focus of my research to macroeconomics and to take a closer look into possible links between distributional changes and business cycles. This monograph is the end-product of a research programme on this issue over the last five years. Needless to say, I am indebted to Ravi Batra.

The reason I have opted for this unconventional approach of writing a monograph out of unpublished research, rather than trying to publish a few articles first, is that after years of work I can now see some unity among the pieces, although the level of unity may not be comparable to that in a standard monograph which integrates some already-existing and accepted thoughts. Further, I felt that I could express myself more effectively this way and that the message would get into print faster in a book than if I were to wait till all the relevant articles were published.

I cannot say that the effort and time that have gone into this book have been without a significant opportunity cost. Apart from the enormous pressure on family life that such an endeavour is expected to exert, I had to incur the fixed cost of learning about some of the frontiers of macro and business-cycle research – by no means a simple task – and at the same time forgo my usual research output in the field of international trade.

During these intense years, I was fortunate to draw support from two sources that kept me going. One is from family and friends – especially my wife, Mita, who is an economist and also my colleague. This is more remarkable than usual because, being untenured and under the pressure of 'publish or perish' herself, she needed more support from me than vice versa. I am also thankful to other members of our families, especially my mother-in-law, who stayed with us for long periods of time and helped us, so that I was able to concentrate on this project more than would otherwise have been possible.

The other source of support was totally unexpected. I sent out to various individuals in the field of macroeconomics and business cycles working papers whose final versions form some of the individual chapters of this monograph, and I was hoping to hear back from some of them. I did; and to my surprise, the most encouraging words came from William A. Brock. He has offered many insightful comments. Chapter 4 is born out of his suggestion that I pursue the inequality–business-cycle link in terms of political pressure theory. I am grateful to him for his support.

I am also thankful to David Wildasin and especially Bill Witte for detailed comments on various parts of the manuscript. I have immensely benefited from reviews by the referees both in terms of style and content. I am indebted to them for the time they took to study the draft chapters closely, suggest changes and raise many interesting issues.

This book is mainly but not only aimed toward macroeconomists and I am an outsider to them. Being an outsider has its disadvantages as well as some advantages. I was not dogmatic about any particular school of thought and was at liberty to pick my own teachers. The problem was well defined. Different models, to me, were just different means to focus different aspects of the same general problem. There were no assumptions or frameworks to which I felt fundamentally attached. I regarded all authors cited in the references as my teachers, although they constitute a proper subset of teachers from whom I have benefited. My debt is owed to them in differing magnitudes.

1 Introduction

I Motivations
The subject matter of this monograph has been motivated in different ways.

Need for new perspectives on business cycles
Most severe recessions have been responsible for the emergence of new ideas or explanations for business cycles and functioning of the macroeconomy. Keynesian macroeconomics and business-cycle theory were born in the aftermath of the Great Depression. Recurring recessions in the 1970s formed the *raison d'être* for rational expectations and the new classical equilibrium approach to business cycles. Lately, the American economy has experienced a severe downturn and there are indications that the world economy, including that of the US, is currently braced for a slowdown, if not a downturn. Economists trained since the mid-seventies, who tend to think of recessions as resulting from some adverse shock, must be hard-pressed for a convincing example of such a shock. Very few seem to understand or have the conviction deep down as to why the downturn started in the absence of any apparent major external shock to the system and why it cut so deep and was unlike previous recessions in the postwar period (although most of us would lose no chance to impart our own impressions). It is clearly not the Gulf war, nor any external price shock, nor a bad winter. For most other possible factors a forceful argument can be made that they are endogenous rather than exogenous to the economic-political system.

At the same time, there is a strong feeling growing amongst macroeconomists that the discipline is at a crossroads with no consensus on the right approach to deal with important macroeconomic issues. As Mankiw (1991) writes: 'In fact, one can fairly say that academic macroeconomics is in a state of disarray.' And, 'Today, macroeconomists are much less sure of themselves [compared to twenty years ago].' Of course, unity of approach has never been a strong point of macroeconomics, but the disunity is more glaring now than ever.

All this suggests that this is probably one of the most opportune times to entertain new perspectives on business cycles. The time may be ripe to de-emphasize external-shock hypotheses and to explore new internal mechanisms in some rigorous way. This monograph can be viewed as an attempt in that direction.

However, I did not embark upon this project with such a broad, sweeping mission. I was initially motivated by a more specific concern.

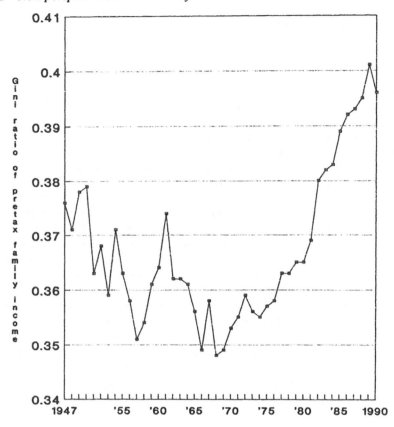

Source: US Census, *Population Studies*, P–60 series, various issues.

Figure 1.1   Trend in income inequality in the US, 1947–90

Concern about growing inequality in the US

This was my original motivation. It is a fact that economic inequities have been growing in the US for a few decades in terms of both income distribution and wealth distribution. Figure 1.1 depicts the Gini ratio of pre-tax income inequality across families in the US in the postwar period. (The data on post-tax income inequality measures are not available on a continuous annual basis.) During 1947–68 the trend was toward greater equality, although there were a few years during which inequality significantly increased. Since 1968 the trend has reversed. The 5 per cent increase from 0.348 in 1968 to 0.396 in 1990 is indeed quite substantial. The Report by the Joint Economic Committee to the US Congress (1990) characterizes as dramatic the growing gap between the richest families and others. It states that 'the income of the top 1% of all families rose by an estimated 75% between 1980 and 1990' (p. 12). This was highlighted by the news media during the 1992 spring presidential primaries campaign in the US. See, for example, the front-page news item in the *New York Times* on 5 March 1992, 'The 1980s: a Very Good Time for the Very Rich', and the editorial on 19 April 1992, 'The Rich Get Richer'.

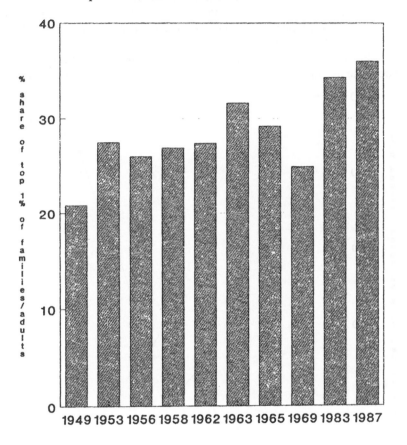

Source: Batra (1988, p.233).

Figure 1.2   Trend in wealth inequality in the US, 1949–87

The data on wealth inequality in the US is very sparse compared to that of income inequality. However, from what is available, the increase in wealth inequality is even more glaring. As Figure 1.2 shows, the wealth share of the top 1 per cent of families/adults has shown an increasing trend since 1949. In 1987 this share was equal to 36 per cent, which is nearly the same as the previous peak of 36.3 per cent in 1929 just before the Great Depression. True, changes in the wealth share of the top 1 per cent do not in principle give a true indication of the overall changes in wealth inequality, but the figures are consistent with recent changes in income inequality.

Similar patterns of growing inequities in recent years may be true for other advanced countries, although there is a general lack of availability of data to verify this. However, data are available on the recent trend in income inequality in the UK. As Figure 1.3 shows, the trend is again positive. In fact, the correlation between the trends in income inequality in the US and the UK over 1970–89 is 0.97.

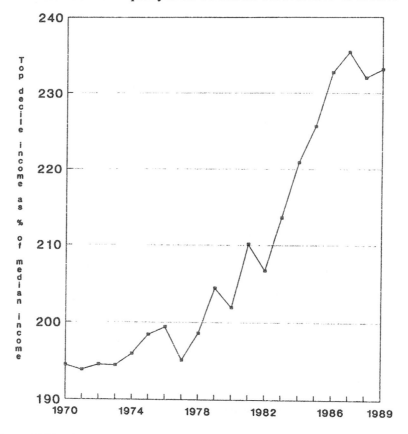

Source: UK Dept of Employment, *Family Expenditure Surveys*, annual issues.

Figure 1.3   Trend in income inequality in the UK, 1970–89

A number of books have appeared recently that raise grave concerns regarding many adverse consequences – economic, political and social – of the massive build-up of income and wealth inequality. Batra (1987) argues that extreme concentration of wealth is the harbinger of major downturns (depressions) in market economies. Winnick (1989) talks about the adverse implications in terms of 'simple humanitarianism' as well as social and political unrest and foreign perceptions. Phillips (1990) analyses the redistribution of power and wealth and its political–economic ramifications in the US, especially in the 1980s. Braun (1991) attributes the shrinking of the middle class, the declining consumer base, the threat to democracy and deteriorating family life to the increase in economic inequality.

None of these works, however, has developed a formal theoretical framework, and consequently their claims cannot be examined in a rigorous, axiomatic manner. This was the source of my own motivation for this monograph. I do not, however, address the non-economic effects of wealth and income disparities.

Adieux to the representative agent
From a methodological viewpoint, this monograph can be seen as an attempt to get away from an assumption which is pervasively used but seldom justified in macroeconomics, namely, the existence of a 'representative agent'. In a standard macro model, there is always a representative household and a representative firm, or the assumption that technology and preference are alike and homothetic, so that all households or firms in the economy can be lumped together as one entity. But where does the representative household live? Where is the representative firm located? One can tear apart this assumption on the ground of its being highly unrealistic. But this is, I think, quite unwarranted and unfair. Any discipline, such as economics, which is prepared to use the assumption that people/agents live indefinitely or are immortal – for the good reasons of analysing certain classes of problems – has no right to criticize *any* assumption solely on the ground of realism. A ridiculous assumption does not necessarily mean that it is useless. What it can do is to suppress certain issues so as to let other issues be better focused. This can indeed be useful. So the real question is to identify the issues which are hidden under the assumption of a 'representative agent' and ask whether they can be important for the issues which are being raised in the first place. It is evident that the representative household and firm assumption hides the implications of distributional changes or heterogeneity across households and firms. Could these be important for the central query of macroeconomics, namely, fluctuations in aggregate output and employment?

If you ask a sample of macroeconomists, the majority will probably give a negative answer directly or indirectly, depending on how diplomatic they are. The conventional wisdom seems to hold that, if there is any significant link, aggregate fluctuations influence distributional changes rather than vice versa.

From the discussions I have had with many colleagues I have observed that when I start with distributional changes and try to arrive at any of their possible effects, the counter-arguments are that the distributional changes, to begin with, may be partly reflecting something else, for example, unemployment or unanticipated inflation. Maybe so. However, the reverse could be equally true. A variable x influencing or 'causing' y does not rule out that y may influence x. Hence the issue of heterogeneity and distributional changes in macro activity can hardly be dismissed *a priori*. Whether and how they are important for fluctuations in aggregate output and employment is the subject matter of this monograph.

However, there is a growing realization that heterogeneity of agents may be quite important in understanding macro behaviour. Geweke (1985) and Stoker (1986) demonstrate the pitfalls of using the representative-agent model and aggregate data to explain aggregate behaviour. Campbell and Mankiw (1989, 1990, 1991) have shown that the behaviour of aggregate consumption over time is better explained in a model of heterogeneous rather than homogeneous households. Using micro data, Mankiw and Zeldas (1991) show that consumption behaviour differs between stockholding households and non-stockholding households. It is also being increasingly understood that the impact of various shocks differs significantly between firms of different sizes. For example, Gertler and Gilchrist (1991) show that small manufacturing firms are more sensitive than large firms to changes in monetary policy. The empirical analysis by Calomiris and Hubbard (1991) of firm response to the undistributed profit tax of 1936–7 in the US finds that the change in investment behaviour due to this shock varied widely between firms of different sizes. Moreover, Davis and Haltiwanger (1992) observe that gross rates of simultaneous job creation and job destruction are remarkably large in US manufacturing industries and are related to cyclical swings, and they point out that such phenomena can be effectively explained only through models that allow for firm heterogeneity. Very recently, Kirman (1992) has provided a critical essay on the limitations of the representative-agent models and some of the recent literature on the implications of heterogeneity.[1]

While these studies provide ample indication that heterogeneity and distributional changes can be important in understanding macro activities and business cycles, the objective of this monograph is more ambitious and direct in that it is shown that heterogeneity itself is a factor contributing to aggregate output fluctuations. In doing so, it attempts to bring heterogeneity and distributional changes to the centre stage of business-cycle analysis.

II An overview

The central concern of business-cycle analysis is the variation in aggregate output. There can be many sources of variation in aggregate output. Although inter-related, it seems useful to classify them according to whether they arise on the supply side or on the demand side of a macro system. They can also be grouped depending on whether they are exogenous or endogenous to the system. Exogenous sources of variation refer to the direct impact of changes in the parameters of a macro system, whereas endogenous sources refer to changes in the endogenous variables (originally due to changes in parameters) which also affect positions and slopes of aggregate supply and demand curves.

On the supply side, the exogenous sources are the once-for-all productivity shocks of various kinds. The endogenous sources include capital accumulation and utilization, employment of labour, and other inputs and endogenous components of organizational and technological changes.

Given that there are nominal rigidities, aggregate output can be influenced from the demand side. Preference shocks and policy-induced shocks, monetary or fiscal, are examples of exogenous shocks on the demand side.[2] Endogenous sources would include changes in aggregate wealth and income, their distribution and changes in asset returns.

Turning to wealth and income distribution, there are different sources of variation, such as heterogeneity in preferences, heterogeneity in individual efficiency and various types of social and legal institutions.

Thus, in principle, the role of inequality and heterogeneity in influencing aggregate output can be examined in numerous frameworks or models. A single study cannot hope to be all-encompassing. This is particularly true since the literature on the link between inequality and heterogeneity and business cycles is quite limited, even though, on these subjects individually, it is vast.

The chapters in this monograph represent my endeavour over the last few years to obtain some understanding of this issue. There is some unity across different chapters, but not as much as one would expect in a typical monograph that for the most part synthesizes and refines existing thoughts on particular issues. Each chapter may be seen as an essay in its own right.

This monograph contains four parts. Part I contains five essays, Chapters 2–6. The main theme is how, in the presence of heterogeneous agents, distributional changes can interact with aggregate activities to generate business cycles. The business cycle is a very broad concept. Current research emphasizes external shocks and the implied observed patterns of correlation among macro variables over time as the main features of business cycles. It does not highlight or stress how the internal mechanism of a macro system may itself generate ups and downs – or, in other words, an oscillatory or fluctuating dynamic path of an economy. But in the essays in Part I the business cycle is interpreted mainly in terms of its internal mechanism. It must, however, be made clear that alternative interpretations of what we mean by business cycles are *not* mutually exclusive. They merely reflect the complexity or multidimensionality of the business-cycle phenomenon and testify that no single approach can ever hope to accommodate all or most of the important facets of business cycles.

Chapter 2 begins with a sketch of the historical background and alternative approaches to business cycles. The specific approach undertaken in the subsequent chapters is then spelt out. Namely, it is the emphasis on the internal mechanism of a macro system which is capable of producing an oscillatory or fluctuating time-path of aggregate output. This is by no means inconsistent with external-shock-based models of business cycles.

Explaining the observed correlation between macro variables is de-emphasized as the litmus test of the theoretical models. There are two reasons. First, given the extremely limited and highly aggregative time-series data available on wealth and income distribution, there is currently very little information on the distribution of behavioural parameters across households in actual economies, including that of the US. There is considerable scope for observed correlations among standard aggregates, such as GNP, employment and the like, and aggregate measures of inequality – or stylized facts about their interrelationships – to be 'manufactured' by choosing *a priori* the 'right' distribution of parametric values. Hence this would not serve any meaningful purpose. Secondly, even if there were information on parametric values at disaggregated levels, the models developed here are much less mature than the standard, representative-agent models of the business cycle. So their 'time' for facing more stringent tests *vis-à-vis* the data is yet to come.

Having described the approach, the general intuition is developed as to how inequality and heterogeneity may contribute to oscillatory dynamics. Chapter 2 also discusses the particular basis of inequality and heterogeneity modelled in the subsequent chapters.

Formal modelling begins in Chapter 3. A capital-accumulation model is probably the most common type of dynamic model explored in macro theory. I examine two versions of the standard one-sector capital-accumulation model, with the important modification that households are heterogeneous in terms of their time preference. Preference heterogeneity implies endogenous wealth and income distribution. I begin with a simple Solow–Stiglitz model with a rule-of-thumb savings function. Next, I develop a Ramsey-type fully optimizing, infinite-horizon model of capital accumulation. The main result is that in an economy with heterogeneous households, capital accumulation by one household generates an asymmetric pecuniary externality effect on the income and savings of, and hence capital accumulation by, another household. This asymmetry, if strong enough, implies oscillatory dynamics of individual capital stocks as well as the aggregate capital stock and output.

Similar to Chapter 3, Chapter 4 develops models in which output variations arise from the supply of resources by households for productive activity. However, the decision-making of households or the household behaviour analysed in this chapter is novel from the perspective of existing business-cycle theory. Specifically, a public-choice approach is developed to endogenize the share of total resources which are directed to productive activities.

The public-choice theory holds that policy-makers do not always set policies consistent with maximizing social welfare. They behave partly as individuals who attempt to enhance their own welfare too. Hence they are subject to lobbying and political pressure by interest groups. It is well known that such activities often use resources which could be otherwise utilized in directly productive activities and hence result in the loss of aggregate output (Bhagwati, 1980, 1982). Chapter 4 explores dynamic models in which redistributive taxes are raised by the government, and households lobby by using real resources to influence the transfers they receive or the tax rates they face. In the process, the aggregate output can vary even if the total endowment of the economy is fixed. Oscillatory or fluctuating dynamics of aggregate output are shown to result in this environment.

In a comparative light, the implications of lobbying for economic growth have been recently studied by Magee, Brock and Young (1989, ch. 8), Terrones (1990) and Alesina and Rodrick (1991). Chapter 4 analyses the implications of lobbying for business cycles rather than growth. There is also a rich literature on political business-cycle theory. The gist of this theory is that incumbent politicians or political parties attempt to pursue a more expansionary macro policy, in terms of consumption and employment, near election time than at other times in order to swing the voters in their favour. This induces a source of fluctuation in the economy of a democratic nation. Relative to this literature, the distinguishing feature of Chapter 4 is that households actively try to influence political decision-making by using resources in lobbying for policy changes that will benefit them, rather than merely revealing their preferences through voting. Moreover, the emphasis is on household heterogeneity implying differential incentives to lobby by different households, rather than on the interaction between the incumbent on one hand and the electorate as a group on the other.

As in Chapters 3 and 4, the models in Chapter 5 exhibit output variations from the supply side. But again, model frameworks or the mechanisms are novel compared to existing business-cycle theory. Two partial equilibrium models of firm heterogeneity are developed. This is in contrast to the general equilibrium models with household heterogeneity in Chapters 3 and 4. In each model the firms are heterogeneous in terms of their marginal costs of production. The first model examines an oligopolistic industry in which the discount rate facing firms is variable and the dynamics arise in the presence of an adjustment cost of changing output or capacity from the previous period.

In the field of industrial organization – both theoretical and empirical – increasing efforts are being made to analyse the evolution process of an industry, for example, Jovanovic (1982), Pakes and Ericson (1990), Dunne, Roberts and Samuelson (1988), Lambson (1991) and Das and Das (1991). Firm heterogeneity is a hallmark of this literature. While its emphasis is on the evolution of the internal structure of the industry, the profitability and life-span of firms, and the pattern of entry and exit of firms, I use an industry-evolution model to concentrate on the dynamics of industry output. This is the second model in Chapter 5. In both models, a nonmonotonic path of industry output may arise precisely due to interdependence among heterogeneous firms.

In Chapter 6 I formulate two Keynesian models with nominal rigidities. Aggregate demand plays an active role. I return to household heterogeneity. In contrast to the one-good models in previous chapters, there are three goods: a commodity, money and equities. Apart from household heterogeneity and the equity market, the models in this chapter are similar to the standard IS-LM model. The first model is based on static expectations and wage rigidity, and the second on rational expectations and price rigidity. The models have a ring of the old underconsumption theory of business cycles, but they go far beyond that in terms of rigour, completeness and, in particular, the critical role played by the equity market. It is interesting that the standard 'underconsumption argument' that greater inequality reduces aggregate demand and hence reduces aggregate output in equilibrium – because the rich have a lower marginal propensity to consume than the poor – holds under static expectations. But under rational expectations the impact of greater inequality on aggregate output may be just the opposite. The nature of the internal mechanism is thus different between static and rational expectations. In both cases, however, heterogeneity and inequality may contribute to an oscillatory pattern of aggregate output.

Part II of the book contains two essays, Chapters 7 and 8, on the implications of distributional changes for financial markets. There exists a large literature on financial markets and real activity, including landmark contributions by Gurley and Shaw (1955), Minsky (1975), and, recently, several models of informational asymmetry in the loan market. A general theme coming out of this literature seems to be that the debt position of firms and borrowers is a critical barometer in business fluctuation. A better financial balance sheet of borrowers results in a more efficient allocation of resources. Distributional changes also figure in this literature. But they pertain to those between borrowers and lenders, or capitalists and workers. I emphasize, instead, the size distribution of wealth and income and my objective is to develop specific testable hypotheses concerning the impact of household inequality on some of the financial markets.

Chapter 7 deals with the impact of distributional changes on the demand for stocks and the demand for money. The importance of the money market in macro analysis is too well known to require any motivation. The stock market is a necessary element in any capitalist economy and its behaviour is an important component of the overall performance of the financial sector. In particular, Chapter 7 develops the hypothesis that an increase in inequality increases the demand for stocks and money. Thus, for example, an increase in the real average price of stocks over time can be attributed in part to growing inequality over time.

Chapter 8 studies the implication of distributional changes for the stability of the banking sector, through changes in the composition of savings supplied by households to banks and its effect on a bank's portfolio of riskless and risky assets. It advances a hypothesis that a more unequal distribution of savings may result in an increase in the ratio of risky to riskless assets held by banks, thereby raising the probability of bank failure.

In Part III there are two empirical essays, Chapters 9 and 10. Chapter 9 is a primer. Time-series data available on distributional changes are documented. In particular, continuous time-series data on wealth inequality are not available. The patterns of contemporaneous and lagged correlations among measures of income inequality and real GNP/GDP in the US and some other countries are estimated and discussed. Empirical regularities that emerge, particularly for the US in the postwar period, are: (a) a negative contemporaneous correlation between innovations in income inequality and real GNP; (b) a negative correlation between innovations in income inequality and lagged innovations in real GNP; and (c) a positive correlation between innovations in real GNP and lagged innovations in income inequality.

More substantive empirical analysis is undertaken in Chapter 10. There are three sets of empirical exercises pertaining to the postwar US. The first deals with the central thesis of this monograph: dynamic interaction between inequality and aggregate output. Using a VAR approach, perhaps the most significant finding is that there is a feedback relationship, in terms of causality, between real GNP and income inequality, while allowing for money stock and interest rate. The term 'causality' may be unappealing to some. But, in substance, the causality test concerns the statistical significance of dynamic relationships across variables – exactly suited for examining the cross effects in the internal mechanism of a dynamic system. Furthermore, in one particular ordering of variables (suggested in part by the data), innovations in inequality account for a 19 per cent variation in real GNP around its expected path, while innovations in money stock and interest rate account for 7 per cent and 35 per cent respectively. Next, I estimate a money demand function (for M1) which not only includes a scale variable and an opportunity-cost variable as usual but also income inequality. In all regressions (in differences), the coefficient of inequality is found to be positive and statistically significant. Finally, I estimate reduced-form stock-price functions which include income return on stocks, total or income return on long-term bonds, real GNP and income inequality as explanatory variables. Again, the coefficient of income inequality turns out to be consistently positive and statistically significant.

These results support the central hypothesis of this monograph on business cycles as well as the hypotheses developed in Chapter 7 on the impact of inequality on demand for money and stocks. This should not be considered definitive, however. Data constraints on inequality measures are severe – especially for time-series analysis – and this precludes more comprehensive empirical analysis at present. But the results strongly suggest that inequality may be one of the key variables in the macro system. It is advocated that more frequent and comprehensive data on distributional measures be collected on a regular basis.

Part IV contains Chapter 11, the concluding chapter.

III Possible misinterpretations
Lest I might appear to promise too much or to mislead, let me quickly guard against possible misinterpretations.

1. First and foremost, *the book does not advocate that any inequality is undesirable or that policies should be designed to eliminate nearly all wealth and income inequalities.* There is no denying that some inequality is absolutely essential in a capitalist economy. The book implicitly advocates that inequalities beyond a certain critical point may be economically harmful. This is really saying that 'unbridled capitalism' or 'capitalism run amok' may not be the most efficient way for a market economy to function.

2. The book is concerned with personal, not functional, distribution of wealth and income. From another angle, there are two types of inequalities: those based on age distribution in an economy and those across the same cohorts of families, households or individuals. Presumably, both are important. This monograph, however, deals with the latter.

3. *It is not assumed that distributional changes are exogenous in the economy nor is it claimed that distributional changes unidirectionally 'cause' output or employment.* Preferences, technology and endowments are the primitives which basically dictate the dynamics of the economy; the rest are endogenous. However, the observable counterpart of this is the interaction between aggregate output and distributional changes. In terms of causality, the intended interpretation is that distributional changes and aggregate output cause each other; thus there is a feedback. Obviously, there are many factors other than those captured in the models which can affect wealth and income distribution, aggregate output or both, but there is no reason to believe they explain all or most of the variations in distributional changes and aggregate output.

4. *Distributional changes are neither necessary nor sufficient to cause business cycles.* But this is true of *any* theory. A related point is that in terms of magnitude there is no presumption that distributional changes are more important than all other factors, although it might well be relative to some factors. But being less important does not mean being unimportant.

5. *The basic idea that economic inequality is a contributing factor in the business cycle is not brand new.* There exists a literature arising from Karl

Marx which advocates this (see Sherman and Evans, 1984) but, unlike this literature, (a) the framework of this book is neoclassical in that respective markets and marginal products determine the respective factor rewards; (b) there is absolutely no use of or emphasis on the concept of the 'degree of exploitation'; and (c) personal rather than functional distribution of income/wealth is shown to be important in the generation of business cycles.

Even within the neoclassical framework, the idea that cycles may arise in an economy with heterogeneous households is not new. It is an interesting coincidence that two colleagues of mine here at Indiana University, Robert Becker and Ciprian Foias, have shown this in a two-person, Ramsey-economy with capital accumulation (Becker and Foias, 1987)[3].

There is also a strand of the so-called 'underconsumption theories' that emphasizes distributional changes in business cycles (Valentine, 1987, pp. 331–4). It tells a simple Keynesian tale. As the economy is in the upswing of the business cycle, economic inequities grow. Since the rich have a lower propensity to consume than the poor, this leads to a fall in aggregate demand and triggers an economic downturn. The story, as far as it goes, seems plausible; but surely it does not go far. It only provides an account of the downturn. It does not explain the transition from a downturn to an upturn, nor does it outline any precise mechanism of how distributional changes occur over time. As Valentine (p. 331) aptly remarks, 'The views of many underconsumptionists really do not constitute a complete theory of the cycle since most of them have attempted only to explain the downturn of the cycle and the depression period. A complete analysis of the cycle cannot be based upon such underconsumption theories.'

A number of empirical works have attempted to deal with personal distribution of income and macro activity, such as Blinder and Esaki (1978), Buse (1982), Nolan (1987), Balke and Slottje (1989) and Haslag, Russell and Slottje (1989), among others.

6. This is not a book on the theory of wealth or income distribution *per se*.
7. Lastly, the business-cycle models developed here are not inconsistent with external-shock-based theories of business cycles. But their emphasis is different. As a general remark, it is seldom the case that any particular theory is logically false. It is essentially the difference in emphasis which distinguishes one theory from another. This is exactly how the theory espoused here is fundamentally different from the external-shock-based theories of business cycles.

IV   What is new then?

Very few contemporary ideas in economics can claim to be brand new. As they say, if you dig hard, you will find traces of almost any idea from Smith, Ricardo, Mills, Marshall, Keynes, Fisher, Pigou, Schumpeter or other economists of similar rank. The idea pursued in this volume – namely that distributional changes may interact with aggregate activities to generate business cycles – is no exception. In this case, you may not even have to go that far back. However, there is an obvious difference between the inkling or traces of an idea and the development of its potential and scope. I believe this is where the novelty of this volume lies. The idea of linking heterogeneity and distributional changes to business cycles may not be new, but the exact *mechanisms* through which they interact to generate business cycles, as well as the level of emphasis at which these are pursued, are claimed to be new.

Also, I must add that I do not know of any work which deals with firm heterogeneity as a factor contributing to output fluctuation (Chapter 5), or the type of linkage between household heterogeneity and banking behaviour hypothesized in Chapter 8.

Concerning the empirical work, the crucial difference lies in the maintained hypotheses. The existing literature largely treats the link between macro activity and inequality as a one-way street from the former to the latter. Most studies on macro activities or policies and distributional changes ask how unemployment or inflation or some macro policy affects distribution of income. But seldom vice versa.[4] The root cause of this obviously lies in an *a priori* general belief that it is mostly unidirectional.

As Blinder and Esaki (1978) write, 'there is no reason to expect any important reverse causation from income distribution to unemployment or inflation'. However, it is shown in Chapter 10 that income distribution does 'cause' output and unemployment in postwar US. The empirical analysis, although limited in scope due to the scarcity of relevant data, is generally supportive of the hypotheses developed in the monograph.

V   Nature of the essays

Let me say a little about the general nature of the essays. Each essay is partly open-ended in the sense that one could think of other related issues that could have been examined, more generality could have been achieved and conclusions could be based on firmer grounds. How far one goes is a function of one's preference, orientation, ability and time constraint. In my case I have always felt that I could work further to make it a better product, but only at the cost of enormous time and effort. I cannot afford this at this point of writing. Thus I can easily imagine that the level of rigour may disappoint a purist. But on the other hand, it is not primarily addressed to non-economists or meant as supplementary reading for an introductory economics course. The rigour in my judgement is at the level of an advanced undergraduate or a graduate course in economics. The seed ideas are there and they are developed in ways which are not too loose or too tight. I can only hope that I have not erred much in my judgements and that the monograph has something positive to offer.

Finally, if the reader finds the language a bit conversational, it is meant to be so.

Notes

1. In general equilibrium theory, heterogeneity leading to more – rather than less – regular aggregate behaviour has been shown by Hildenbrand (1983) and Grandmont (1987). Lippi (1988) illustrates how simple behaviour of heterogeneous agents may lead to complicated aggregate behaviour.
2. Fiscal policy may affect the supply side as well. See, for example, Barro (1990) for an endogenous growth model in which government spending enters the production function as a 'public service'.
3. A recent paper by Phelan (1991) also links income distribution to business cycles, but it does not analyse how distributional changes may contribute to nonmonotonic dynamic path of aggregate output.
4. See, for example, Blinder and Esaki (1978) and Nolan (1987). Balke and Slottje (1989) is an exception. It develops a VAR model in which the time-series of both inequality measures and macro variables are endogenous. But their specification of the contemporaneous-residuals model – which is critical in the VAR analysis – is *a priori* biased to inequality being the most endogenous variable.

PART I

MODELS OF OUTPUT FLUCTUATION

2 Basic premises and methodology

I General approach to business cycles: external shocks or the internal mechanism?

What does it take to show theoretically that a particular factor contributes to business cycles? The methodology of current business-cycle research does not provide a unique answer to this question. Earlier models of the business cycle, starting with the celebrated multiplier–accelerator model of Samuelson (1939), emphasized the *internal mechanisms* or the *propagation mechanisms* of an economy as important to the business-cycle phenomenon. It underscored how various components of aggregate output interact with each other to generate an oscillatory pattern of aggregate output over time. External shocks were in the background, and were required only to trigger a dynamic process. There were a few models, notably Kaldor (1940) and Goodwin (1951), that produced deterministic cycles without explicit dependence on external shocks. The emphasis on the internal mechanism continued into the 1960s, although the business-cycle theory itself seemed to lose some of its prominence amidst the high growth rates of developed economies.

Then came the turbulent seventies with high rates of inflation, the oil price shocks and recessions hitting the world economy. Business-cycle theory was back in business. However, the emphasis shifted from the internal mechanism to the external shocks – clearly guided by the events of the seventies. 'Supply shocks' and 'demand shocks' became the buzz words for macroeconomists. Internal mechanisms as a contributing factor of business fluctuation took a back seat – so much further back as practically to imply that it may not be important at all. With few exceptions, professional articles dealing with business cycles or even explicitly using the term 'business cycles' in their titles would deal with the short-run and long-run impacts of supply or demand shocks, but would contain hardly anything resembling cycles or oscillations. The presumption was that such shocks occur randomly over time following some non-i.i.d. stochastic process so as to produce an oscillatory pattern of macro variables. In addition, the assumption of rational expectations became an integral feature of macro modelling.

Although the framework of business-cycle analysis that developed in the seventies continues to dominate today, the eighties witnessed a return to the old theme emphasizing the internal mechanism, albeit using new mathematical tools and with a new degree of emphasis. On one hand, there were numerous papers showing the existence of deterministic limit cycles or endogenous cycles in an overlapping generations framework, such as the essays in Grandmont (1986). On the other hand, there were models relying on chaotic dynamics intended to

19

price or quantity rigidities or market power) or behavioural imperfections (such as rules of thumb or static expectations). Finite life-time can also be regarded as a behavioural imperfection in the sense that agents are unable to arbitrage between all future periods. But imperfections or rigidities being necessary conditions for oscillatory or fluctuating dynamics does not imply that they are negligible in real economies. They are facts of any economy. Hence one approach would be to look for factors that contribute to oscillations, *given that some forms of imperfections exist as they are*. I take this approach. In particular, the loan market is shut out in all chapters in Part I. This captures imperfections in the loan market in an extreme fashion. There are other imperfections also, but they vary between different chapters. In general, the scope and magnitude of non-monotonicity are likely to increase with the number and magnitude of distortions. For example, non-monotonicity is more likely to arise or be more pronounced under static expectations than under rational expectations.

Asymmetric cross effects
In most of the models in the following chapters, the relationships lead to a dynamic system of the form:

$$f_1(\mathbf{X}_{t+1}, \mathbf{X}_t) = 0$$
$$\cdots\cdots\cdots\cdots\cdots\cdots$$
$$f_n(\mathbf{X}_{t+1}, \mathbf{X}_t) = 0, \text{ or}$$

$$f(\mathbf{X}_{t+1}, \mathbf{X}_t) = 0, \tag{2.1}$$

where $\mathbf{X}_t \equiv (X_{1t}, X_{2t}, ..., X_{nt})$ is a vector of n variables. We will be concerned with the local dynamics around the steady state: $f(\mathbf{X}^*, \mathbf{X}^*) = 0$. Linearizing $f_i(.)$s at $\mathbf{X}^*$ and implicitly expressing $\mathbf{X}_{t+1} - \mathbf{X}^*$ in terms of $\mathbf{X}_t - \mathbf{X}^*$, the local dynamics are governed by

$$\tilde{\mathbf{X}}_{t+1} = A\tilde{\mathbf{X}}_t, \tag{2.2}$$

where A is an $n \times n$ matrix whose elements are functions of the derivatives of $f_i(.)$s evaluated at $\mathbf{X}^*$, and '~' represents the deviation from the steady state. The solution path of $\mathbf{X}_t$ is the solution to the system of first-order difference equations (2.2).

If m out of n variables are predetermined in the initial period, a unique solution path will exist if and only if A has exactly m roots which are stable, that is, whose moduli are less than one (see, for instance, Laitner, 1989). There is no guarantee that this will be the case, especially if the dimension (n) is high, but the existence of a unique path is not typically ruled out either. Assuming that the solution path is unique, the question is: *When would a system such as (2.2) exhibit an oscillatory solution path?*

Mathematically, oscillatory dynamics are generated by complex conjugate roots which imply trigonometric functions. Hence the question boils down to: When would the matrix **A** possess complex conjugate roots (that are stable)? Of course it can happen that the matrix **A** has other stable roots that are not complex conjugates (that is, real) and if the magnitudes of these roots and their eigenvectors are sufficiently large, then the solution path will not be oscillatory. But, none the less, complex conjugate roots are necessary to generate and hence are at the root of oscillatory solution paths.

A general intuitive understanding of the conditions under which a system of first-order difference (or differential) equations would possess complex conjugate roots is best obtained by considering a two-dimensional system. Suppose $X_t = (X_{1t}, X_{2t})$, so that the system (2.2) reduced to

$$\tilde{X}_{1t+1} = a_{11}\tilde{X}_{1t} + a_{12}\tilde{X}_{2t}$$

$$\tilde{X}_{2t+1} = a_{21}\tilde{X}_{1t} + a_{22}\tilde{X}_{2t}. \tag{2.3}$$

The analytical solutions of the roots of the system (2.3) are:

$$\mu_1, \mu_2 = \frac{1}{2}\left[-(a_{11} + a_{22}) \pm \left\langle (a_{11} - a_{22})^2 + 4a_{12}a_{21} \right\rangle^{1/2} \right].$$

The roots are complex conjugates if and only if

$$(a_{11} - a_{22})^2 + 4a_{12}a_{21} < 0. \tag{2.4}$$

Thus the necessary condition for the existence of complex conjugates is that a_{12} and a_{21} be of opposite signs. This is where the intuition behind oscillations lies. *Two variables interact with each other over time to generate oscillatory time paths only if the cross impact on each other is asymmetric in sign.* Suppose $a_{12} > 0$ and $a_{21} < 0$. Then an increase in X_{2t} tends to increase X_{1t+1} which in turn tends to lower X_{2t+2}. Thus an increase in X_{2t} may result in a decrease in X_{2t+2}, implying an oscillatory path. Inequality (2.4) says that the opposing cross effects have to be strong enough – that is, $-4a_{12}a_{21}$ has to be greater than $(a_{11} - a_{22})^2$ – in order to imply complex conjugate roots and oscillatory time paths.

The intuition that asymmetric cross effects are the key to oscillatory dynamics is further illustrated in Figure 2.1. In order to highlight the cross effects, assume that the own effects are zero, $a_{11} = a_{22} = 0$. The system (2.3) reduces to

$$\tilde{X}_{1t+1} = a_{12}\tilde{X}_{2t}$$

$$\tilde{X}_{2t+1} = a_{21}\tilde{X}_{1t}. \tag{2.3'}$$

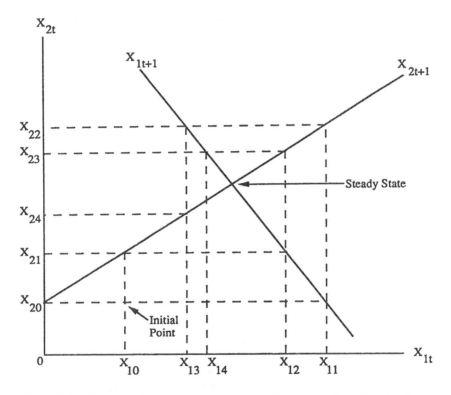

Figure 2.1   Asymmetric cross effects or dynamic reaction functions leading to oscillatory time paths

Supposing as before that $a_{12} > 0$ and $a_{21} < 0$, the system (2.3'), expressed in X_{1t} and X_{2t}, is depicted in Figure 2.1. The intersection point represents the steady state (X_1^*, X_2^*). The dynamics are directly read off the X_{1t+1} and X_{2t+1} schedules which can be viewed as 'dynamic reaction functions'. Starting from an initial, off-the-steady-state, configuration (X_{10}, X_{20}) at $t = 0$, Figure 2.1 traces the dynamics till $t = 4$. The oscillatory paths of X_{1t} and X_{2t} are clear. Such paths result precisely because the cross effects are opposite in sign so that the slopes of X_{1t+1} and X_{2t+1} curves are opposite in sign. Figures analogous to Figure 2.1 will be seen in the following chapters.

This basic intuition of asymmetric cross effects extends to the case of higher dimensions, the only difference being that the asymmetry could be just in magnitude, not necessarily in sign. Hence the general point is that *a first-order difference or differential equation system exhibits oscillatory solutions (locally) only if the cross effects of X_{it} on X_{jt+1} and X_{jt} on X_{it+1} are asymmetric for some i's and j's.*

Put differently, *the presumption of oscillation rides on asymmetry.* This indeed conforms to a well-known result in matrix algebra that a real square matrix possesses complex conjugate roots only if it is an asymmetric matrix (see, for example, Rao, 1973, ch. 1).

Hence in most of the dynamic systems studied in Chapters 3–6, the basic search is on asymmetric cross effects. Only the third model in Chapter 4 and the second model in Chapter 5 contain one predetermined variable in the initial period; the search there is on a negative stable root, which would imply fluctuating dynamics.

I can even tell you at this point the general intuition as to why inequality and heterogeneity may be a key in the business-cycle phenomenon. It is because *heterogeneity implies asymmetric cross effects.*

IV The 'proof' of the existence of oscillations

Deriving analytical conditions under which oscillations may exist locally is nearly impossible unless the dimension of the system is either two or at most three.[3] However, most of the models in the following chapters involve dynamic systems in higher dimensions. Hence there is little choice but to work out numerical examples, and these are my 'proofs' of the existence of oscillatory dynamics.

However, let me quickly add that the parameter values or functional forms chosen in the examples may not be the most 'realistic', but they are plausible and within the restrictions imposed in the respective models. No particular model by itself is meant to resemble or mimic any actual economy. At best, they are considered as some of the individual pieces of a big puzzle.

For the same reason, the degree of oscillation exhibited in some of the diagrams in the following chapters may not be visually impressive. None the less, they exhibit oscillations, and taken together across the models, they may very well imply a major oscillatory pattern for an economy.

V The basis for economic inequality: heterogeneous rate of time preference

As I said in Chapter 1, the theory of wealth and income distribution *per se* is not the subject matter of this monograph. My objective is to use some parts of this theory and link them to business cycles.

There exists a vast literature on the economics of inequality – Meade (1964), Sen (1973), Blinder (1974), Thurow (1976), Atkinson (1983), Atkeson and Lucas (1991) and Banerjee and Newman (1991), among many others. It addresses, theoretically and empirically, the sources and propagation of income and wealth inequality and poverty, and their implications for the economy. It is quite possible that different sources and aspects of inequality could exert important and different implications for macroeconomic activity. However, the essays in Chapters 3, 4 and 6 (except the third model in Chapter 4) consider a single factor for the existence of wealth and income inequality which appears to be the key in generating oscillatory dynamics – namely, difference in the rate of time preference. This is probably one of the most – if not the most – important sources of heterogeneity which may lead to oscillatory dynamics, because it not only implies heterogeneity directly but also makes behavioural relations nonaggregable so that changes in the distribution as well as in the aggregate interact with each other. For example, differences in the productivity of individual agents in the economy endogenize distribution but may not necessarily negate aggregation of behavioural relations, and, to this extent, aggregate changes imply distributional changes but not vice versa (see, for example, Stiglitz, 1969). In any event, it is hoped that future research will eventually look into the implications for the business cycle of other factors, such as the life-cycle of an individual, the differences in endowment, ability, opportunity, marriage, inheritance, individual risk-bearing, temporary productivity or preference shocks facing individuals – which are also thought to be important determinants of inequality.

VI On micro foundations
Finally, some remarks about the micro foundation of macro models and its implication for this study are in order.

From the methodological point of view, there is no doubt that contemporary macro models are better than the traditional Keynesian models on grounds of micro foundation. However, there exist a number of recent macro models which are not micro founded in the household sector. They typically assume rather than deduce from first principles the aggregate demand functions and then proceed to examine the issues they wish to investigate.[4]

Where does one draw the line these days? Of course, in theory the answer is straightforward. The optimal point is where the marginal benefit from micro foundation equals its marginal cost in terms of tractability and focus. As Blanchard and Fisher (1989, p. 558) write, 'Explicit derivation [from first principles] forces one to think more precisely about the specification one intends to use. It may lead, however, for reasons of analytical tractability, to specifications which are unpleasantly contorted and leave out important complexities of the issues at hand.' But there are hardly any guidelines on where this optimal point might be. There is an acute problem of asymmetric information which is rather unfortunate. The researcher would typically have much better information on the marginal cost involved in improving the micro foundation of his or her model, whereas readers who see the work, and who are in a position to evaluate but have not themselves worked out a similar model, may not realize the magnitude of these costs. As a result, there is ample scope to exercise dogmatism – advertently or inadvertently – in evaluating such models.

Why am I elaborating all this? The reason is that I happen to run into this hard choice particularly in Chapter 6 and I wish to forewarn the reader in the hope that he or she will not be dogmatic about it. As will be seen, Chapter 6 works out models with three markets – commodity, money and equity – as well as heterogeneity across households, the combination of which is quite complicated to handle without having to postulate directly the demand functions. This is *ad hoc*, but no more so than the direct assumption of aggregate demand functions in numerous other models. In any event, being *ad hoc* does not imply being useless. The usefulness of a model is mostly an empirical matter.

Notes

1. For an overview of macroeconomics and business cycles and an historical account of recent works on business cycles, see Zarnowitz (1992). See also Gordon (1986) for essays on American business cycles.
2. All the models in the following chapters are of this kind, except the third model in Chapter 4 and the second in Chapter 5, where damped fluctuation rather than damped oscillation is shown to result.
3. See Gabisch and Lorenz (1987, p. 157) for a sufficient condition for the existence of complex roots in a three-dimensional system.
4. Sargent and Wallace (1981), Ball (1988), Stadler (1990) and Waller and VanHoose (1991), to name a few.

3   Inequality, heterogeneity and business cycles in models of capital accumulation

I   Introduction

Capital accumulation is a common source of learning about economic dynamics. For a long time, it has been studied in the context of economic growth. Its implication for business cycles is of relatively recent origin and comes under the purview of the real business-cycle theory. The basic assumptions of the neoclassical growth theory, such as the representative agent, and basic results, such as the monotonic adjustment of aggregate output (or its growth rate) to its steady state, remain unchallenged. The business-cycle aspect involves stochastic specification of model primitives and examinations of the implied correlations among aggregate variables along the adjustment path due to (real) shocks to technology or preferences. The emphasis is on matching the derived correlations with observed correlations in actual economies. An important work on the neoclassical capital-accumulation model as a business-cycle model is due to King, Plosser and Rebelo (1988).

In this chapter, I study two neoclassical models of capital accumulation with the same broad objective: understanding business cycles. But my emphasis is different from – in fact, opposite to – that of the real business-cycle theory. The representative-agent assumption is rejected and my central concern is the monotonicity issue, and for reasons discussed in section II of Chapter 1, I downplay the correlation-matching issue.

Compared to the existing representative-agent models of capital accumulation, the distinguishing feature of these models is that households are heterogeneous in their rate of time preference, so that their savings/consumption behaviour is different. As a result, their capital accumulation behaviour is different, and wealth and income distributions in the economy are endogenous. By design, there is no technological progress, externality, growth of labour force or any other source of long-term growth.

In section II, I develop a variant of the simplest, Solow–Stiglitz type, capital-accumulation model in which the savings function is directly postulated.[1] Households differ in their marginal propensities to save, that is, in thriftiness. In section III, the model is extended to a Ramsey-type optimizing, perfect-foresight framework with households living indefinitely.

The main result is that oscillatory dynamics can arise in such economies, which otherwise do not arise in the absence of household heterogeneity. Thus household heterogeneity and distributional changes are a factor of the business cycle on their own. As was shown in Chapter 2, some sort of asymmetric cross effect is crucial for oscillatory dynamics, and in the present context this translates itself into what is called 'the asymmetric pecuniary externality effect'. Heterogeneity in savings propensity or time preference implies unequal distribution of capital-holding across households, and, in the presence of inequality, the cross impacts of capital-accumulation behaviour by one household on another's incentive to accumulate capital via changes in factor rewards and income are asymmetric. This asymmetry is the key to the oscillatory dynamics in these models.

II   A simple Solow–Stiglitz model

Consider a one-commodity, full-employment economy. The commodity can be either consumed or saved. The households undertake the task of transforming savings into capital at constant marginal cost. Each household behaves as one entity. There are two households in the economy, 1 and 2, although the model can be generalized to more than two households. Production is carried out by labour and capital. All markets are competitive.

At time t, household h ($= 1, 2$) faces the budget constraint

$$C_{ht} + K_{ht+1} = y_{ht} + (1-\delta)K_{ht}, \text{ or}$$

$$K_{ht+1} = S_{ht} + (1-\delta)K_{ht}, \tag{3.1}$$

where C_{ht} (S_{ht}) $\equiv$ the household's consumption (savings), $K_{ht} \equiv$ the capital stock held by it at the beginning of period, $y_{ht} \equiv$ its income, and $\delta \equiv$ the rate of capital depreciation.

Savings functions are directly specified. Let us consider the simplest savings function in which savings are proportional to income.[2] Let

$$S_{1t} = s_1 y_{1t}, \quad S_{2t} = s_2 y_{2t}, \tag{3.2}$$

where s_h's are positive constants between zero and one. It is interesting that after the beating this rule-of-the-thumb savings or the corresponding consumption function has taken during the seventies and eighties, empirical evidence partially supporting it is now emerging (see, for example, Campbell and Mankiw, 1989, 1990, 1991).

It is supposed that household 1 is thriftier than household 2, that is,

$$s_1 > s_2. \tag{3.3}$$

The income of household h consists of labour earnings and rental income from owning capital. Each household's labour endowment is constant, equal to 1/2, so that the total labour endowment of the economy is normalized to 1. Denoting the wage rate by w_t, household h's labour earnings are equal to $w_t/2$ at time t.

Let the aggregate production function be neoclassical: $Q_t = \tilde{Q}(K_t, 1) \equiv Q(K_t)$, with positive and diminishing returns, and constant returns to scale. Factors are paid their marginal products. Let $r(K_t)$ be the marginal product of capital.

The capital rental income of household h equals $r(K_t)K_{ht}$ and its total income:

$$y_{ht} = \frac{w_t}{2} + r(K_t)K_{ht} = \frac{1}{2}Q(K_t) + r(K_t)\left(K_{ht} - \frac{K_t}{2}\right). \qquad (3.4)$$

Thus the wealthier household also earns higher income.

Substituting (3.4) in the savings functions (3.2), and substituting the latter into the budget equation (3.1), we obtain the dynamics of the economy:

$$K_{1t+1} = (1-\delta)K_{1t} + s_1\left[\frac{Q(K_t)}{2} + r(K_t)\left(K_{1t} - \frac{K_t}{2}\right)\right] \equiv f_1(K_{1t}, K_{2t}) \qquad (3.5)$$

$$K_{2t+1} = (1-\delta)K_{2t} + s_2\left[\frac{Q(K_t)}{2} + r(K_t)\left(K_{2t} - \frac{K_t}{2}\right)\right] \equiv f_2(K_{1t}, K_{2t}). \qquad (3.6)$$

The description of the model is complete. Apart from the no-growth assumption, the structure of the model is different from the simplest Solow-type equilibrium capital accumulation model only in that the savings propensities vary across households. The difference between this model and Stiglitz's (1969) is that the latter assumed heterogeneity of savings behaviour based on functional distribution, that is, whether one is a capitalist or a worker (Stiglitz, 1969, p. 391) in the tradition of Kaldor (1956), whereas here the heterogeneity is based on personal or household distribution of income.[3]

Steady state and local dynamics
From (3.5) and (3.6) the steady state is defined by

$$s_1\left[\frac{Q(K^*)}{2} + r(K^*)\left(K_1^* - \frac{K^*}{2}\right)\right] = \delta K_1^* \qquad (3.7)$$

$$s_2 \left[\frac{Q(K^*)}{2} + r(K^*)\left(K_2^* - \frac{K^*}{2}\right) \right] = \delta K_2^*, \qquad (3.8)$$

where the asterisks mark the respective steady state values. It is easily verified that $K_1^* > K_2^*$, that is, the thriftier household holds more capital and earns higher income in the long run.[4] We may thus call households 1 and 2 the 'rich' and the 'poor', respectively. It can also be shown that the steady state, if it exists, is unique.[5]

Given the steady state, the local dynamics of the system (3.5)–(3.6) are described by

$$K_{1t+1} - K_1^* = f_{11}\left(K_{1t} - K_1^*\right) + f_{12}\left(K_{2t} - K_2^*\right) \qquad (3.5a)$$

$$K_{2t+1} - K_2^* = f_{21}\left(K_{1t} - K_1^*\right) + f_{22}\left(K_{2t} - K_2^*\right), \qquad (3.6a)$$

where the partials are evaluated at the steady state. Denoting by $(K_1^* - K_2^*)/2$ by z^*, the expressions for the partials are:

$$f_{11} = 1 - \delta + s_1\left(r^* + z^* r'\right); \quad f_{12} = s_1 z^* r' < 0 \qquad (3.9a), (3.9b)$$

$$f_{21} = -s_2 z^* r' > 0; \quad f_{22} = 1 - \delta + s_2\left(r^* - z^* r'\right). \qquad (3.9c), (3.9d)$$

Existence of oscillation

It is seen from (3.9a)–(3.9d) that in the *absence* of heterogeneity and inequality (that is, if $z^* = 0$), f_{12} and f_{21} are zero, and f_{11} and f_{22} are positive; thus, the dynamic path of $K_{1t} = K_{2t}$ would be monotonic. However, in the *presence* of heterogeneity and inequality, the cross effects, f_{21}, and f_{12}, are non-zero. Moreover, they are of the opposite sign – which, as explained in Chapter 2, is a necessary condition for oscillations. Hence oscillations can arise in this model. Holding constant the own effects, the lagged cross effects or the dynamic reaction functions are illustrated in Figure 3.1, which is analogous to Figure 2.1. An increase in the capital stock in the hands of the poor has a negative effect on the capital accumulation of the rich, whereas an increase in the capital stock in the hands of the rich has a positive effect on the capital accumulation of the poor.

The economics of why f_{12} and f_{21} are opposite in sign is therefore important in understanding why oscillation may arise in this model. As K_{it} increases, it tends to increase the aggregate capital stock, change the wage rate as well as the rental to capital and hence exert a pecuniary externality effect on household j's income and savings. This externality has a positive component through an increase in the real wage, but a negative component through a decrease in the rent. Particularly, since the rich household holds more capital than the average, as the capital stock in the hands of the poor (K_{2t}) increases, its negative pecuniary externality effect through the decrease in rent earned by the rich outweighs the positive pecuniary externality effect through the increase in their wage earnings; in the net, the rich household's income goes down and hence it saves less. This explains why $f_{12} < 0$. On the other hand, the poor household gains in terms of its total income as the capital stock of the rich increases, because the negative pecuniary externality effect on its total income is smaller (as it owns less capital) and it is dominated by the positive pecuniary externality effect through the increase in wage earnings. Thus $f_{21} > 0$. These opposite cross effects constitute the potential source of oscillation in this economy. This is called 'the asymmetric pecuniary externality effect'.

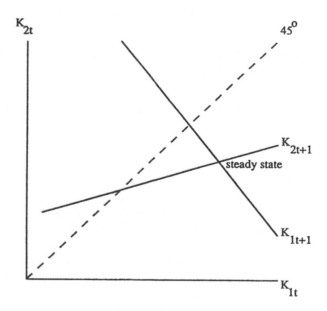

Figure 3.1   Asymmetric cross effects of capital accumulation

Although the sign reversal between f_{12} and f_{21} is a necessity, the necessary and sufficient condition for oscillation in this two-dimensional model is: $(f_{11} - f_{22})^2 + 4f_{12}f_{21} < 0$ (see (2.4) in Chapter 2). Substituting the expressions (3.9a)–(3.9d) in it, it reduces to[6]

$$\left(s_1 - s_2\right)\left[s_1\left(r^* + z^* r'\right)^2 - s_2\left(r^* - z^* r'\right)^2 \right] < 0. \qquad (3.10)$$

Although this model is *ad hoc* in that savings functions are directly specified rather than derived from first principles, it illustrates that the existence of oscillation hinges on three factors: (a) heterogeneous savings behaviour; (b) a nontrivial distribution of capital in the steady state; and (c) direct dependence of savings on current income. A more general model will also contain the presumption of oscillation as long as these features are present.

An example
Consider an economy in which the aggregate production function is CES:

$$Q(K_t, L_t) = \left(L_t^{-v} + K_t^{-v}\right)^{-1/v} = \left(1 + K_t^{-v}\right)^{-1/v},$$

where the labour endowment is normalized to unity. Choose the following parameter values: $v = 3$; $\delta = 0.30$; $s_1 = 0.49$; $s_2 = 0.13$.

Using the steady state conditions it can be derived that $K_1^* = 0.9$; $K_2^* = 0.1$; $Q^* = 0.79$; $r^* = 0.40$; $r' = -0.79$, and that the oscillation condition (3.10) is satisfied. The complex conjugate roots are equal to $0.76 \pm (0.07)i$ and their modulus 0.77. Thus a temporary or a permanent shock to technology or preferences will trigger a damped-oscillation path of adjustment to the steady state. (Simulations of such shocks are presented for the model developed in section III).

III An infinite horizon Ramsey-type model
The basic objection to a model of the above kind is that the savings function is directly postulated rather than derived from first principles. This is a behavioural imperfection. In this section, I develop a Ramsey-type infinite horizon model with fully rational, optimizing households, which eliminates the above imperfection. Compared to the standard representative-household, one-sector model of capital accumulation, there are two crucial differences: (a) households are different in terms of their rate of time preference; and (b) there is an imperfection in the capital-formation sector or activity (to be explained). Hence there is a different kind of imperfection here compared to the previous model. It is shown that the propagation or the internal mechanism of this model is also capable of producing oscillatory paths basically for the same reason – namely, the asymmetric pecuniary externality effect. After developing the model I present, for illustration, a numerical model economy in which the parametric configuration is such as to produce an oscillatory path of adjustment. The dynamics of

aggregate output and wealth and income inequality are traced following permanent and temporary technological shocks.

Elements of the model and equations governing the dynamics of the system

Let the production function be $Q_t = AF[K_t, 1]$ where A is a neutral technological parameter. A change in A would constitute a permanent technological shock. A will be made a function of time while considering a temporary technological shock.

It is assumed that there are H households ($h = 1, 2, ..., H$) with different rates of time preference or patience, β_h. Let households be indexed in decreasing order of patience, that is, $\beta_i > \beta_j$ if $i < j$; hence household 1 is the most patient and household H the least. Each household maximizes

$$\sum_{t=0}^{\infty} \beta_h^t U_h(C_{ht}), \quad h = 1, ..., H \tag{3.11}$$

subject to its budget constraint.

It is well known that if households face a budget constraint such as (3.1), the problem leads to an implication that in the steady state the most patient household ends up holding all the capital and the others none (see Becker, 1980). It is shown by Becker and Foias (1987) that oscillations and cycles can arise in such an economy. However, as Epstein and Hynes (1983) point out, such a long-run distribution of capital is 'unappealing'. Moreover, I am interested in showing oscillations based on variations in capital-holding across households, which cannot be handled in this framework since all capital is owned by one household.

One solution to this problem is to assume a recursive utility function with a variable rate of time preference, such as in Epstein and Hynes (1983) and Lucas and Stokey (1984). But it is shown already by Benhabib, Jafarey and Nishimura (1988) that oscillations cannot arise in this model (see their one-sector model). This is because there are no imperfections in their model.[7]

In what follows, I develop an alternative solution concept which implies some market or behavioural imperfection, a nontrivial distribution of capital in the steady state and that savings are directly dependent on current income. Hence the asymmetric pecuniary rent externality effect is present and oscillations may arise.

Note that a one-sector production model such as this does not allow for market production of capital through hiring factors of production. It is implicit that households undertake the task of transforming savings into capital and that the marginal rate of transformation is constant (equal to one). It can also be interpreted as a constant-cost storage technology *à la* Wallace (1980) and Sargent

(1987, ch. 7). Although there is no market-storage or capital-producing sector, it is *not* an imperfection because the marginal rate of transformation across households is the same. Assume instead an increasing-cost or diminishing-returns household storage technology – which does not seem any less plausible than a constant-cost technology. This assumption, as will be seen, generally leads to a nontrivial steady-state distribution of capital and is my proposed solution. Increasing costs introduce an imperfection in that across households different levels of savings imply different marginal costs of obtaining new capital.

Apart from the storage technology, this solution concept can be motivated in the context of market production of capital. Suppose that capital is heterogeneous and there are m types of capital, where m is some large number. Let the production function of the final good be

$$Q_t = f\left[\left(\sum_{i=1}^{m} K_{it}^{(v-1)/v}\right), L_t\right], \; v > 1,$$

where v is the elasticity of substitution between any two types of capital. Since each capital is different, suppose that it is produced by a separate plant or technology. However, let the technology of producing capital be symmetric. Let there be diminishing returns to the production of capital by consumption goods (savings) – which is my proposed solution. On the input supply side (of the production of capital), suppose that there are private transaction costs preventing a household from supplying its savings to all different (m) plants. In other words, there are private costs of diversification of portfolio of capital. For convenience, assume that $m = H$, that is, the number of types of capital equals the number of households, and that the transactions costs are sufficiently high for it to be optimal for each household to 'invest' in one type of capital. Thus, in equilibrium, each household owns a unique type of capital and as long as the levels of savings by two households are different, the marginal rates of transformation from savings to capital will be different because of diminishing returns. This will be a case of behavioural imperfection, in that households are unable to diversify completely due to private transactions costs and hence, in the presence of diminishing returns, are subject to unequal marginal rates of transformation of their savings into ownership of new capital.

Returning to the original solution concept, let I_n stand for new capital goods formed, that is, gross investment. In view of the preceding discussion, let $I_{nht} = g(S_{ht})$, with $g' > 0 > g''$. Instead of budget (3.1), we then have

$$K_{ht+1} = g(S_{ht}) + (1-\delta)K_{ht} = g\left(\frac{1}{H}w_t + r_t K_{ht} - C_{ht}\right) + (1-\delta)K_{ht}, \quad (3.1')$$

where w_t/H is a household's labour income, assuming that each household owns labour endowment equal to $1/H$.

Maximizing (3.11) subject to (3.1') yields the following first-order conditions:

$$\beta_h^t U'\,_h\left(C_{ht}\right) = \eta_{ht} g'\left(S_{ht}\right); \quad \eta_{ht-1} = \eta_{ht}\left[g'\left(S_{ht}\right)r_t + 1 - \delta\right], \quad (3.12)$$

where $\eta_{ht}s$ are the multipliers associated with the budget constraints. Defining $\mu_{ht+1} \equiv \eta_{ht}\beta_h^{-t}$, equations (3.12) imply

$$U'_h\left(C_{ht}\right) = \mu_{ht+1} g'\left(S_{ht}\right) \qquad (3.13)$$

$$\beta_h \mu_{ht+1}\left[g'\left(S_{ht}\right)r(K_t) + 1 - \delta\right] = \mu_{ht}. \qquad (3.14)$$

Equations (3.1'), (3.13) and (3.14) describe the dynamics of the system.

Steady state
As before, let the steady-state values be denoted by asterisks. Equations (3.1'), (3.13) and (3.14) reduce respectively to

$$\delta K_h^* = g\left(S_h^*\right) \qquad (3.1'')$$

$$U'_h\left(C_h^*\right) = \mu_h^* g'\left(S_h^*\right) \qquad (3.13^*)$$

$$\beta_h\left(g'\left(S_h^*\right)r\left(A,K^*\right) + 1 - \delta\right) = 1. \qquad (3.14^*)$$

Since $g'' < 0$ and $\beta_i > \beta_j$ for $i < j$, it follows from (3.14*) that $S_i^* > S_j^*$ for $i < j$. In view of (3.1''), $S_i^* > S_j^*$ implies that $K_i^* > K_j^*$. Hence, in the long run, a more patient household saves more, holds more capital and earns higher income than a less patient household.[8] Unlike when the marginal storage cost is constant, it is not necessarily the most patient that ends up with all the capital in the long run. In view of (3.14*), this outcome is ruled out unless the range of the $g'(.)$ function is too small relative to the dispersion of $\beta_h s$.[9]

Presence of oscillation
The aim is to show that along the optimal, perfect-foresight path, damped oscillations can exist.

To see this intuitively, let us turn to equation (3.13). Noting that $C_{ht} = y_{ht} - S_{ht}$ and U_h'' and g_h'' are negative, equation (3.13) implicitly defines

$$S_{ht} = S_h \left(\underset{+}{y_{ht}}, \underset{+}{\mu_{ht+1}} \right), \tag{3.15}$$

which is indeed very similar to the *ad hoc* savings functions (3.2), except that it has an intertemporal substitution effect term. Thus, to the extent that savings are affected by current income via (3.15), the asymmetric pecuniary external-ity effects on savings are present in this model too. Just as in the earlier model, in a two-household economy, the cross effect of capital accumulation by one household on the other's income, savings and hence on capital accumulation is opposite in sign. Algebraically, $\partial y_{1t}/\partial K_{2t} = z^* r' < 0$ and $\partial y_{2t}/\partial K_{1t} = -z^* r' > 0$, exactly as in the earlier model.

Local dynamics

Because y_{ht} is a function of K_{1t} and K_{2t}, equation (3.15) implicitly defines

$$S_{ht} = S_h[K_{1t}, K_{2t}, \mu_{ht+1}, A]. \tag{3.15'}$$

Next, substituting (3.15') into the budget equations (3.1') and the first order conditions, equations (3.1') and (3.14) can be regarded as a system of first-order difference equations in $2H$ variables, K_{ht} and μ_{ht}. These equations define implicitly

$$K_{ht+1} = k_h[K_{1t}, \ldots, K_{Ht}, \mu_{1t}, \ldots, \mu_{Ht}; A] \tag{3.16a}$$

$$\mu_{ht+1} = u_h[K_{1t}, \ldots, K_{Ht}, \mu_{1t}, \ldots, \mu_{Ht}; A]. \tag{3.16b}$$

The local (linearized) dynamics can be expressed in vector form:

$$\mathbf{J}_{t+1} = \mathbf{M}\mathbf{J}_t, \tag{3.17}$$

where $\mathbf{J}_t \equiv [K_{1t} - K_1^*, \ldots, K_{Ht} - K_H^*, \mu_{1t} - \mu_1^*, \ldots, \mu_{Ht} - \mu_H^*]'$ is a $2H$-element vector of deviations from the steady state and $\mathbf{M}$ is the Jacobian of the system (3.16a)–(3.16b) evaluated at the steady state. There are H initial conditions: $K_{h0} - K_h^*$ for $h = 1, \ldots, H$.

Seeking numerical examples or simulations of matrix $\mathbf{M}$ and its character-istic roots does not require analytical solutions of the elements of this matrix (partials of k_h and u_h functions). However, for $H = 2$, I have derived them for the sake of illustrating how complicated these are even for $H = 2$. Appendix 3.2 lists them. It shows that the expectation of a completely analytical solution of dynamic models with heterogeneity of agents is bound to be unrealistic in most cases.

Existence and uniqueness of the solution to (3.17)
Since the system (3.17) has H initial conditions, the existence of a solution requires that at least H out of the $2H$ roots of M have a modulus less than one. Given existence, uniqueness requires that exactly H roots have a modulus less than one. Given the dimension of M, nothing much could be said in general on the sign and magnitude of the roots. In terms of a specific example with $H = 2$, it was found that for certain ranges of parametric values, less than two roots have a modulus less than one, that is, a solution does not exist, while for other ranges it is not a problem. As I discussed in Chapter 2, my aim is to show that a model economy exists whose solution path is unique and which exhibits damped oscillation.

A two-household model economy
Consider an economy with two households: 1 and 2. Assume a Cobb–Douglas production function, $Q_t = AK_t^\theta$, $0 < \theta < 1$; a gross investment technology, $g_h(.) = vS_h^\gamma$, $0 < \gamma < 1$; and a constant-absolute-risk-aversion utility function:

$$U_h(C_{ht}) = -(\sigma_h / \xi_h)\exp[-\xi_h C_{ht}], \sigma_h, \xi_h > 0.^{10}$$

The steady-state conditions (3.1") and (3.14*) analytically solve for K_1^*, K_2^*, S_1^* and S_2^*. Defining

$$a \equiv \left(\frac{1/\beta_1 - 1 + \delta}{1/\beta_2 - 1 + \delta}\right)^{-\gamma/(1-\gamma)} \quad \text{and} \quad b \equiv \ln\left(\frac{vA\gamma\theta(1+a)^{-(1-\theta)}}{1/\beta_2 - 1 + \delta}\right),$$

it turns out that

$$K_1^* = a.\exp\left(\frac{\gamma b - (1-\gamma)\ln(\delta/v)}{1 - \gamma + \gamma(1-\theta)}\right); \quad K_2^* = \exp\left(\frac{\gamma b - (1-\gamma)\ln(\delta/v)}{1 - \gamma + \gamma(1-\theta)}\right);$$

$$S_1^* = a^{1/\gamma}.\exp\left(\frac{b + (1-\theta)\ln(\delta/v)}{1 - \gamma + \gamma(1-\theta)}\right); \quad S_2^* = \exp\left(\frac{b + (1-\theta)\ln(\delta/v)}{1 - \gamma + \gamma(1-\theta)}\right).$$

Given these expressions, K^*, w^*, r^*, C_1^* and C_2^* are given by $K^* = K_1^* + K_2^*$, $w^* = (1-\theta)AK^{*\theta}$, $r^* = \theta AK^{*-(1-\theta)}$, $C_1^* = w^*/2 + r^*K_1^* - S_1^*$ and $C_2^* = w^*/2 + r^*K_2^* - S_2^*$. (The parameters of the utility functions do not affect these steady-state values.)

Choosing $A = 300$, $\theta = 0.1$, $\gamma = 0.87$, $\delta = 0.5$, $\beta_1 = 0.84$ and $\beta_2 = 0.65$, we find the steady-state values:

$$K_1^* = 33.31, \ K_2^* = 2.17, \ S_1^* = 25.35, \ S_2^* = 1.10, \ C_1^* = 207.79, \ C_2^* = 194.42.$$

In the utility function, ξ_h is taken equal to 0.80 and σ_h such that the $U_h' = 1$ at the steady state. We then calculate the $\mathbf{M}$ matrix and its roots. The roots are equal to 1.96, 1.11 and $0.93 \pm (0.03)i$. Thus there are exactly two roots whose moduli are less than one and these are complex conjugates. As a result, the system will exhibit an oscillatory transition path toward the steady state.

A permanent technological shock
A permanent technological shock of $A = 299$ to $A = 300$ was simulated. The local dynamics initiated by this shock are governed by (3.17), where $\mathbf{M}$ is evaluated at the new steady-state values and the initial conditions are given by $K_{10} - K_1^* \neq 0$ and $K_{20} - K_2^* \neq 0$, where K_{h0} and K_h^* are the old and new steady-state values respectively.

The simulated time paths, in terms of percentage deviation from the steady state, of the share of wealth held by the rich (household 1) and its share in total income and the total output –which are trigonometric functions resulting from the stable complex conjugate roots – are graphed in Figures 3.2A–C. As seen, the positive technological shock has a positive impact on the wealth and income share of the rich and aggregate output in the initial phase of the transition path. The oscillatory paths of these variables are confirmed in the diagram by either the smooth non-monotonicity or their crossing with the x-axis (the steady state). Numerically, each variable oscillates around and asymptotically converges with the x-axis. The oscillatory pattern may not be prominent graphically because of large differences in scale between deviations in the initial and subsequent periods.

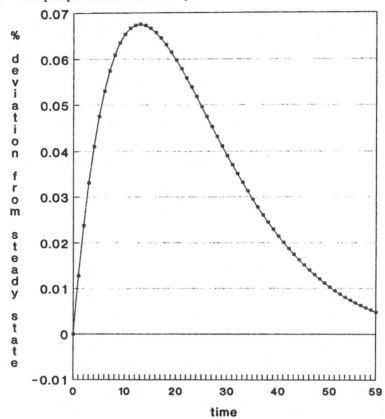

Figure 3.2A   Wealth share of household 1: permanent productivity shock,
A = 299 to 300

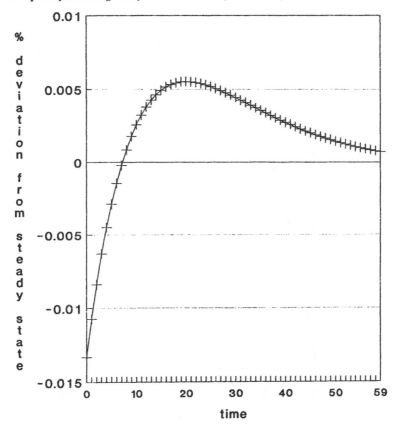

Figure 3.2B   Income share of household 1: permanent productivity shock,
A = 299 to 300

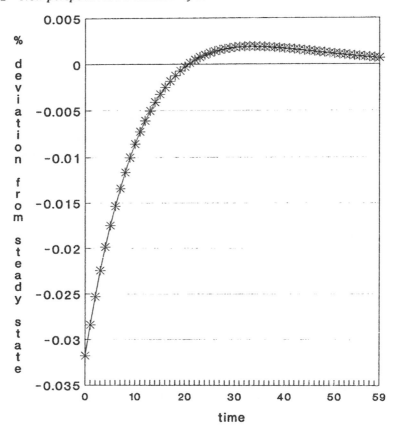

Figure 3.2C   Aggregate output: permanent productivity shock, A = 299 to 300

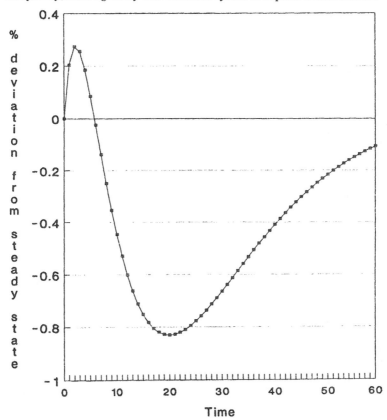

*Figure 3.3A   Wealth share of household 1: temporary productivity shock,
A = 300 to 301, persistence parameter = 0.7*

Temporary shocks
Suppose that the parameter, A, instead of being time invariant, follows a
stochastic AR(1) process:

$$A_{t+1} = B + \rho A_t + \varepsilon_{t+1}, \qquad (3.18)$$

where A_0 is given, $0 \leq \rho < 1$ and ε_t's are i.i.d. with $E(\varepsilon_t) = 0$ for all t.

Thus it is a stationary process with the long-run average equal to $B/(1-\rho)$.

A stochastic process such as (3.18) implies stochastic processes of other state
and control variables. However, as discussed in King, Plosser and Rebelo

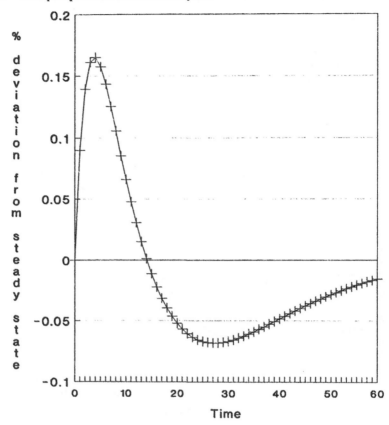

Figure 3.3B   Income share of household 1: temporary productivity shock, A = 300 to 301, persistence parameter = 0.7

(1988, p. 211), the burden of computing the stationary distribution of all relevant variables is enormous. As they do, I invoke certainty equivalence, based on two approximations: (a) the steady-state values of other variables in the nonstochastic model with $A = B/(1-\rho)$ are taken as their approximate solutions near the stationary point; and (b) the local dynamics are posited by expanding the linearized system (3.17) (for $H = 2$) to include A_t, that is

$$\tilde{\mathbf{J}}_{t+1} = \tilde{\mathbf{M}}\tilde{\mathbf{J}}_t + \begin{bmatrix} \mathbf{0}_{4\times1} \\ \varepsilon_{t+1} \end{bmatrix}, \qquad (3.17')$$

where $\tilde{\mathbf{J}}_t \equiv \left[K_{1t} - K_1^*, K_{2t} - K_2^*, \mu_{1t} - \mu_1^*, \mu_{2t} - \mu_2^*, A_t - B/(1-\rho) \right]$, and

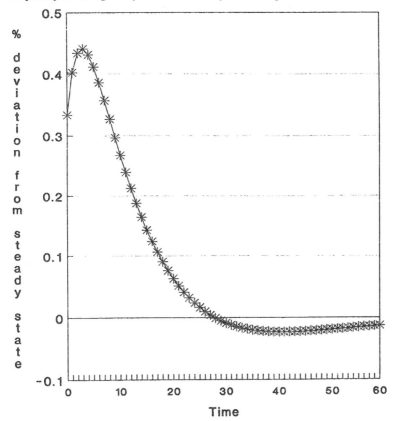

Figure 3.3C   Aggregate output: temporary productivity shock, A = 300 to 301, persistence parameter = 0.7

$$\tilde{M} \equiv \begin{bmatrix} M_{4\times4} & \dfrac{\partial(k,u)}{\partial A}_{\,4\times1} \\ 0 & \rho \end{bmatrix}^{11,\ 12}.$$

The impacts of temporary shocks are the impulse response functions generated by $A_0 - B/(1-\rho) \equiv \varepsilon_0 \neq 0$, conditional on information available at $t = 0$.

The adjustment path following a temporary shock of $\varepsilon_0 = 1$ was simulated for two specifications: $\rho = 0.7$ and $\rho = 0$ (no persistence). In each case, B was chosen so as to yield $B/(1-\rho)$ equal to 300, the value of the technological parameter in the nonstochastic case. Thus the eigen roots of $\tilde{M}(5\times5)$ are the four

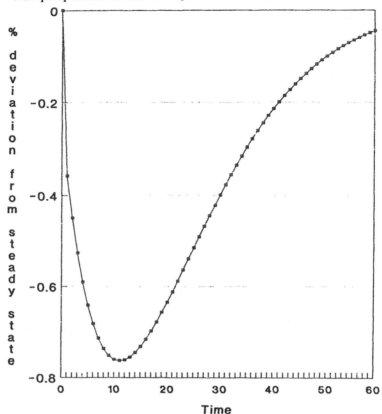

*Figure 3.4A   Wealth share of household 1: temporary productivity shock,
A = 300 to 301, no persistence*

eigen roots in the nonstochastic case plus ρ. The resulting paths are plotted in
Figures 3.3A, B, C and Figures 3.4A, B, C respectively.[13] The oscillatory
patterns are confirmed again.

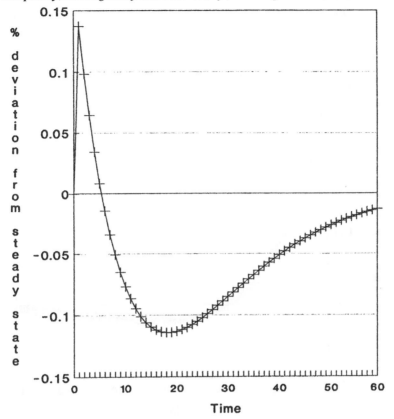

Figure 3.4B   Income share of household 1: temporary productivity shock,
A = 300 to 301, no persistence

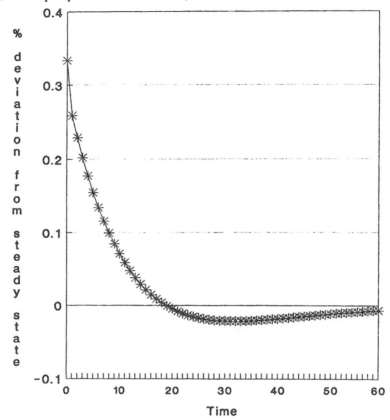

Figure 3.4C   Aggregate output: temporary productivity shock, A = 300 to 301, no persistence

IV Concluding remarks

This chapter has presented two models of capital accumulation in the presence of household heterogeneity in thriftiness or rate of time preference. The main result is that oscillations can arise because of heterogeneity and the implied changes in wealth and income distribution. The asymmetric pecuniary externality effect is the key behind the oscillatory dynamics, and this effect is present as long as there is a nontrivial distribution of capital in the economy and savings are directly dependent on current income (along with other determinants). The models also illustrate some of the behavioural or market distortions on which these features depend and hence in the presence of which the interaction of distributional changes and capital accumulation behaviour can generate oscillatory dynamics of aggregate output. The first model contained a behavioural distortion in the form of a rule-of-thumb savings function rather than a savings function derived from first principles. The second model assumed a market distortion in the capital-building sector.

Dynamics of capital accumulation and distributional changes can be studied in the overlapping generations framework with heterogeneous households and bequest motive. The finiteness of life can be interpreted as an imperfection and therefore oscillatory dynamics can arise (see the essays in Grandmont, 1986). While the bequest motive contributes toward inequality and presence of oscillations, the change in preferences or savings behaviour of a given household or family over generations is a factor toward equality, weakening the presumption of oscillatory dynamics. One may also investigate a capital accumulation model with heterogeneous households with some households facing credit constraints, in which oscillations are likely to arise because credit constraints would imply that current savings are directly dependent on current income.

Appendix 3.1 Derivation of inequality (3.10)

Direct substitution of (3.9a)–(3.9d) yields

$$
\begin{aligned}
(f_{11} - f_{22})^2 &+ 4f_{12}f_{21} \\
&= -4s_1 s_2 (zr')^2 + \left[s_1(r+zr') - s_2(r-zr') \right]^2 \\
&= -4s_1 s_2 (zr')^2 + \left[s_1(r+zr') \right]^2 + \left[s_2(r-zr') \right]^2 - 2s_1 s_2 \left[r^2 - (zr')^2 \right] \\
&= \left[s_1(r+zr') \right]^2 + \left[s_2(r-zr') \right]^2 - 2s_1 s_2 \left[r^2 + (zr')^2 \right] \\
&= \left[s_1(r+zr') \right]^2 + \left[s_2(r-zr') \right]^2 - s_1 s_2 \left[(r+zr')^2 + (r-zr')^2 \right] \\
&= s_1(r+zr')^2 (s_1 - s_2) + s_2(r-zr')^2 (s_2 - s_1) \\
&= (s_1 - s_2)\left[s_1(r+zr')^2 - s_2(r-zr')^2 \right], \text{ the left-hand-side of (3.10)}.
\end{aligned}
$$

For notational simplicity, asterisks are ignored in all appendices.

Appendix 3.2   Elements of matrix H

Substituting (3.13) in (3.14) we eliminate μ_{ht+1} and express dS_{ht} as a function of dy_{ht}, dK_t and $d\mu_{ht}$:

$$\left(\mu_h g_h'' - \beta_h U_h' r g_h'' + U_h''\right) dS_{ht} = U_h'' dy_{ht} + \beta_h U_h' g_h' r' dK_t - g_h' d\mu_{ht}. \text{(3.A1)}$$

Next we substitute $\partial y_{1t}/\partial K_{1t} = r+zr'$, $\partial y_{1t}/\partial K_{2t} = zr'$, $\partial y_{2t}/\partial K_{1t} = -zr'$ and $\partial y_{2t}/\partial K_{2t} = r-zr'$ in (3.A1), use $dK_t = dK_{1t}+dK_{2t}$ and substitute dS_{ht} in (3.1') and (3.14) to obtain

$$k_{11} \equiv \frac{\partial K_{1t+1}}{\partial K_{1t}} = g_1' \cdot \frac{U_1''(r+zr') + \beta_1 U_1' g_1' r'}{\mu_1 g_1'' - \beta_1 r U_1' g_1'' + U_1''} + 1 - \delta \underset{<}{\overset{>}{=}} 0;$$

$$k_{12} \equiv \frac{\partial K_{1t+1}}{\partial K_{2t}} = g_1' \cdot \frac{U_1'' zr' + \beta_1 U_1' g_1' r'}{\mu_1 g_1'' - \beta_1 r U_1' g_1'' + U_1''} \underset{<}{\overset{>}{=}} 0;$$

$$k_{13} \equiv \frac{\partial K_{1t+1}}{\partial \mu_{1t}} = - \frac{\left(g_1'\right)^2}{\mu_1 g_1'' - \beta_1 r U_1' g_1'' + U_1''} > 0;$$

$$k_{14} \equiv \frac{\partial K_{1t+1}}{\partial \mu_{2t}} = 0;$$

$$k_{21} \equiv \frac{\partial K_{2t+1}}{\partial K_{1t}} = g_2' \cdot \frac{-U_2'' zr' + \beta_2 U_2' g_2' r'}{\mu_2 g_2'' - \beta_2 r U_2' g_2'' + U_2''} > 0;$$

$$k_{22} \equiv \frac{\partial K_{2t+1}}{\partial K_{2t}} = g_2' \cdot \frac{U_2''(r-zr') + \beta_2 U_2' g_2' r'}{\mu_2 g_2'' - \beta_2 r U_2' g_2'' + U_2''} + 1 - \delta > 0;$$

$$k_{23} \equiv \frac{\partial K_{2t+1}}{\partial \mu_{1t}} = 0;$$

$$k_{24} \equiv \frac{\partial K_{2t+1}}{\partial \mu_{2t}} = - \frac{\left(g_2'\right)^2}{\mu_2 g_2'' - \beta_2 r U_2' g_2'' + U_2''} > 0;$$

$$u_{11} \equiv \frac{\partial \mu_{1t+1}}{\partial K_{1t}} = -\beta_1 \mu_1 \left[g_1' r' + r g_1'' \cdot \frac{U_1''(r+zr') + \beta_1 U_1' g_1' r'}{\mu_1 g_1'' - \beta_1 r U_1' g_1'' + U_1''} \right] \underset{<}{\overset{>}{=}} 0;$$

$$u_{12} \equiv \frac{\partial \mu_{1t+1}}{\partial K_{2t}} = -\beta_1 \mu_1 \left[g_1' r + r g_1'' \cdot \frac{U_1'' zr' + \beta_1 U_1' g_1' r'}{\mu_1 g_1'' - \beta_1 r U_1' g_1'' + U_1''} \right] \gtrless 0;$$

$$u_{13} \equiv \frac{\partial \mu_{1t+1}}{\partial \mu_{1t}} = 1 + \beta_1 \mu_1 r g_1'' g_1' \cdot \frac{1}{\mu_1 g_1'' - \beta_1 r U_1' g_1'' + U_1''} > 0;$$

$$u_{14} \equiv \frac{\partial \mu_{1t+1}}{\partial \mu_{2t}} = 0;$$

$$u_{21} \equiv \frac{\partial \mu_{2t+1}}{\partial K_{1t}} = -\beta_2 \mu_2 \left[g_2' r + r g_2'' \cdot \frac{-U_2'' zr' + \beta_2 U_2' g_2' r'}{\mu_2 g_2'' - \beta_2 r U_2' g_2'' + U_2''} \right] > 0;$$

$$u_{22} \equiv \frac{\partial \mu_{2t+1}}{\partial K_{2t}} = -\beta_2 \mu_2 \left[g_2' r + r g_2'' \cdot \frac{U_2''(r - zr') + \beta_2 U_2' g_2' r'}{\mu_2 g_2'' - \beta_2 r U_2' g_2'' + U_2''} \right] \gtrless 0;$$

$$u_{23} \equiv \frac{\partial \mu_{2t+1}}{\partial \mu_{1t}} = 0;$$

$$u_{24} \equiv \frac{\partial \mu_{2t+1}}{\partial \mu_{2t}} = 1 + \beta_2 \mu_2 r g_2'' g_2' \frac{1}{\mu_2 g_2'' - \beta_2 r U_2' g_2'' + U_2''} > 0.$$

Appendix 3.3   Elements of $\partial(k, u)/\partial A$

The elements of the $\partial(k, u)/\partial A$ matrix in (3.17') are the following:

$$\frac{\partial k_1}{\partial A} = \frac{U_1''(Q_A / 2 + z r_A) + \beta_1 U_1' g_1' r_A}{\mu_1 g_1'' - \beta_1 U_1' r g_1'' + U_1''}, \text{ where } Q_A = F(K_t, 1)$$

$$\frac{\partial k_2}{\partial A} = \frac{U_2''(Q_A / 2 - z r_A) + \beta_2 U_2' g_2' r_A}{\mu_2 g_2'' - \beta_2 U_2' r g_2'' + U_2''}$$

$$\frac{\partial u_1}{\partial A} = -\beta_1 \mu_1 \left[g_1' r_A + r g_1'' \cdot \frac{U_1''(Q_A / 2 + z r_A) + \beta_1 U_1' g_1' r_A}{\mu_1 g_1'' - \beta_1 U_1' r g_1'' + U_1''} \right]$$

$$\frac{\partial u_2}{\partial A} = -\beta_2 \mu_2 \left[g_2' r_A + r g_2'' \cdot \frac{U_2''(Q_A / 2 - z r_A) + \beta_2 U_2' g_2' r_A}{\mu_2 g_2'' - \beta_2 U_2' r g_2'' + U_2''} \right]$$

Appendix 3.4   Solution of undetermined coefficients and the initial values of jump variables when $\rho = 0$

Given the discrete shock ε_0 at $t = 0$, the transition of the system from $t = 0$ to $t = 1$ is given by

$$\mathbf{J}_1 = \mathbf{MJ}_0 + \frac{\partial(k,\mu)}{\partial A}\varepsilon_0. \qquad (3.A2)$$

On the other hand, given $\mathbf{J}_1$, the system, *expected as of $t = 0$*, evolves according to (3.17) from $t = 1$ onwards. Let the stable roots be denoted by λ_3 and λ_4, which are complex conjugates, and let the respective normalized eigenvectors be $(1, v_{j2}, v_{j3}, v_{j4})$ for $j = 3, 4$. Hence the general solution of the system for $t \geq 1$ (expected as of $t = 0$) is given by

$$\mathbf{J}_t = \sum_{j=3}^{4} \begin{pmatrix} b_j \\ b_j v_{j2} \\ b_j v_{j3} \\ b_j v_{j4} \end{pmatrix} \lambda_j^t, \; t \geq 1, \qquad (3.A3)$$

where b_j's are undetermined coefficients. Thus at $t = 1$,

$$\mathbf{J}_1 = \sum_{j=3}^{4} \begin{pmatrix} b_j \\ b_j v_{j2} \\ b_j v_{j3} \\ b_j v_{j4} \end{pmatrix} \lambda_j. \qquad (3.A4)$$

Equations (3.A2) and (3.A4) constitute eight equations and solve for eight entities: all four elements of $\mathbf{J}_1$, $K_{11}-K_1^*$, $K_{21}-K_2^*$, $\mu_{11}-\mu_1^*$ and $\mu_{21}-\mu_2^*$; two elements of $\mathbf{J}_0$, $\mu_{10}-\mu_1^*$ and $\mu_{20}-\mu_2^*$ (the other two elements of $\mathbf{J}_0$ are zero as the temporary shock leaves $K_{10}-K_1^*$ and $K_{20}-K_2^*$ equal to zero); and the two undetermined coefficients, b_3 and b_4.

Notes

1. Solow (1956) and Stiglitz (1969).
2. Wealth effects can be introduced without any change of results. See Das (1991).
3. It is interesting that other parts of Stiglitz's (1969) paper deal with personal distribution but do not assume heterogeneity in preferences.
4. Equations (3.7) and (3.8) can be expressed as $s_h(w^*/2 + r^*K_h^*) = \delta K_h^*$, or $s_h w^*/2 = (\delta - s_h r^*)K_h^*$, $h = 1, 2$. Taking the ratio, $K_1^*/K_2^* = (s_1\delta - s_1 s_2 r^*)/(s_2\delta - s_1 s_2 r^*) > 1$, as both the numerator and the denominator are positive and $s_1 > s_2$.

5. Totally differentiating equation (3.7) and denoting $-(K_1^* - K_2^*)r'/(2r^*)$ by ω (>0) yields

$$\left[s_1 r^* (1-\omega)-\delta\right]dK_1^* = s_1 r^* \omega dK_2^*.$$

Equation (3.7) can also be expressed as $\delta = s_1 y_1^*/K_1^*$. Using this, we can deduce

$$\left[\lambda_1 (1-\omega)-1\right]dK_1^* = \lambda_1 \omega dK_2^*,$$

where $\lambda_h \equiv r^* K_h^*/y_h^* < 1$. Since $dK_1^* + dK_2^* = dK^*$, the above expression reduces

$$\frac{dK^*}{dK_1^*} = -\frac{1-\lambda_1}{\lambda_1 \omega}.$$

This is equivalent to equation (3.7) implicitly defining a function $K^* = \upsilon_1(K_1^*)$ such that $\upsilon_1' = -(1-\lambda_1)/(\lambda_1 \omega)$.

Similarly, it can be derived that equation (3.8) implicitly defines $K_1^* = \upsilon_2(K^*)$ such that $\upsilon_2' = -[\lambda_2(1+\omega)-1]/(1-\lambda_2)$. If we now define $\upsilon_3(K_1^*) \equiv \upsilon_2(\upsilon_1(K_1^*)) - K_1^*$, then $\upsilon_3(K_1^*) = 0$ defines the steady state K_1^*. However,

$$\upsilon_3'\left(K_1^*\right) = \upsilon_2' \upsilon_1' - 1 = -\frac{1-\lambda_1}{\lambda_1}\left[\frac{\lambda_1}{1-\lambda_1} - \frac{\lambda_2}{1-\lambda_2} + \frac{1}{w}\right] < 0,$$

since $0 < \lambda_h < 1$, $\lambda_1 > \lambda_2$ and $\omega > 0$. Thus the $\upsilon_3(K_1^*)$ function is strictly monotonic. This implies that $\upsilon_3(K_1^*) = 0$ yields a unique solution. It is then immediate that the solution to K_2^* is unique also.

6. The derivation of this expression is given in Appendix 3.1.

7. Scheinkman and Weiss (1986) also present an optimizing, heterogeneous-agent model of production. But the source of variation in production is labour supply, not capital accumulation. Moreover, the inequality of income arises due to random productivity shocks to agents, not due to heterogeneity in preference.

8. The more patient household also consumes more. This is seen by noting that in the steady state $C_i^* - C_j^* = r^*(K_i^* - K_j^*) - (S_i^* - S_j^*) = (r^*/\delta)[g(S_i^*) - g(S_j^*)] - (S_i^* - S_j^*)$. By strict concavity of the $g(.)$ function, $g(S_j^*) - g(S_i^*) < g'(S_i^*)(S_j^* - S_i^*) <=> g(S_i^*) - g(S_j^*) > g'(S_i^*)(S_i^* - S_j^*)$. Hence $C_i^* - C_j^* \geq (S_i^* - S_j^*)[r^* g'(S_i^*) - \delta]/\delta$. However, in view of (3.14*), $r^* g'(S_h^*) - \delta = 1/\beta_h - 1 > 0$. It is already shown that for $i < j$, $S_i^* > S_j^*$. Hence $(S_i^* - S_j^*)[r^* g'(S_i^*) - \delta]/\delta > 0$, implying that $C_i^* - C_j^* \geq 0$ for $i < j$.

9. Given existence, it is straightforward to show that the steady state is unique. Equation (3.14*) implies

$$\frac{g'\left(S_i^*\right)}{g'\left(S_j^*\right)} = \frac{1/\beta_i - 1 + \delta}{1/\beta_j - 1 + \delta} = \text{a positive constant.}$$

This, in turn, implies that for any given i, S_j^* ($j \neq i$) is an increasing function of S_i^*, i.e. $S_j^* = \Gamma_{ji}(S_i^*)$, $\Gamma_{ji}' > 0$. Summing (3.1") over all households and using the $\Gamma_{ji}(.)$ functions,

$$\delta K^* = g\left(S_1^*\right) + .. + g\left(S_i^*\right) + .. + g\left(S_H^*\right) = g\left(\Gamma_{1i}\left(S_i^*\right)\right) + .. + g\left(S_i^*\right) + .. + g\left(\Gamma_{Hi}\left(S_i^*\right)\right)$$

$$\equiv \upsilon\left(S_i^*\right), \upsilon_i' > 0.$$

This equation generates a positive locus between S_i^* and K^*. Note that equation (3.14^*) implies a negative locus between S_i^* and K^*. Hence there can be only one intersection between these loci, implying the uniqueness of S_i^* and K^*. Uniqueness of other solutions follows immediately.

10. See Blanchard and Fisher (1989, p. 44) for a discussion on the use of such a utility function in macroeconomics.

11. The analytical expressions of $\partial(k,u)/\partial A$ are given in Appendix 3.3.

12. This is equivalent to the transition from the dynamics in the nonstochastic model given in (3.7) of King, Plosser and Rebelo (1988) to the dynamics in the stochastic model given in (4.1) of their paper.

13. In the case of $\rho > 0$, it is straightforward to solve the undetermined coefficients of the general solution equations of (3.17') and the initial values of jump variables. But it is not so in the case of $\rho = 0$, since the shock is discrete: nonzero at $t = 0$ and zero elsewhere. The method of solution in this case is outlined in Appendix 3.4.

4 Heterogeneity, redistributive lobbying and business cycles

I Introduction

This chapter links household inequality to business cycles through the political market. There is of course the political business-cycle theory which recognises that business fluctuations may be partly due to the attempts by incumbent politicians or political parties to engage in immediate consumption, output or job-oriented policies, that is, choose a high-inflation cum low-unemployment point along the Phillips curve near election times compared to other times. There is a rich literature on this theory, starting with the seminal work of Nordhaus (1975), for example, Lindbeck (1976), Hibbs (1977), McRae (1977), Tufte (1978), Minford and Peel (1982), Cukierman and Meltzer (1986), Alesina and Sachs (1988), Rogoff and Sibert (1988), Alesina (1989) and Rogoff (1990), among many others. While the earlier political business-cycle models assumed adaptive expectations, a permanent tradeoff between inflation and unemployment, voter myopia and nominal rigidities, the recent models incorporate rational expectations and the cycles are based on some form of asymmetric information about the environment between voters and the incumbent politicians. For example, Rogoff and Siebert (1988) and Rogoff (1990) assume asymmetric information about the incumbent's competence in providing public goods.

A particular strand of the political business-cycle theory stresses the ideological affiliation of politicians or political parties and its implications for the inflation–output tradeoff. Some parties are more concerned about unemployment and income distribution and less about inflation than other parties. Again, the earlier models of this kind, notably Hibbs (1977), assumed adaptive expectations and a permanent tradeoff along the Phillips curve, while later models, such as Alesina and Sachs (1988), assume rational voters.

The commonalty among the political business-cycle models is that the behaviour of politicians or political parties is influenced by the electorate to the extent that the latter votes. Election or the expected outcome of an election is the only medium through which politicians and households (voters) connect with each other. There is no 'active' participation by potential voters in the form of lobbying to influence policies, particularly redistributive policies. Such activities however are a common practice in democracies and often require real resources which could be otherwise utilized in direct production. The objective of this chapter is to develop business-cycle models with heterogeneous households and their incentive to engage in lobbying by expending real resources so as to influence redistributive policies. Compared to the political business-cycle theory in which politicians and the electorate interact only in some voting process and the policies themselves have direct implications for variation in aggregate output, here there is (a) more direct and active interaction in terms of 'influence peddling' and voting remains only in the background; (b) variation in output resulting from variations in the amount of real resources used in the influence peddling or the lobbying process; and (c) the emphasis on the effect of heterogeneity on the incentive to lobby.

Of course, the notion of political lobbying, the use of real resources in the lobbying process and its implication for aggregate efficiency, is not new. A variety of static models that deal with lobbying and the related issue of endogenous policy exist, particularly in the field of international trade, for example, Krueger (1974), Brock and Magee (1978), Bhagwati (1980, 1982), Young and Magee (1986), Magee (1987), and Das (1990), to name but a few. The ramifications of lobbying for economic growth have been studied recently by Magee, Brock and Young (1989, ch. 8), Terrones (1990) and Alesina and Rodrik (1991).

The purpose of this chapter is to link household heterogeneity to business cycles through redistributive lobbying.

In a capitalist economy, interest groups engage in lobbying to shape different types of government policies such as various regulatory schemes, taxes, distribution of tax proceeds and the like. The models in this chapter consider lobbying in the context of an income tax and the distribution of its proceeds. Specifically, I present three models. In order to focus as sharply as possible on the variation in output due to the substitution of real resources away from production and toward lobbying, the models assume given factor endowments and no savings.

In the first two models developed in sections II and III, the rate of income tax is treated as exogenous – that is, not explained – while the distribution of tax proceeds is endogenously determined by lobbying. The third and last model in section IV endogenizes the tax rate but the mechanism of the distribution of the proceeds is kept exogenous. More specifically, section II presents a model of zero-sum lobbying in the sense that the tax revenues are fully distributed among the lobbying households. Hence the net gain to the lobbyists as a group is zero.[1] Section III develops a model of positive-sum lobbying in the following sense. There are two groups of households. One is poor – or below some poverty line – which is subsidized, does not pay any taxes and does not lobby. Households in the other group are above the poverty line, pay taxes and lobby in order to receive some transfers. Lobbying by any particular household in the tax-payer group has two effects. First, it has the *externality effect* of increasing the total transfers to the tax-payers as a group, thereby reducing the amount of total transfer to the poor. Second, given the total transfer to this group, it increases that household's share in the total transfers. Put differently, lobbying affects the distribution *as well as* the size of the pie of total gross transfers to the tax-payers. The critical assumption in both these models is that the tax-paying households have heterogeneous time preference. This implies asymmetric cross effects of lobbying by one household on optimal lobbying by another and these are instrumental in generating the oscillatory time path of individual as well as total lobbying and output.

In contrast, the model in section IV assumes that the tax-payers are alike in their preference and they lobby to affect the tax rate. As in section III, there is a non-tax-paying group which is poor, does not lobby but receives the tax proceeds as transfers. The heterogeneity in this economy lies in the difference in the endowments which separates the tax-paying households from the non-tax-paying households (the poor). For simplicity, it is assumed that tax-paying households do not receive any transfers; in other words, the tax rate subject to lobbying is interpreted as the net tax rate. The model is shown to imply a non-monotonic path of lobbying and total output, but for a different reason compared to the previous models.

Before getting into the models, however, it seems useful to delineate the imperfections the models presume, that constitute the environment in which non-monotonicity of output may result. These are (a) the presence of distortionary taxes; (b) use of real resources in the directly unproductive or 'DUP' uses; (c) absence of a perfect political market; and (d) some form of technological rigidity.

II   A model of zero-sum lobbying and business cycles
In general, owners of specific factors across different sectors of an economy lobby to protect or enhance their net income. In the context of income taxes and the tax proceeds, they may lobby toward reducing the tax rate or schedule facing tax-payers as a whole, or they may lobby toward increasing the factor-specific subsidies that they receive out of the total tax proceeds. I assume that there is one-to-one correspondence between the number of households and the number of specific factors of production. There is an aggregate one-sector production which requires specific factors but no generic factors. Furthermore, the specific factors enter production symmetrically and linearly. Thus they can be aggregated and interpreted as a single factor or resource. None of these assumptions is required, but together they reduce the production side of the economy to the minimum, enabling the model to focus on the distributional aspects in the economy.

Let there be H households, indexed by $h = 1,..., H$. Each household is endowed with $\bar{K}_h$ units of the resource. The total amount of the resource available to the economy is

$$\bar{K} = \sum_h \bar{K}_h.$$

A part of it, equal to L_t, is used in the lobbying process at time t (to be elaborated shortly). Thus the total amount of the resource used productively at t equals $K_t = \bar{K} - L_t$. In addition to the already specified assumptions on the production side, let there be technological rigidities in the form of a one-period gestation lag between factor employment and output (as, for example, in the real business-cycle model of Long and Plosser, 1983). Thus we can write

$$Q_{t+1} = rK_t, \tag{4.1}$$

where r is independent of K_t. (Recall that the specific factors enter the production function linearly.) The product market is assumed to be competitive and there is free entry and exit. Hence the unit reward to the factor equals r. The productivity coefficient r is taken as time-invariant except while considering a temporary productivity shock.

Each household lives indefinitely and has the same instantaneous utility function, $u(c_{ht})$, $u' > 0 > u''$. But the rate of time preference varies across the households. Let β_h be the discount factor of household h. Its income, y_{ht}, is taxed at the rate τ, which – as mentioned earlier – is exogenous. The total tax proceeds at time t equal

$$T_t = \tau \sum_h y_{ht},$$

which is redistributed among the H households. Let s_{ht} be the share of household h in the total transfer, T_t. It is assumed that s_h depends on lobbying by household h, L_{ht}, as well as lobbying by other households:

$$s_{ht} = s_h\left(L_{ht}, \{L_{-ht}\}\right), \tag{4.2'}$$

where $\{L_{-ht}\}$ denotes the vector of lobbying by other households. Lobbying requires resource use and let the unit of L_{ht} be normalized as one unit of the resource. Thus

$$\sum_h L_{ht} = L_t.$$

It seems reasonable to suppose that

(a) s_h is subject to positive but diminishing returns, that is, $s_{hh} > 0$ and $s_{hhh} < 0$;
(b) s_h is a negative function of $\{L_{-ht}\}$, that is, $\partial s_h/\partial\{L_{-ht}\} < 0$;
(c) s_h is homogeneous of degree zero, that is, if all households step up their lobbying by a common factor, s_h is unchanged; and finally,
(d) s_h must be such that

$$\sum_h s_h = 1.^2$$

A particular function which satisfies (a)–(d) and which will be used below is:

$$s_{ht} = \frac{L_{ht}}{\sum_h L_{ht}} \equiv \frac{L_{ht}}{L_t}.^3 \tag{4.2}$$

This function states that the proportion of the total transfer allocated to a household is equal to the proportion of its lobbying to total lobbying by all households.

This essentially completes the description of the model. It should be noted that it highlights the technological rigidity as a source of dynamics in the economy. This is not necessary. Alternatively, one can appeal to the sluggishness in the political system and specify a delayed effect of lobbying, for example, $s_{ht+1} = s_h(L_{ht}, \{L_{-ht}\})$.

Household optimization and equations governing the dynamics of the model
The one-period lag in production implies a one-period lag in the factor payment, which makes the household problem of allocating the resource between lobbying and productive use an intertemporal one. The perfect foresight, intertemporal problem facing household h is to maximize

$$\sum_{t=0}^{\infty} \beta_h^t u(c_{ht}),$$

subject to

$$c_{ht} \leq (1-\tau)rK_{ht-1} + s_h\left(L_{ht}, \{L_{-ht}\}\right)T(.)_t$$

$$K_{ht} \leq \overline{K}_h - L_{ht}.$$

Its control variables are the sequence of $\{c_{ht}, L_{ht}$ and $K_{ht}\}$. It treats the sequence $\{L_{-ht}\}$ as exogenous, which amounts to assuming an open-loop, Nash strategy in the lobby space.

It is slightly easier to use the transformation, $z_{ht} \equiv K_{ht-1}$, where z_{ht} can be interpreted as the productive resource use by h at the *beginning* of period t. The household problem can be restated as

$$\text{Maximize} \quad \sum_{t=0}^{\infty} \beta_h^t u(c_{ht})$$
$$c_{ht}, L_{ht}, z_{ht} \quad t=0$$

subject to

$$c_{ht} \leq (1-\tau)rz_{ht} + s_h\left(L_{ht}, \{L_{-ht}\}\right)T(.)_t \tag{4.3}$$

$$z_{ht+1} \leq \overline{K}_h - L_{ht}. \tag{4.4}$$

Given $u' > 0$, (4.3) and (4.4) will be satisfied with equality.

From the viewpoint of interpretation, it is important to observe that lobbying is similar to *negative investment*.[4] This is because an increase in lobbying, on one hand, increases a household's share in the total transfer and hence increases its current consumption, but, on the other hand, it decreases its future income and consumption by reducing the amount of the resource to be rented out for production.

The Euler equations of this constrained optimization are given by

$$\beta_h u'\left(c_{ht+1}\right)(1-\tau)r = u'\left(c_{ht}\right)s_{hh}(.)T(.)_t, \quad h = 1,\dots, H, \tag{4.5}$$

where $s_{hh}(.) \equiv \partial s_h(.)/\partial L_{ht}$. In view of the particular lobby function (4.2),

$$s_{hh}(.) = \frac{L_t - L_{ht}}{L_t^2}$$

and by definition, $T(.) = \tau r z_t$, where $z_t = \Sigma z_{ht}$.

Equation (4.5) is easy to interpret. A household lobbies to the point where the marginal loss in terms of future consumption (l.h.s. of (4.5)) equals the marginal benefit in terms of current consumption (r.h.s. of (4.5)).

Equations (4.3)–(4.5) describe the dynamics of the model. These are $3H$ equations containing $3H$ variables: c_{ht}, L_{ht} and z_{ht} for $h = 1,\ldots, H$. There are H initial conditions: $z_{h0} = \bar{z}_{h0}$ for $h = 1,\ldots, H$.

Steady state
In the steady state, equations (4.3)–(4.5) reduce to

$$c_h^* = (1-\tau)rz_h^* + \frac{L_h^*}{L^*}\tau r z^* \qquad (4.3^*)$$

$$z_h^* = \bar{K}_h - L_h^* \qquad (4.4^*)$$

$$\beta_h(1-\tau) = \frac{L^* - L_h^*}{L^{*2}}\tau z^*, \qquad (4.5^*)$$

where the asterisks denote the steady-state values.

A fundamental implication of (4.5*) is that for any two households, i and j,

$$\frac{\beta_i}{\beta_j} = \frac{L^* - L_i^*}{L^* - L_j^*}, \qquad (4.6)$$

so that $L_i^* > L_j^*$ if and only if $\beta_i < \beta_j$. In other words,

Proposition 4.1: Compared to any given household, a more impatient household lobbies more.

This is readily explained by noting that lobbying is analogous to negative investment. A more impatient household naturally engages in more negative investment or more lobbying.

If we denote the relative lobbying by household h, L_{ht}/L_t, by ℓ_{ht}, equation (4.6) can be directly solved to yield

$$\ell_h^* = 1 - \frac{(H-1)\beta_h}{H\bar{\beta}}, \qquad (4.6')$$

where $\bar{\beta} \equiv \Sigma\beta_h/H$ is the average discount factor. Hence

Proposition 4.2: The distribution of lobbying in relative terms across households is dependent only on the distribution of preferences.

Another implication is that

Proposition 4.3: Household ranking in terms of wealth and gross income may not be the same.

Proposition 4.3 follows since differential lobbying responses imply differences in gross income. Even if the endowments were identical, the less-patient household would earn less gross income as it lobbies more. Thus there will be income inequality even in the absence of any wealth inequality. Still another implication is that

Proposition 4.4: Household ranking in terms of gross and disposable incomes may not be the same.

This is because, while a less-patient household would tend to earn less gross income, it receives more transfer by lobbying more. It is interesting to note that in contrast to models of capital accumulation with heterogeneous households, such as Epstein and Hynes (1983), it is quite possible that a less-patient household may consume more in the steady state.

The general solution of the steady state is given by aggregating (4.4*) and (4.5*) over the households to obtain respectively

$$z^* = \overline{K} - L^* \tag{4.7}$$

$$H(1-\tau)\overline{\beta} = \frac{H-1}{L^*}\tau z^*. \tag{4.8}$$

Equations (4.7) and (4.8) determine L^* and z^*. Aggregate output is equal to rz^*. Given L^*, the individual lobbying levels are obtained from (4.6'). Equation (4.3*) then solves for the individual consumption levels. The solution of L^* and z^* is illustrated in Figure 4.1, in which AA and BB schedules represent equations (4.7) and (4.8) respectively. Clearly, the solution of the steady state is unique.

Various comparative statics can be done.[5] We note here only the one which would be relevant for understanding the source of oscillations.

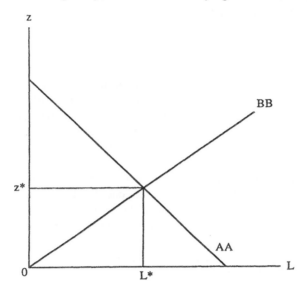

Figure 4.1   Steady state solution

Proposition 4.5: A change in the distribution of the resource across households (with the total amount of the resource unchanged) does not affect lobbying at the household or aggregate level and does not affect the aggregate output.

In other words, a change in the distribution of $\bar{K}_h$ with $\bar{K}$ unchanged does not affect L_h^* or z^*. It only affects resource use for production at the household level.

Local dynamics
It is shown that while household heterogeneity – implied by the heterogeneity in preferences – is not necessary to generate a nonmonotonic path of aggregate output in this model, it is a contributing factor on its own.[6]

To see this, consider for a moment the above model without household heterogeneity, that is, assume that β_h and $\bar{K}_h$ are the same across the households. In equilibrium, $c_{ht} = Q_t/H$. Accordingly, equations (4.3)–(4.5) would imply

$$\beta_h u'\left(rz_{t+1}/H\right)(1-\tau) = \frac{u'\left(rz_t/H\right)(H-1)\tau z_t}{\left(\bar{K}-z_{t+1}\right)H}. \qquad (4.9)$$

Equation (4.9) implicitly defines

$$z_{t+1} = f(z_t). \tag{4.9'}$$

The path of z_t is monotonic or fluctuating according to whether f' is positive or negative. By differentiating (4.9), it follows that f' is positive or negative according to whether the measure of relative risk aversion, $\eta \equiv -c_h u''(c_h)/u'(c_h)$, is greater or less than one. Thus, *without heterogeneity*, the time path of total lobbying and hence that of total output can be nonmonotonic. This happens if η is less than one.

It will be argued now that in the presence of heterogeneity an oscillating path of aggregate output can arise when η exceeds one. The local dynamics are characterized by the linearized versions of (4.3), (4.4) and (4.5). Totally differentiating these equations and noting that $\Sigma c_{ht} = r\Sigma z_{ht}$ at any t, we obtain

$$-\frac{\tau z^*}{L^*}\left(1-\ell_h^*\right)\tilde{z}_{ht+1} + \frac{\tau z^*}{L^*}\ell_h^*\sum_{j\neq h}\tilde{z}_{jt+1} = \frac{1}{r}\tilde{c}_{ht} - \left(1-\tau+\tau\ell_h^*\right)\tilde{z}_{ht} - \tau\ell_h^*\sum_{j\neq h}\tilde{z}_{jt},$$

$$h = 1,\ldots,H-1 \tag{4.10}$$

$$\sum_h \tilde{c}_{ht+1} - r\sum_h \tilde{z}_{ht+1} = 0, \ h = 1,\ldots,H \tag{4.11}$$

$$\xi_h \tilde{c}_{ht+1} + \frac{2}{L^*}\tilde{z}_{ht+1} + \sum_{j\neq h}\left(\frac{2}{L^*} - \frac{1}{L^*-L_h^*}\right)\tilde{z}_{jt+1}$$

$$= \xi_h \tilde{c}_{ht} - \frac{1}{z^*}\sum_h \tilde{z}_{ht} - \frac{1}{z^*}\sum_{j\neq h}\tilde{z}_{jt}, \ h = 1,\ldots,H, \tag{4.12}$$

where ξ_j is the measure of absolute risk aversion and '~' denotes the deviation from the respective steady state value. (By definition, the measures of relative and absolute risk aversion are related by $\eta_j = \xi_j c_j$.)

The system (4.10)–(4.12) can be written in the matrix form:

$$\mathbf{A}\mathbf{J}_{t+1} = \mathbf{B}\mathbf{J}_t, \text{ or } \mathbf{J}_{t+1} = \mathbf{M}\mathbf{J}_t,$$

where $\mathbf{J}_t \equiv [\tilde{c}_{1t},\ldots,\tilde{c}_{Ht},\tilde{z}_{1t},\ldots,\tilde{z}_{Ht}]'$ and $\mathbf{M} = \mathbf{A}^{-1}\mathbf{B}$. A unique perfect foresight solution path will exist if $\mathbf{M}$ has H non-zero (stable) roots whose moduli are less than one and $H-1$ (unstable) roots whose moduli exceed one.[7] Due to the high dimension of the model, a unique perfect foresight may not always exist with the restrictions imposed. As in Chapter 3, my objective is not to formally investigate the existence or the uniqueness issue, but to show the existence of oscillatory dynamics along a perfect foresight path.

Existence of oscillations

The rationale behind the existence of an oscillatory path lies again in some form of asymmetry, and here it is the asymmetric cross effect of lobbying by one household on the marginal effectiveness of lobbying by another at the equilibrium. This arises because of heterogeneity in the relative resource use in lobbying, ℓ_h^*, which, in turn, stems from heterogeneous rates of time preference.

The logic of the asymmetry is most clearly seen in the special case of a two-household economy. From (4.2), the marginal effectiveness of lobbying by household h is given by $s_{hh} = (L_t - L_{ht})/L_t^2$. In the two-household case, it reduces to $s_{11} = L_{2t}/(L_{1t} + L_{2t})^2$ and $s_{22} = L_{1t}/(L_{1t} + L_{2t})^2$. Now suppose that $\beta_1 > \beta_2$, so that in the steady state $L_1^* < L_2^*$. It is then easily derived that in the neighbourhood of the steady state $\partial s_{11}/\partial L_{2t} = (L_1^* - L_2^*)/L^{*3} < 0$ and $\partial s_{22}/\partial L_{1t} = (L_2^* - L_1^*)/L^{*3} > 0$. Hence there is an asymmetry precisely due to $L_1^* \neq L_2^*$. Although the more patient household lobbies less, the effectiveness of its lobbying *at the margin* is higher and it decreases as the other household lobbies more. Just the opposite happens to the marginal effectiveness of lobbying by the more impatient household as the more patient household intensifies its lobbying. If we call household 1 the 'patient' and household 2 the 'impatient' or 'Mr Hyper', then, in terms of the implicit reaction functions, it means that an increase in the lobbying by Mr Hyper induces the patient household to lobby less, whereas an increase in the lobbying by the patient household induces Mr Hyper to lobby more.

These opposing cross effects, if sufficiently strong, can reinforce each other sufficiently to generate an oscillatory time path of lobbying, productive resource use and aggregate output. It should be noted that the difference in lobbying along the steady state, that is, the difference in ℓ_h^* is due to the heterogeneity in the time preference, not due to difference in endowment (see Proposition 4.2). Hence heterogeneity in the time preference is the key.

In what follows, an extreme but simple numerical example of a two-household economy is constructed in which the steady-state configuration is such as to imply a unique, oscillatory time path of adjustment. As illustrations, two simulations are conducted: a permanent tax shock and a temporary productivity shock.

A two-household economy

Let the endowments and the discount factors be $\overline{K}_1 = \overline{K}_2 = 375$, $\beta_1 = 0.95$ and $\beta_2 = 0.05$. Thus household 1 is highly patient and household 2 highly impatient. Let the technological parameter be $r = 0.05$ and the tax rate be $\tau = 20$ per cent. Given these specifications, the steady state values can be solved as: $L_1^* = 7.5$, $L_2^* = 142.5$, $L^* = 150$, $z^* = 600$, $Q^* = rz^* = 30$, $c_1^* = 15$ and $c_2^* = 15$.

Finally, let the instantaneous utility function satisfy constant absolute risk aversion with $\xi_1 = \xi_2 = 1$. These values are chosen so as to rule out fluctuations in the *absence* of heterogeneity. It is because the implied measures of relative risk aversion in the steady state in this case exceed one: $\eta_1 = \xi_1 c_1^* > 1$ and $\eta_2 = \xi_2 c_2^* > 1$.

The local dynamics are characterized by (4.10)–(4.12) which, in this case, is a 4×4 system. The matrices $\mathbf{A}$ and $\mathbf{B}$ equal symbolically,

$$
\mathbf{A} = \begin{bmatrix}
0 & 0 & -\dfrac{L_2^* \tau z^*}{L^{*2}} & \dfrac{L_1^* \tau z^*}{L^{*2}} \\[2mm]
1 & 1 & -r & -r \\[2mm]
\xi_1 & 0 & \dfrac{2}{L^*} & \dfrac{L_2^* - L_1^*}{L^* L_2^*} \\[2mm]
0 & \xi_2 & \dfrac{L_1^* - L_2^*}{L^* L_1^*} & \dfrac{2}{L^*}
\end{bmatrix}
$$

$$
\mathbf{B} = \begin{bmatrix}
\dfrac{1}{r} & 0 & \tau - 1 - \ell_1^* \tau & -\ell_1^* \tau \\[2mm]
0 & 0 & 0 & 0 \\[2mm]
\xi_1 & 0 & -\dfrac{1}{z^*} & -\dfrac{1}{z^*} \\[2mm]
0 & \xi_2 & -\dfrac{1}{z^*} & -\dfrac{1}{z^*}
\end{bmatrix}.
$$

As it turns out, the roots are 0, 2.39, and $0.49 \pm 0.26i$. There are two initial conditions, and note that the two non-zero stable roots are complex conjugates. Thus, given that the system is out of the steady state initially, the adjustment path is unique and – importantly, for our purpose – oscillatory.

I now present the results of two simulations.

A permanent tax shock of $\tau = 17$ per cent to $\tau = 20$ per cent
The results of this simulation are graphed in Figures 4.2A–C for z_1, z_2, and the total output Q_t, equal to rz_t. A permanent tax increase implies more lobbying activities in the long run and hence less productive factor use by each household. Thus, initially, the productive factor use by each household declines. Also the response of household 2 – the impatient household – is greater in the initial periods, compared to household 1.

The oscillatory time paths of z_{1t}, z_{2t}, and the total output are confirmed by the nonmonotonic curves and their crossing of the horizontal axis – the steady state.

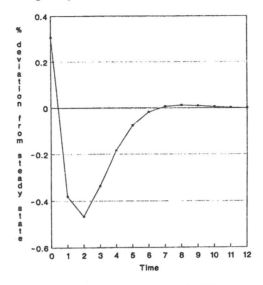

Figure 4.2A   Productive resource use by household 1: permanent tax increase from τ = 17 per cent to 20 per cent

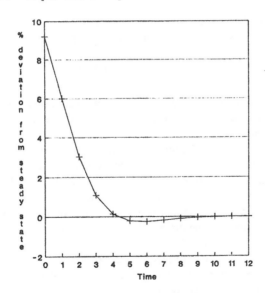

Figure 4.2B   Productive resource use by household 2: permanent tax increase from τ = 17 per cent to 20 per cent

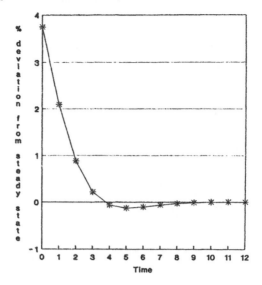

Figure 4.2C   Aggregate output: permanent tax increase from $\tau = 17$ *per cent to 20 per cent*

A temporary productivity shock of 1 per cent from r = 0.05

Consider now an AR(1) stochastic process of the productivity parameter r:

$$r_{t+1} = B + \sigma r_t + \varepsilon_{t+1},$$

where r_0 is given, $0 \leq \sigma < 1$ and ε_t's are i.i.d. with zero mean. It is a stationary process with the long-run average equal to $B/(1-\sigma)$. A temporary shock would constitute a change in r_0.

As in Chapter 3, the assumption of certainty equivalence is invoked here. In the two-household example, the augmented system would have five first-order difference equations with five variables z_{1t}, z_{2t}, c_{1t}, c_{2t} and r_t. Choosing B in the AR(1) process equal to $0.05(1-\sigma)$, so that the steady state r equals 0.05 as before, there are five eigen roots – the four roots in the nonstochastic model and σ. The dynamics are spanned by the three stable roots: the complex conjugates and σ.

This model was simulated for a temporary productivity shock of 1 per cent starting with $r = 0.05$. The parameter σ was chosen equal to 0.01, that is, there is almost zero persistence. The results are graphed in Figures 4.3A–C. The oscillatory time path is confirmed again.

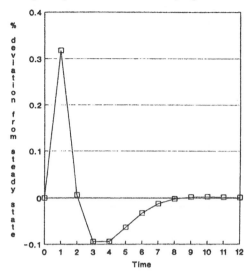

Figure 4.3A   Productive resource use by household 1: temporary productivity increase by 1 per cent, persistence parameter = 0.01

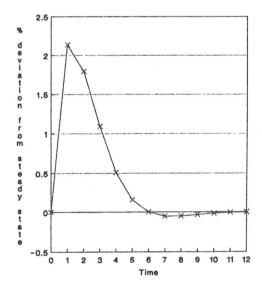

Figure 4.3B   Productive resource use by household 2: temporary productivity increase by 1 per cent, persistence parameter = 0.01

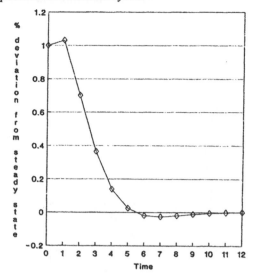

Figure 4.3C   Aggregate output: temporary productivity increase by 1 per cent, persistence parameter = 0.01

III A model of positive-sum lobbying and business cycles

In the previous model, lobbying was a zero-sum game in that all households were lobbying and the net gain to the lobbyists together was zero. In reality, there are households in the lower end of the wealth distribution – the 'poor' – who, because of equity concerns, are subsidized and do not pay taxes. Needless to say, they have little means to engage in lobbying activities. In this situation, lobbying by the tax-payers may not be a zero-sum activity. In the course of using influence activities in order to secure more (gross) transfer to themselves, the total amount of net transfer to the poor may also be affected. Thus, lobbying by an individual tax-payer would have a substitution effect of the kind explored in the previous model and may also have an *externality effect* of reducing the total net transfer to the poor or equivalently increasing the total transfer to the tax-payers as a group.

This idea is captured by specifying

$$s_{ht} = \frac{L_{ht}}{L_t} \tag{4.2}$$

$$T = BL_t^{\alpha}, \, B > 0, \, 0 < \alpha < 1, \tag{4.13}$$

where $h = 1, \ldots, H$ now denotes a tax paying household and T is the total gross transfer to the tax-payer group. Thus the total gross transfer to the tax-payers is a strictly concave, increasing function of total lobbying by the tax-payers. An individual tax-payer does not however internalize the effect of his lobbying on T.

Let the endowment and preference structure of tax-payers be the same as before. The endowment of the poor is not crucial at all. Hence, it is assumed that they have zero endowment, so their total consumption equals the total net transfer they receive, equal to $\tau Q_t - BL_t^\alpha$. The technology of production is described by (4.1) as before. This completes the description of the model.

The budget constraint of a tax-paying household now reads as

$$c_{ht} \leq (1-\tau)rz_{ht} + \frac{L_{ht}}{L_t}BL_t^\alpha, \tag{4.3'}$$

and the first-order condition of its optimization problem is an analogue of (4.5):

$$\beta_h u'\left(c_{ht+1}\right)(1-\tau)r = Bu'\left(c_{ht}\right)\left(\frac{L_t - L_{ht}}{L_t^2}\right)L_t^\alpha. \tag{4.5'}$$

Equations (4.3'), (4.4) and (4.5') describe the dynamics of this economy.

The steady state conditions are given by

$$c_h^* = (1-\tau)rz_h^* + BL_h^* L^{*\alpha-1} \tag{4.14}$$

$$z_h^* = \overline{K}_h - L_h^* \tag{4.4*}$$

$$\beta_h(1-\tau)r = B\left(L^* - L_h^*\right)L^{*\alpha-2}. \tag{4.15}$$

The steady state is similar to that of the previous model with one exception: Propositions 4.1–4.5 hold and the steady state is unique. However, it is not only the proportion of lobbying (L_h^*/L^*) which is independent of endowment; so is total lobbying. This is seen by summing (4.15) over h to obtain

$$L^* = \left\{\frac{(1-\tau)rH\overline{\beta}}{B(H-1)}\right\}^{1/(\alpha-1)},$$

which is independent of $\overline{K}$.

The local dynamics are dictated by the linearized versions of (4.3'), (4.4) and (4.5'):

$$\left[(1-\alpha)\ell_h^* - 1\right]\tilde{z}_{ht+1} + (1-\alpha)\ell_h^* \sum_{j\neq h} \tilde{z}_{jt+1} = \upsilon\tilde{c}_{ht} + \gamma\tilde{z}_{ht}, h=1,\ldots,H \quad (4.16)$$

$$\xi_h\tilde{c}_{ht+1} + \frac{2-\alpha}{L^*}\tilde{z}_{ht+1} + \sum_{j\neq h}\left(\frac{2-\alpha}{L^*} - \frac{1}{L^* - L_j^*}\right)\tilde{z}_{jt+1} = \xi_h\tilde{c}_{ht}, h=1,\ldots,H, \quad (4.17)$$

where $\upsilon \equiv L^{*1-\alpha}/B$ and $\gamma \equiv -(1-\tau)r\upsilon$.

The existence of an oscillatory adjustment path rests basically on the same ground – asymmetric cross effect of lobbying by one tax-payer on the marginal effectiveness of lobbying by another arising due to heterogeneous time preference. However, the heterogeneity in time preference is in a sense a stronger factor in generating the oscillatory path compared to the previous model in that, unlike in the latter, a nonmonotonic path cannot arise in this model without heterogeneity.

The argument proceeds as follows. If all tax-paying households were alike, equations (4.3'), (4.4) and (4.5') would reduce to

$$z_{t+1} = \overline{K} - \left\{\frac{c_t - (1-\tau)rz_t}{B}\right\}^{1/\alpha} \quad (4.18)$$

$$\theta u'(c_{t+1}/H) = \frac{u'(c_t/H)}{(\overline{K} - z_{t+1})^{1-\alpha}}, \quad (4.19)$$

where $\theta \equiv \beta_h(1-\tau)rH/[B(H-1)]$. Equations (4.18) and (4.19) implicitly define

$$z_{t+1} = g(z_t, c_t), \ g_z > 0, \ g_c < 0 \quad (4.20)$$

$$c_{t+1} = f(z_{t+1}, c_t), \ f_z < 0, \ f_c > 0. \quad (4.21)$$

Substituting the $g(.)$ function in $f(.)$,

$$c_{t+1} = \phi(z_t, c_t), \ \phi_z = f_z g_z < 0, \ \phi_c = f_z g_c + f_c > 0. \quad (4.22)$$

Equations (4.20) and (4.22) determine the dynamics of z_t and c_t. It is easy to check that both roots of this system are real and positive. Thus, if a solution path exists, it must be monotonic.

Hence, unlike in the previous model, household heterogeneity is a necessary factor in generating a nonmonotonic path of the aggregate output.

A two-household model economy

Consider a similar example as in section II. Let the resource endowments and time preferences by $\bar{K}_1 = \bar{K}_2 = 200$, $\beta_1 = 0.95$ and $\beta_2 = 0.10$. Let the tax rate be 30 per cent. The technological parameters are $r = 0.10$ in the production function, and $B = 0.50$ and $\alpha = 0.50$ in the lobby function. The instantaneous utility function satisfies constant absolute risk aversion with $\xi_1 = \xi_2 = 3$.

Given this configuration, the steady-state values can be solved as : $L^* = 46$, $z^* = 354$, $z_1^* = 196$, $z_2^* = 158$, $c_1^* = 14.01$ and $c_2^* = 14.15$. (An interesting feature of this example is that the less-patient household consumes more.) The net taxes paid by households 1 and 2 are 5.54 and 1.67 respectively. The poor households as a group consume 7.21.

The eigen roots of the system (4.16)–(4.17) turn out to be $1.95 \pm (0.23)i$ and $0.68 \pm (0.11)i$. So there are two stable roots and they are complex conjugates. Hence, this economy exhibits a unique oscillatory adjustment path to the steady state.

IV   A model of endogenous tax rate

Consider now an economy consisting of tax-paying households and a fringe of non-tax-paying poor households. Unlike in the previous models, the tax rate is influenced by the lobbying efforts of tax-paying households, tax-paying households' preferences are alike, and moreover, there is no lag in production but a lag in the impact of lobbying on the tax rate. Let

$$\tau_{t+1} = f\left(L_{1t} + \dots + L_{ht} + \dots + L_{Ht}\right) \equiv f(L_t), \ f' < 0 < f'', \quad (4.23)$$

be the tax rate function.[8] Thus, an increase in total lobbying reduces the tax rate in the next period and $f'' > 0$ reflects diminishing returns in lobbying. Let the productivity parameter, r, be unity. A tax-paying household's disposable income at t then equals $(1-\tau_t)(\bar{K}_h - L_{ht})$. Letting β denote the common rate of time preference, its optimization problem is to:

$$\text{Maximize} \sum_{t=0}^{\infty} \beta^t (1-\tau_t)(\bar{K}_h - L_{ht})$$

subject to (4.23) and the initial condition that τ_0 is given. As before, an open-loop, Nash-strategy is assumed. The Euler equations for this problem are:

$$\beta(\bar{K}_h - L_{ht+1}) f'(L_t) = -(1-\tau_t), \ h = 1,\dots, H. \quad (4.24')$$

Thus, a household chooses optimal lobbying such that the marginal benefit from lobbying in terms of future consumption (l.h.s. of (4.24')) equals the marginal sacrifice in terms of current consumption (r.h.s. of (4.24')).

Summing (4.24') over the tax-paying households,

$$\beta\left(\overline{K} - L_{t+1}\right)f'\left(L_t\right) = -\left(1 - \tau_t\right)H,$$

or

$$L_{t+1} = \overline{K} + \frac{1 - \tau_t}{\hat{\beta}f'\left(L_t\right)}, \tag{4.24}$$

where $\hat{\beta} \equiv \beta/H$. Equations (4.23) and (4.24) govern the dynamics. The steady state is defined by

$$\tau^* = f\left(L^*\right) \tag{4.23*}$$

$$\hat{\beta}\left(\overline{K} - L^*\right)f'\left(L^*\right) = -\left(1 - \tau^*\right).^9 \tag{4.24*}$$

Linearizing (4.23) and (4.24) around the steady state, the local dynamics are described by $\mathbf{J}_{t+1} = \mathbf{M}\mathbf{J}_t$, where $\mathbf{J}_t = [\tau_t - \tau^*, L_t - L^*]'$ and

$$\mathbf{M} = \begin{bmatrix} 0 & f' \\ -\dfrac{1}{\hat{\beta}f'} & -\dfrac{\left(1 - \tau^*\right)f''}{\hat{\beta}(f')^2} \end{bmatrix},$$

where the derivatives are evaluated at the steady state. It is seen that the determinant of $\mathbf{M}$ (the product of the roots) is positive, and the sum of the diagonal elements (the sum of eigen roots) is negative. Hence, if the roots are real – which is necessary for the existence of a solution, since there is only one initial condition – they are both negative. In other words, *if a unique perfect foresight path exists, it must be fluctuating over time.* The presumption of a nonmonotonic path of total output is thus strongest in this model among the three models considered in the chapter.

Recall that the tax-payers in this model are homogeneous units. Hence the source of fluctuation is something other than heterogeneous time preference. Specifically, it is the negative impact of L_t on L_{t+1} (that is, $-(1-\tau^*)f''/[\hat{\beta}(f')^2] < 0$) which implies a fluctuating time path of the adjustment process. The economic reasoning behind this is contained in the Euler equation (4.24'). An increase in lobbying in period $t+1$ tends to reduce the gross income or the tax base in period $t+1$. This reduces the marginal benefit from lobbying in period t (as lobbying in period t affects net income in period $t+1$) and induces a household to lobby less. Hence, in the aggregate, more lobbying at $t+1$ is associated with less lobbying at t.

Example The only function that needs to be specified is $f(L_t)$. Let

$$f(L_t) = \frac{1}{1+L_t}.$$

Let $\beta = 0.95$, $H = 100$ and $\bar{K} = 500$. The steady state is the solution to the following equations:

$$\tau^* = \frac{1}{1+L^*}; \qquad -0.095\left[\frac{500 - L^*}{\left(1+L^*\right)^2}\right] = -\left(1 - \tau^*\right).$$

The explicit solutions are $\tau^* = 37$ per cent and $L^* = 1.73$. The matrix $\mathbf{M}$ equals

$$\mathbf{M} = \begin{bmatrix} 0 & -0.13 \\ 785.89 & -364.71 \end{bmatrix},$$

which has two roots: -0.29 and -364.42. Thus, there is exactly one stable root, -0.29. Hence the adjustment path to the steady state is unique. The solution path of L_t is $L_t = 1.73 + (2.16) (\tau_0 - 0.37)(-0.29)^t$. The total output equals $Q_t = \bar{K} - L_t = 498.27 - (2.16) (\tau_0 - 0.37) (-0.29)^t$. The stable root being negative, a shock in endowment, preference or lobby technology would generate a fluctuating time path of total output according to the above solution equation.

V Concluding remarks

This chapter has presented three models linking household heterogeneity to business cycles through the political market. The analysis is, however, much different from the political business-cycle theory. The standard political business-cycle models emphasize variation in output due to the incentive of the incumbent politicians or political parties to engage in more liberal macro policies near election times. Election or some form of voting is typically the medium through which households or voters and the politicians are interdependent. Apart from household heterogeneity, the distinguishing features of the models explored in this chapter are that households actively influence the behaviour of politicians through lobbying, and the variation of output stems from the fact that lobbying requires real resources which can be otherwise used for directly productive activities.

It is interesting that the implications of lobbying for economic growth have been a subject of recent research. The models of this chapter relate lobbying to business cycles rather than growth, and emphasize how household hetero-geneity contributes to business cycles through lobbying with regard to distributive policies.

The requirement of real resources in lobbying implies that in an economy in which factor endowments are exogenous, output can still vary as factor use for production varies. In such an economy, given the tax rate and given that the tax-paying households lobby to secure a larger share in the redistribution of the tax proceeds, if the tax-paying households have unequal rates of time preference, their supply of lobbying would be different, implying an asymmetric cross effect of lobbying by one household on the marginal effectiveness of lobbying by another. This asymmetry, if sufficiently strong, can produce oscillatory dynamic paths of lobbying and output. Even when the tax-paying households' preferences are alike, a fluctuating time path of total lobbying and output emerges in so far as lobbying is directed toward reducing the future tax rate.

Nonmonotonicity of aggregate output results in the presence of distortions such as distortionary taxes, imperfect political markets and some rigidity either in the technology of production or in the lobbying technology.

In closing, may I remark that in reality the dynamics of changes in redistributive policies are probably significantly slower than those of standard macro variables. The models and the logic behind oscillations should therefore be judged in the light of changes over long periods rather than from one quarter or year to the next.

Notes

1. The model is similar to the story of inequality, lobbying and aggregate fluctuation in Brock (1991).
2. More generally, one could think of a lagged effect of s_{ht-1} on s_{ht}, which would capture a stock effect of lobbying on the transfers.
3. A slightly more general function will be

$$s_{ht} = \frac{L_{ht}^{\gamma}}{\sum_h L_{ht}^{\gamma}}$$

where $0 < \gamma \le 1$.

4. Of course, the difference is that investment adds to a stock, while the effect of lobbying in this model is a one-time loss of future consumption.
5. For example, an increase in the total endowment increases aggregate output as well as total lobbying. An increase in the tax rate shifts the *BB* curve out and results in more lobbying and less aggregate output.

6. In the positive-sum lobbying model in the next section, heterogeneity in preferences is necessary to generate a nonmonotonic path of the aggregate output.
7. This is because one of the roots of this system is always zero, implied by (4.11) which is *not* a difference equation.
8. More generally, τ_{t+1} could be made dependent on τ_t also.
9. Equations (4.23*) and (4.24*) respectively generate a decreasing and an increasing locus between τ^* and L^*. Hence these loci cannot intersect more than once and the steady state is uniquely determined at the intersection point.

5   Firm heterogeneity and business cycles

I   Introduction

In Chapters 3 and 4, household heterogeneity was portrayed as a factor contributing to business cycles. This chapter, as the title suggests, concerns the role
of firm heterogeneity. As noted in Chapter 1, there already exists some literature
attempting to establish that firms of different sizes respond differently to
common shocks, suggesting that firm heterogeneity may be important in understanding the impact of various shocks on output and employment. My objective
here is beyond this -- namely, to argue that firm heterogeneity itself may
contribute to an oscillatory or a fluctuating dynamic path of industry output. Two
models are explored. In each model firm heterogeneity is represented by the
difference in the marginal cost of production. In the first model the market
structure is oligopolistic, the discount rate is variable and there is no entry and
exit. The output dynamics result from adjustment cost in changing output from
the previous period. In the second model, firms operate in a competitive market
(although the analysis can be easily extended to a monopolistically competitive
market), the discount rate is constant and there is no adjustment cost of the above
type. The dynamics arise from simultaneous entry and exit of firms, as in an
industry evolution model.

II   An oligopoly model with heterogeneous firms and adjustment costs

Consider an industry with n firms producing a homogeneous good in an
oligopoly market. Let

$$p_t = A x_t^{-\varepsilon} = A \left(\sum_j^n x_{jt} \right)^{-\varepsilon}$$

be the inverse demand function facing the industry, where $x_t \equiv$ the industry output
at t, $x_{jt} \equiv$ the output of firm j at t, and $1/\varepsilon \equiv$ the (constant) price elasticity of
demand. Each firm faces a constant but different marginal cost of production,
c_j. There is no entry or exit.

There are adjustment costs in the variation of output from the previous
period, given by

$$\frac{1}{2} m \left(x_{jt} - x_{jt-1} \right)^2, \ m > 0.$$

These costs may arise from adjusting to variation in employment (Sargent, 1979) or to a different plant size or equipment. The instantaneous profit of firm j is equal to

$$\pi_{jt} = \left(Ax_t^{-\varepsilon} - c_j\right)x_{jt} - \frac{1}{2}m\left(x_{jt} - x_{jt-1}\right)^2. \qquad (5.1)$$

The presence of the adjustment costs makes the decision-making by firms dynamic.

A critical assumption is that different firms may face different discount factors, β_j. In the theory of the firm it is common to assume that the discount rate facing the firms is constant. But this is more on the grounds of simplicity and tractability than realism. Firm owners care eventually about their consumption. It is natural that different agents with different levels of consumption and utility may weigh the future differently. An important paper by Uzawa (1968) proposes that the discount *factor* (inverse of the discount *rate*) may be an increasing function of utility from consumption. In the case of a risk-neutral firm, this translates into a discount factor function which is nondecreasing in profits:

$$\beta_j = \beta\left(\pi_{jt}\right). \qquad (5.2)$$

I assume a discount factor function such as (5.2). This would presume that firms face an imperfect capital market.

For simplicity, I assume further that (5.2) is a stepwise rather than a smoothly increasing function in π_{jt}, as shown in Figure 5.1. There is no empirical evidence to guide which type of a discount factor function may be preferable, and *a priori*, a stepwise function appears as plausible as a smoothly increasing function.

The optimization problem facing firm j is to

$$\text{Maximize } \sum_{t=1}^{\infty} \prod_{s=0}^{t} \beta\left(\pi_{js}\right)\pi_{jt},$$

with respect to x_{jt} for $t \geq 1$, subject to x_{j0} being given, where Π is the product function. The $\beta(.)$ function not being smooth, it is complicated to write all the necessary optimality conditions. But this is not needed if we restrict ourselves to local dynamics around the steady state and presume for technical convenience that each firm's profit in the steady state corresponds to the interior of a flat portion of the $\beta(.)$ function.

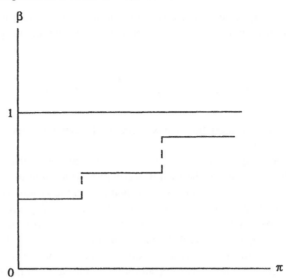

Figure 5.1. β(.) *function*

Assuming an open-loop, Nash strategy in output and noting that β_j's are constant in the neighbourhood of the steady state, the first order conditions (the Euler equations) are:

$$Ax_t^{-\varepsilon}\left(1-\frac{\varepsilon x_{jt}}{x_t}\right) - c_j - m\left(x_{jt} - x_{jt-1}\right) + \beta_j m\left(x_{jt+1} - x_{jt}\right) = 0 \quad (5.3)$$

or

$$r_j\left(x_{jt}, \{x_{-jt}\}\right) - c_j - m\left(x_{jt} - x_{jt-1}\right) + \beta_j m\left(x_{jt+1} - x_{jt}\right) = 0, \quad (5.3')$$

where

$$r_j(.) \equiv Ax_t^{-\varepsilon}\left(1-\frac{\varepsilon x_{jt}}{x_t}\right)$$

is the marginal revenue of firm j and $\{x_{-jt}\}$ stands for the vector of outputs by all other firms.

Steady State
It is evident that in the steady state

$$Ax_t^{*-\varepsilon}\left(1 - \frac{\varepsilon x_j^*}{x^*}\right) = c_j, \qquad (5.3*)$$

which is a static rule saying that marginal revenue equals marginal cost. (Asterisks denote steady state values.) Adjustment costs matter only during the periods of adjustment to the steady state.

Given model specifications, it is straightforward to obtain explicit analytical solution of the steady state. Summing (5.3*) over the firms solves for the industry output:

$$x^* = \left[\frac{\sum c_j}{A(n - \varepsilon)}\right]^{-1/\varepsilon}.$$

For a positive solution, it is necessary that $\varepsilon < n$, that is, the price elasticity is greater than the inverse of the number of firms. Given x^*, p^* is solved from the inverse demand function. From (5.3*), the market shares are equal to $s_j^* = (1 - c_j/p^*)/\varepsilon$. Finally, individual outputs are solved from the industry output and market shares. It is easy to prove that, compared to any given firm, a more efficient firm produces more and earns higher profit. There is a non-positive correlation between c_j on one hand and π_j^* or β_j on the other.

I assume that the support of the distribution of c_j is not too small, so that in the steady state there are at least two firms whose profits correspond to two levels of β in Figure 5.1.

Local dynamics and the existence of oscillations
Specifically, I show that heterogeneity in efficiency cannot by itself produce oscillatory outcome but, together with heterogeneity in discount factor or rate of time preference, it can.

Suppose, contrary to the model, β_j's were constant and the same for all firms, equal to $\bar{\beta}$, but c_j's were still different. Then equation (5.3) can be aggregated over firms to obtain

$$Ax_t^{-\varepsilon}(n - \varepsilon) - \sum c_j - m(x_t - x_{t-1}) + \bar{\beta}m(x_{t+1} - x_t) = 0. \qquad (5.4)$$

This is a second-order difference equation in the industry output. It is straightforward to deduce that the linearized version of this equation has two roots, both of which are real and positive and one of them is less than one. Hence a unique perfect foresight path exists and it is monotonic. Thus oscillation or non-monotonicity does not arise just because firms are heterogeneous in efficiency.

However, given that β_j is variable, equation (5.3) cannot be aggregated, and the distribution of firms influences the industry output. There are asymmetric cross effects, which are necessary, and, if strong enough, sufficient for generating oscillatory paths.

To see this, I first express equation (5.3) in terms of a system of first-order equations. Define $y_{jt+1} \equiv x_{jt+1} - x_{jt}$. Substituting this into (5.3),

$$r_j\left(x_{jt}, \left\{x_{-jt}\right\}\right) - c_j - my_{jt} + \beta_j my_{jt+1} = 0. \tag{5.5}$$

This, together with

$$y_{jt+1} = x_{jt+1} - x_{jt}, \tag{5.6}$$

constitutes $2n$ first-order difference equations with $2n$ variables: x_{jt} and y_{jt} for $j = 1, 2, ..., n$.

Differentiating (5.5) and (5.6) and solving for x_{jt+1} and y_{jt+1}, the local dynamics are expressed as

$$\tilde{x}_{jt+1} = \left(1 - \frac{r_{jj}}{\beta_j^* m}\right)\tilde{x}_{jt} - \left(\sum_{h \neq j}^{n} \frac{r_{jh}}{\beta_j^* m}\right)\tilde{x}_{ht} + \frac{1}{\beta_j^*}\tilde{y}_{jt} \tag{5.7}$$

$$\tilde{y}_{jt+1} = -\left(\frac{r_{jj}}{\beta_j^* m}\right)\tilde{x}_{jt} - \left(\sum_{h \neq j}^{n} \frac{r_{jh}}{\beta_j^* m}\right)\tilde{x}_{ht} + \frac{1}{\beta_j^*}\tilde{y}_{jt}, \tag{5.8}$$

where '~' marks the respective deviation from steady state and r_{jh} is the partial of r_j with respect to x_{ht}.[1] Evaluated at the steady state,

$$r_{jj} = -\frac{p^*\varepsilon}{x^*}\left[2 - (1+\varepsilon)s_j^*\right]; \quad r_{jh} = -\frac{p^*\varepsilon}{x^*}\left[1 - (1+\varepsilon)s_j^*\right]. \tag{5.9}$$

The system (5.7) and (5.8) can be expressed in the matrix form

$$\mathbf{J}_{t+1} = \mathbf{M}\mathbf{J}_t, \tag{5.10}$$

where $\mathbf{J}_t \equiv [\tilde{x}_{1t}, ..., \tilde{x}_{nt}, \tilde{y}_{1t}, ..., \tilde{y}_{nt}]'$.

The asymmetries are implicit in the 'reaction functions' – that is, in the sign and magnitude of r_{jh}, $j \neq h$, which captures the effect of output by firm h at t on the output of firm j at $t+1$ in (5.7). They can best be illustrated in a duopoly example with $\varepsilon = 1$. Let $c_1 < c_2$, so that $x_1^* > x_2^*$. Consider first the marginal revenue of firm 1. In view of (5.9), $r_{12} = A(x_1^* - x_2^*)/(x_1^* + x_2^*)^3 > 0$ and $r_{21} = -A(x_1^* - x_2^*)/(x_1^* + x_2^*)^3 < 0$. In other words, an increase in the output of the less efficient firm tends to have a positive impact on the output of the more efficient firm in the next period, whereas an increase in the output of the more efficient firm tends to have a negative impact on the output of the less efficient firm in the next period. These dynamic reaction functions or lagged cross effects are depicted in Figure 5.2, which, similar to Figure 2.1, ignores the own effects. The asymmetry – which is necessary for oscillatory dynamics – is indicated by the opposite slopes of x_{1t+1} and x_{2t+1} curves around the steady state.

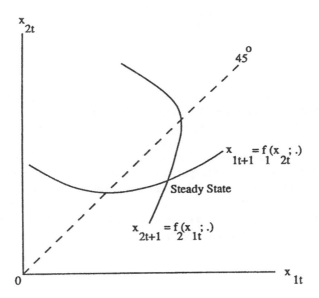

Figure 5.2 Asymmetric cross effects when $\varepsilon = 1$

Before I present a numerical example, it is noteworthy that the asymmetric cross effects will not be present, despite heterogeneity, if the market demand function were linear. Because, in this case, both r_{12} and r_{21} will be negative. Hence, a nonlinear demand function is also a part of the necessary environment in which firm heterogeneity is capable of producing oscillatory dynamics of the industry output.

A numerical example

Consider a duopoly in which $c_1 = 1$ and $c_2 = 10$, that is, firm 1 is more efficient than firm 2. Let $A = 3000$ and $\varepsilon = 0.91$. The steady state outputs and profits are solved as $x_1^* = 516.88$, $x_2^* = 5.21$, $\pi_1^* = 4699$ and $\pi_2^* = 0.48$. We can also interpret firm 1 and firm 2 as the large firm and the small firm respectively. Let the $\beta(.)$ function be such that $\beta_1^* = \beta(4699) = 0.95$ and $\beta_2^* = \beta(0.48) = 0.30$. Finally, let the adjustment coefficient be $m = 0.50$. The matrix $\mathbf{M}$ equals

$$
\mathbf{M} = \begin{bmatrix}
1 - \dfrac{r_{11}^*}{\beta_1^*} & \dfrac{r_{12}^*}{\beta_1^* m} & \dfrac{1}{\beta_1^*} & 0 \\[2ex]
-\dfrac{r_{21}^*}{\beta_2^* m} & 1 - \dfrac{r_{22}^*}{\beta_2^* m} & 0 & \dfrac{1}{\beta_2^*} \\[2ex]
-\dfrac{r_{11}^*}{\beta_1^* m} & -\dfrac{r_{12}^*}{\beta_1^* m} & \dfrac{1}{\beta_1^*} & 0 \\[2ex]
-\dfrac{r_{21}^*}{\beta_2^* m} & -\dfrac{r_{22}^*}{\beta_2^* m} & 0 & \dfrac{1}{\beta_2^*}
\end{bmatrix},
$$

and its roots are equal to 3.65, 1.14 and $0.91 \pm (0.07)i$. Thus there are two stable roots ensuring the existence of a unique perfect foresight path. Moreover, the stable roots being complex conjugates, an external shock can initiate an oscillatory dynamic adjustment path to the steady state.

For illustration, a permanent demand shock from $A = 2900$ to $A = 3000$ was simulated. The time paths of output by individual firms and the industry output are graphed in Figures 5.3A–5.3C. It is interesting how differently the large firm and the small firm react to the command demand shock. In particular, the oscillatory dynamics of industry output is confirmed in Figure 5.3C (by the crossing of the curve with the x-axis).

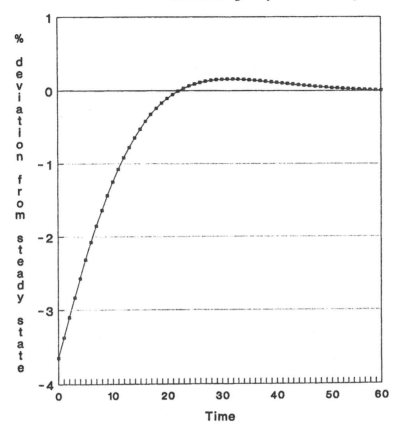

Figure 5.3A   Output of firm 1: permanent demand shock, A = 2900 to 3000

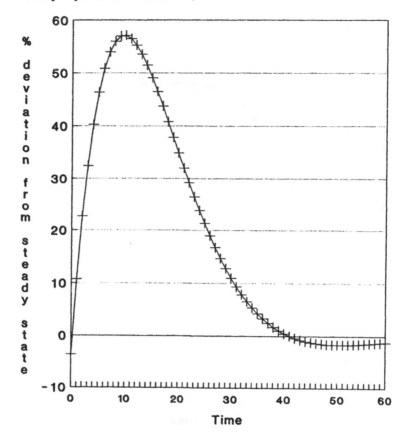

Figure 5.3B   Output of firm 2: permanent demand shock, A = 2900 to 3000

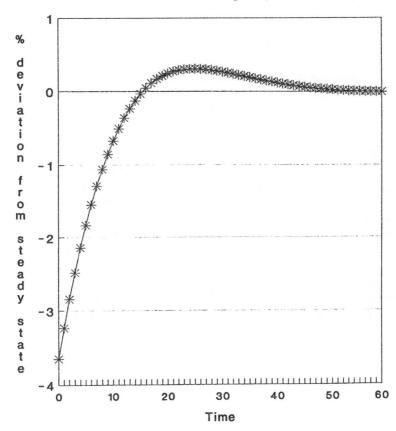

Figure 5.3C   Industry output: permanent demand shock, A = 2900 to 3000

III   An industry evolution model with simultaneous entry and exit

In the field of industrial organization, firm heterogeneity is an integral feature of a recent, fast-growing literature which is concerned with how firms and industry evolve over time as a system, for example, Jovanovic (1982), Dunne, Roberts and Samuelson (1988), Ericson and Pakes (1989), Pakes and Ericson (1990), Lambson (1991) and Das and Das (1991).

The industry evolution process is a very complex phenomenon. There is entry and exit of firms, and entry and exit may take place simultaneously.[2] There can be firm dynamics in the form of investment in capital, R&D activity or some form of passive or active learning (as in Jovanovic, 1982, or Ericson and Pakes, 1989). Moreover, there are inherent uncertainties facing firms regarding the evolution of their costs, outcome of R&D and market conditions. All these are potentially important determinates of the industry evolution process. In what follows, a simple heterogeneous-firm industry evolution model is developed, similar to Das and Das (1991), in which there is entry and exit of firms but no firm dynamics except for the randomness in the evolution of costs.[3] It is shown that a fluctuating pattern of industry output over time may emerge if firms are sufficiently heterogeneous. Thus firm heterogeneity shows up again as a contributing factor in the business-cycle phenomenon.

The Model

Consider a perfectly competitive industry with increasing marginal cost. The marginal cost function varies across firms. Let it be of the form, $bx + (1/2)c_j x^2$, b, $c_j > 0$, where x is the output and c_j may be different across firms. For simplicity, assume that c_j take two possible values, c_H and c_L with $c_H < c_L$. Firms experiencing c_H are the high-efficiency (H-) firms and those experiencing c_L are the low-efficiency (L-) firms. It is presumed that c_L is sufficiently larger than c_H (to be made precise later). Firms however face uncertainty over time regarding their marginal cost. There is a positive probability that an H-firm (L-firm) at t may become an L-firm (H-firm) at $t+1$. It is supposed that c_j follows a discrete, first-order Markov process with the transition probabilities given by

$$
\begin{array}{ccc}
 & \text{At } t+1 & \\
 & c_H & c_L \\
c_H & \rho & 1-\rho \\
\text{At } t & & \\
c_L & 1-\rho & \rho
\end{array}
\qquad (5.11)
$$

where $0.5 \leq \rho < 1$. If $\rho = 0.5$, it means that there is no persistence in the evolution of the marginal cost, while $\rho > 0.5$ indicates some persistence or firm-specific effects. The case of $\rho = 0.5$ may be treated as a benchmark case – not from an empirical perspective but in that it illustrates in the most extreme fashion the role of randomness in costs in the industry evolution process.

Moreover, it is assumed that any entry process takes one period. If there is entry, the entrants face the distribution (c_H, c_L: 0.5, 0.5) in the next period when production begins. It would imply that the potential entrants do not include plants built by the existing firms; they are totally 'new' to the industry. Data indicates that this is by far the most significant type of entry as relative to existing firms entering through the construction of new plants or through changes in the mix of outputs they produce in their existing plants (see Dunne *et al.*, 1988, p. 504).

Instantaneous equilibrium

It is assumed that firms discover their type at the beginning of each period. A firm j of type i (which stays) maximizes $\pi_{ji} = p_t x_{jt} - b x_{jt} - (1/2) c_i x^2_{jt}$, taking p_t as given. The optimal outputs equal $(p_t - b)/c_H$ and $(p_t - b)/c_L$ for H- and L-firms respectively. The reduced-form profit expressions are:

$$\pi_H = \frac{(p_t - b)^2}{2c_H}, \quad \pi_L = \frac{(p_t - b)^2}{2c_L}. \tag{5.12}$$

Denoting the number of firms of each type by n_{Ht} and n_{Lt}, the total quantity supplied at t equals $X_t = (p_t - b)(n_{Ht}/c_H + n_{Lt}/c_L)$. Assuming a linear market demand function, $D_t = \alpha - p_t$, we can explicitly solve p_t as

$$p_t = \frac{\alpha + b(n_{Ht}/c_H + n_{Lt}/c_L)}{1 + n_{Ht}/c_H + n_{Lt}/c_L} \equiv p(n_{Ht}, n_{Lt}). \tag{5.13}$$

One particular property of the $p(.)$ function which will be used later is:

$$\frac{\partial p_t / \partial n_{Ht}}{\partial p_t / \partial n_{Lt}} = \frac{c_L}{c_H} > 1. \tag{5.13'}$$

Entry and exit processes and the industry dynamics

It is assumed that during any period t, events follow this sequence:

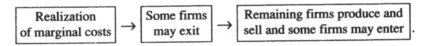

As mentioned before, the entry process takes one period. Let the sunk cost per entry have a fixed component, k, and a variable component proportional to the number of entrants, mn_{Wt}, where $m > 0$ and n_{wt} is the number of entrants.[4] If there is entry, the entry equilibrium is given by the value of an entering firm, v_{Wt}, being equal to the sunk cost per entry:

$$v_{Wt} = k + mn_{Wt}. \tag{5.14}$$

In view of the transition probability matrix (5.11), the values of existing and entering firms are given by the following Bellman equations:

$$v_{Ht} = \pi_{Ht} + \beta[\rho \max(s, v_{Ht+1}) + (1-\rho) \max(s, v_{Lt+1})] \tag{5.15a}$$

$$v_{Lt} = \pi_{Lt} + \beta\left[\rho \max(s, v_{Lt+1}) + (1-\rho)\max(s, v_{Ht+1})\right] \quad (5.15b)$$

$$v_{Wt} = \beta\left[(0.5)\max(s, v_{Lt+1}) + (0.5)\max(s, v_{Ht+1})\right], \quad (5.15c)$$

where β is the common, constant discount factor and s is the opportunity cost of being in the industry net of exit costs if any. Heterogeneity in β would introduce a further element of heterogeneity of firms but would complicate the model considerably. It is shown that output fluctuation can arise even in the absence of differences in β. It is also assumed that the opportunity cost is the same for all firms and strictly positive.

There are four possible paths regarding entry and exit: (a) no entry or exit; (b) no entry but exit; (c) entry but no exit; and (d) entry and exit.[5] However, we will be concerned with local dynamics around the steady state.

Along a steady state, the size of the industry – the total number of firms – is constant, implying that the rate of entry must equal the rate of exit. There are then two possibilities: either these rates are both zero or both positive. Since the model is meant to emphasize entry and exit, it will be natural to analyse dynamics around the steady state with positive entry and exit. Hence, effectively, we deal with the dynamics of case (d).

As long as there is some exit, we need to differentiate between (i) the exit rate being 'moderate' in the sense that some of the L-firms quit and all of the H-firms stay, and (ii) the exit rate being 'too high' in that not only all L-firms quit (i.e., $n_L(t) = 0$), but so do some of the H-firms. In case (i), the exit equilibrium is given by

$$v_{Ht} > s$$

$$v_{Lt} = s, \quad (5.16)$$

the rationale being that before any exit takes place, v_{Lt} is less than the opportunity cost s and thus some L-firms are motivated to quit and in equilibrium the value of being an L-firm just equals the opportunity cost. Since all H-firms stay, v_{Ht} must exceed s. Similarly, in case (ii), the exit equilibrium is given by $v_{Ht} = s$. It is, however, easy to see that too high an exit rate is inconsistent with entry, because otherwise it means that an entering firm can at best earn the opportunity cost and so there will be no motivation to enter and incur the sunk cost of entry. Thus it follows that entry is consistent only with moderate exit – that is, only some of the L-firms quit. Equation (5.16) is then the relevant exit equilibrium condition.

Since there is entry, equation (5.14) holds also. Morever, using (5.16), equations (5.15a)–(5.15c) reduce to

$$v_{Ht} = \pi_{Ht} + \beta\left[\rho v_{Ht+1} + (1-\rho)s\right] \qquad (5.17)$$

$$s = \pi_{Lt} + \beta\left[(1-\rho)v_{Ht+1} + \rho s\right] \qquad (5.18)$$

$$v_{Wt} = \frac{\beta}{2}\left[v_{Ht+1} + s\right]. \qquad (5.19)$$

Lastly, because no high-efficiency firms quit, the number of high-efficiency firms is a state variable. It evolves according to

$$n_{Ht+1} = \rho n_{Ht} + (1-\rho)n_{Lt} + \frac{1}{2}n_{Wt}.^{6} \qquad (5.20)$$

Equations (5.14) and (5.17)–(5.20) govern the industry dynamics.[7] These are five first-order difference equations in five variables: v_{Ht}, v_{Wt}, n_{Ht}, n_{Lt} and n_{Wt}. There is one initial condition, n_{H0}.

Before proceeding further, it is noteworthy that the model predicts an empirically testable hypothesis that *the rate of entry is procyclical.*[8] The proof is as follows. In equilibrium, (a) the industry output, X_t, and market price, p_t, are negatively related by the market demand curve; (b) p_t and π_{Lt} are positively related (see (5.12)); (c) π_{Lt} and v_{Ht+1} are negatively related (see (5.18)); (d) v_{Ht+1} and v_{Wt} are positively related (see (5.19)); and (e) v_{Wt} and n_{Wt} are positively related (see (5.14)). The chain from (a) to (e) implies that X_t and n_{Wt} are positively correlated.[9]

I now simplify the system by using the expressions (5.12) and (5.13). First, by using (5.12), equations (5.17) and (5.18) solve for v_{Ht+1}:

$$v_{Ht+1} = -\frac{1}{\beta z}v_{Ht} + \frac{\eta(1-\beta\rho) + \beta(1-\rho)}{\beta z}s \equiv g(v_{Ht}), \qquad (5.21)$$

where $\eta \equiv c_L/c_H > 1$ and $z \equiv \eta(1-\rho) - \rho$. Next we substitute (5.21) into (5.19) and use (5.14) to eliminate v_{Wt}, and obtain

$$n_{Wt} = -\frac{k}{m} - \frac{1}{2zm}v_{Ht} + \left[\frac{\eta(1-\beta\rho) + \beta(1-\rho)}{2zm} + \frac{\beta}{2m}\right]s \equiv n_W(v_{Ht}). \quad (5.22)$$

Moreover, in view of (5.12), (5.13) and (5.21), equation (5.18) can be rewritten as

$$(1-\beta\rho)s = \frac{\left[p(n_{Ht}, n_{Lt}) - b\right]^2}{2c_L} - (1-\rho)\left[\frac{1}{z}v_{Ht} - \frac{\eta(1-\beta\rho) + \beta(1-\rho)}{z}s\right],$$

which implicitly defines

$$n_{Lt} = n_L\left(\underset{?}{v_{Ht}}, \underset{-}{n_{Ht}}\right).$$ (5.23)

Finally, if we substitute (5.22) and (5.23) into (5.20), then

$$n_{Ht+1} = \rho n_{Ht} + (1-\rho)n_L(v_{Ht}, n_{Ht}) + \frac{1}{2}n_W(v_{Ht}) \equiv h(v_{Ht}, n_{Ht}).$$ (5.24)

Equations (5.21) and (5.24) are two first-order difference equations in two variables, v_{Ht} and n_{Ht}.

Steady state, local dynamics and the existence of fluctuation
The steady state values can be explicitly solved. From equation (5.21),

$$v_H^* = \frac{\eta(1-\beta\rho) + \beta(1-\rho)}{1 + \beta z}s.$$ (5.21*)

Given v_H^*, n_W^* is solved from (5.22), and equations (5.23) and (5.24) reduce to

$$n_L^* = n_L\left(v_H^*, n_H^*\right)$$ (5.23*)

$$(1-\rho)n_H^* = (1-\rho)n_L^* + \frac{1}{2}n_W^*.$$ (5.24*)

Given v_H^*, these equations solve for n_H^* and n_L^*.

The local dynamics around the steady state are dependent crucially on the sign and magnitude of the eigen roots of (5.21) and (5.24). Since the system is recursive, the eigen roots are equal to the diagonal elements of the Jacobian. Denoting the partials by subscripts, the expressions for the eigen roots are:

$$g_v = -\frac{1}{\beta z} = \frac{1}{\beta[\rho - \eta(1-\rho)]}$$

$$h_n = \rho + (1-\rho)\frac{\partial n_{Lt}}{\partial n_{Ht}} = \rho + (1-\rho)\left[-\frac{\partial p / \partial n_{Ht}}{\partial p / \partial n_{Lt}}\right] = \rho - \eta(1-\rho),\ \text{using (5.13').}$$

Since there is one initial condition, n_{H0}, a unique perfect foresight path exists if and only if either $|g_v| < 1$ or $|h_n| < 1$ but not both. Particularly, the path is fluctuating if the stable root is negative. Hence, we take a closer look at the sign and magnitude of g_v and h_n. Figure 5.4 depicts g_v and h_n as functions of ρ. Recall that $0.5 \leq \rho < 1$, and $\eta > 1$ as $c_L > c_H$. Let η be 'sufficiently large' or equivalently H- and L-firms be 'sufficiently heterogeneous' such that

$$\frac{2}{\beta(\eta - 1)} < 1. \tag{5.25}$$

Then it readily follows that $0 > g_v|_{\rho = 0.5} = -2/[\beta(\eta-1)] > -1$ and $h_n|_{\rho = 0.5} < -1$, and g_v and h_n schedules are as shown in Figure 5.4. (The scales of horizontal and vertical axes are different.) From Figure 5.4, it can be inferred that

A. $0.5 \leq \rho < \dfrac{\eta - 1/\beta}{\eta + 1}$ $\Rightarrow -1 < g_v < 0, h_n < -1$ $\Rightarrow$ unique fluctuating path

B. $\dfrac{\eta - 1/\beta}{\eta + 1} < \rho < \dfrac{\eta - 1}{\eta + 1}$ $\Rightarrow g_v, h_n < -1$ $\Rightarrow$ no perfect foresight path

C. $\dfrac{\eta - 1}{\eta + 1} < \rho < \dfrac{\eta}{\eta + 1}$ $\Rightarrow g_v < -1, -1 < h_n < 0$ $\Rightarrow$ unique fluctuating path

D. $\rho > \dfrac{\eta}{\eta + 1}$ $\Rightarrow g_v > 1, 0 < h_n < 1$ $\Rightarrow$ unique monotonic path.

Thus fluctuating dynamics can arise. If C is true, then (5.19) implies that there is an instantaneous adjustment of v_{Ht} to its steady state as $|g_v| > 1$. In view of (5.17) and (5.18), the current profits also jump instantly to their steady state and remain constant. Since current profits are unique functions of p_t, and industry output in equilibrium is a unique function of p_t (via the demand curve facing the industry), the price as well as the industry output adjust immediately to their steady state values and remain constant. However, h_n being negative, the number of H-firms and that of L-firms fluctuate over time. In sum, the composition of firms within the industry fluctuates but the total industry output does not.

However if the parametric configuration A is true, g_v is the stable root implying that the value function follows a fluctuating time path. Accordingly, instantaneous profits, price and industry output fluctuate. (The composition of firms fluctuates as well.) As a numerical example, suppose that $\beta = 0.95$, and $\eta = 5$, that is, the slope coefficient of the marginal cost function of an L-firm

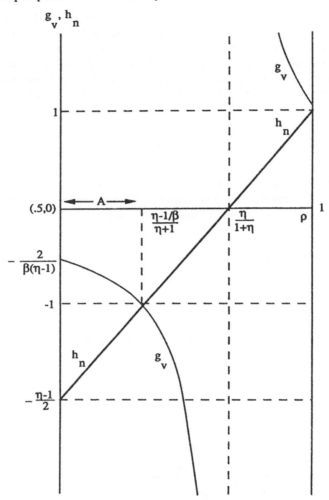

Figure 5.4   Eigen root functions

is five times as high as that of an *H*-firm It is easy to verify that the condition
(5.25) is met and configuration A holds as long as the persistence parameter,
ρ, does not exceed 0.65. From the perspective of the business cycle, this is the
main result: industry output may follow a fluctuating time path. The parametric
configuration A reflects the following general conditions under which this
happens: (a) firms are sufficiently heterogenous ((5.25) holds); and (b) firm-
specific effects or persistence in the evolution of costs are not too strong (i.e.,
$\rho - 0.5$ is not too high).

Intuition

There is, however, no one-line explanation for industry output fluctuation in this model. I have said in the preface that being an outsider to macro economic research has been of some advantage. Let me say that being a trade theorist in particular has helped me in acquiring the intuition here. I will proceed in a roundabout way which I think is useful. In trade theory, there is a theorem in the Heckscher–Ohlin trade model called the 'Rybczinski Theorem', which is a source of many a paradox. It goes as follows. Suppose there are two sectors, say 1 and 2, in a small open economy. Both sectors require two factors, say labour and capital, in production. Assume that the factor coefficients, a_{L1}, a_{K1}, a_{L2} and a_{K2} are given. (L and K denote labour and capital, and the constancy of factor coefficients follows from the country being small, perfect competition and constant returns to scale.) Assuming further that both factors are fully employed and their endowments fixed (at $\bar{L}$ and $\bar{K}$), we can write the full employment conditions as

$$a_{L1}Q_1 + a_{L2}Q_2 = \bar{L}$$

$$a_{K1}Q_1 + a_{K2}Q_2 = \bar{K},$$

where Q_i is the output of sector i. If factor proportions are different between the two sectors, i.e., if $a_{L1}/a_{K1} \neq a_{L2}/a_{K2}$, then the Rybczinski Theorem states that an increase in the endowment of one factor, say labour, leads to an increase in the output of one (labour-intensive) sector but reduces the output of the other sector. This is a paradox because both sectors use labour, yet the output of one sector falls as labour endowment increases. However, you can sense the paradox if you just look at the full employment equation for capital and realize that if the coefficients are fixed and $\bar{K}$ is given, both outputs cannot increase. The paradox arises because (a) factor intensities are *heterogeneous* across sectors, and (b) the increase in labour endowment has to be consistent with full-employment condition of labour *as well as* that of capital.

Our model of industry evolution has similar features. Turning to equations (5.17) and (5.18), it is seen that the evolutions of instantaneous profits and the value function are interdependent and must be consistent with each other, just as the two outputs in the Heckscher–Ohlin model are interdependent and must satisfy the full employment conditions of both factors. Assume for the moment that $\rho = 0.5$, so that equations (5.17) and (5.18) reduce respectively to

$$v_{Ht} = \pi_{Ht} + \frac{\beta}{2}\left(v_{Ht+1} + s\right) \tag{5.17'}$$

$$s = \pi_{Lt} + \frac{\beta}{2}\left(v_{Ht+1} + s\right). \tag{5.18'}$$

Consider now an increase in v_{Ht}. How does it affect v_{Ht+1}? Suppose that v_{Ht+1} increases. Then equation (5.18') implies that π_{Lt} must decrease by the amount $\beta\Delta/2$ where Δ is the magnitude of the increase in v_{Ht+1}. But in view of (5.12), π_{Ht} and π_{Lt} are related by $\pi_{Ht} = \pi_{Lt}c_L/c_H$ – which is an artefact of firm heterogeneity. Thus a decrease in π_{Lt} must be accompanied by a greater decrease in π_{Ht} since $c_L > c_H$. To summarize, if v_{Ht+1} increases by Δ, then π_{Ht} must decrease by more than $\beta\Delta/2$, implying that $\pi_{Ht} + (\beta/2)v_{Ht+1}$ must decrease. In view of (5.17') then, v_{Ht} must decrease. But this is a contradiction as we began with an increase in v_{Ht}. By continuity, the same argument holds if $\rho > 0.5$ but $\rho - 0.5$ is not too large. Hence, paradoxically, an increase in the current value, v_{Ht}, has a negative impact on the future value, v_{Ht+1} if ρ is not too much higher than 0.5. This negative relation implies that v_{Ht} follows a fluctuating path of adjustment.[10] In view of equation (5.18) which shows a one-to-one relationship between v_{Ht+1} and π_{Lt}, it follows that the latter follows a fluctuating time path too. π_{Lt} and p_t are uniquely related by definition, and industry output and p_t are uniquely related via the industry demand curve. Thus it follows that the industry output obeys a fluctuating path over time.

Apart from the difference between ρ and 0.5 being not too large, the key behind this result lies in firm heterogeneity reflected in the difference between c_L and c_H, just as the difference in sectorial factor intensities is critical in generating the Rybczinski Theorem.

IV   Concluding remarks

In contrast to household heterogeneity in earlier chapters, in this chapter I have attempted to develop the notion that firm heterogeneity may also contribute to business cycles. I have developed two models of firm and industry dynamics in the presence of heterogeneous firms. Firm heterogeneity basically stems from the difference in the marginal cost of production. In the first model, the dynamics are based on adjustment costs in production – which is a technological imperfection. There is no entry or exit of firms, the discount rates facing the firms are variable, firms operate in an oligopoly market and the market demand curve is nonlinear. The critical asymmetry leading to the emergence of oscillatory dynamics arises from the asymmetric effect of one firm's output on another's marginal revenue – or, equivalently, asymmetric reaction functions of firms – in an oligopoly market with nonlinear demand curve. In the second model, the industry dynamics are based on simultaneous entry and exit and evolution of the marginal cost. Fluctuations in industry output arise if the difference in the marginal cost across firms is sufficiently large and the evolution of the marginal cost is not too persistent. Finally, it may be remarked that the generalization of industry output in partial equilibrium to business cycles in terms of aggregate output in general equilibrium would presume that shocks are common to most important sectors of an economy, not sector-specific, and that the demands for output produced in different sectors are positively correlated.

Notes

1. $\bar{y}_j$'s are zero in the steady state.
2. An interesting and seemingly counter-intuitive empirical evidence is that the rates of entry and exit are positive correlated over time as well as across industries (see Dunne *et al.*, 1988).
3. The emphasis in Das and Das (1991) is in explaining the observed positive correlation between entry and exit, although fluctuations also arise in their model. The difference between the model below and Das and Das lies in the assumptions on the market structure and the form of the entry cost function.
4. This would capture the costs of resources needed for initial set-up which are imperfectly elastic in supply. They increase as the number of entrants increases. These costs are also present in Ericson and Pakes (1989), for example.
5. Equations and conditions governing each of these possibilities are outlined in Das and Das (1991).
6. It is presumed that there is no aggregate uncertainty.
7. It is assumed that s is high enough so that there is no liquidity constraint facing the L-firms. Otherwise, as shown in Das and Das (1991), the industry dynamics follow a different set of equations.
8. I am grateful to Nobuhiro Kiyotaki for asking whether or not the model predicts entry to be procyclical.
9. The model, however, does not provide a clear prediction as to whether the rate of exit is pro- or counter-cyclical. The rate of exit has a complex expression: $[(1-\rho)n_{Ht-1} + \rho n_{Lt-1} + (1/2)n_{Wt-1}] - n_{Lt}$, where the term in the square brackets equals the total number of L-firms at the beginning of period t. It may very well vary directly or inversely with X_t.
10. Technically, equations (5.17') and (5.18') solve for p_t and v_{Ht+1} in terms of v_{Ht}, and it can be easily derived that $\partial v_{Ht+1} / \partial v_{Ht} < 0$. This result can also be shown graphically by representing these equations in the (p_t, v_{Ht+1}) space.

6 Inequality, heterogeneity and business cycles via aggregate demand

I Introduction

In the business-cycle models explored in Chapters 3, 4 and 5, the variation in aggregate output stemmed basically from the supply side of an economy: through changes in the aggregate capital stock available to the economy by household savings in Chapter 3; through changes in the utilization rate of available resources in productive activity in Chapter 4; and through firm and industry dynamics in Chapter 5. The demand side did not play any active role in influencing the dynamic path of the aggregate output. In this chapter I return to household heterogeneity and inequality, and explore how they can affect aggregate demand and thereby contribute towards fluctuations in the aggregate output. Of course, some form of nominal rigidity must be present for the aggregate demand to influence the aggregate output.

The history of thought in business cycles has a conspicuous slot allocated to the so-called underconsumption theories – a particular strand of which emphasizes how economic inequality affects aggregate demand and thereby may affect aggregate output. As outlined in Chapter 1, the story goes as follows. Economic inequities build up during an upturn of a business-cycle. Since the rich typically have a lower propensity to consume than the poor, a more unequal distribution of income lowers aggregate demand and results in less output in equilibrium. This is how a market economy moves from an upturn to a downturn.

The story seems plausible but, needless to say, grossly incomplete and imprecise. For example, it does not spell out any specific mechanism of how inequities grow as the economy expands or what the sources of inequities are. Even more serious, it is blank on how an economy may move from a downturn to an upturn. Perhaps this explains in part why this strand of the underconsumption theory is mentioned but never taken seriously in modern business-cycle analysis. The objective of this chapter is to pursue this old idea (as they say, old ideas are seldom dead or irrelevant) and provide fully articulated models of business cycle based on it – showing how household inequality in wealth and income may change over time and how the economy may proceed through ups and downs. Specifically, the models of this chapter attempt to demonstrate that it is the heterogeneity in preferences together with household participation in the equity market which constitutes the missing component in the underconsumption theory of business cycles narrated above.

This chapter presents two Keynesian models of business cycles having one commodity market and two asset markets, money and equity. The first one, developed in section II, has some features of a vintage Keynesian model, such as a perfectly competitive market structure, no foresight or static expectations and an extreme form of nominal wage rigidity. The presumption of oscillation hinges on the following asymmetric cross effects: inequality has a negative lagged impact on aggregate output – the underconsumption argument – while an increase in the aggregate output has a positive lagged impact on inequality through participation in the equity market. The second model, developed in section III, is more, but not fully, micro-founded. It assumes a monopolistically competitive product market structure, rational expectations, nominal price rigidity and stochastic components in preference and technology. Interestingly, the asymmetric cross effects capable of producing oscillation in this model are just the opposite of those in the previous model: inequality has a positive lagged impact on aggregate output – the opposite of the underconsumption argument – while an increase in the aggregate output has a negative lagged impact on inequality.

Before getting into the models, however, I must mention that with heterogeneous household behaviour and three markets (apart from the labour market), the models become too complicated to accommodate explicit dynamic optimization problems facing the households and at the same time possess reasonable tractability. Hence, in particular, the asset demand functions will be directly posited rather than derived from first principles (see, for example, Lucas, 1975). This is, however, no more restrictive than directly specifying the aggregate demand function in many stochastic macro models currently in use.[1,2]

II   A Keynesian model with static expectations and nominal wage rigidity

The supply side
This model assumes an extreme form of nominal rigidity: nominal wages are exogenous and constant over time. Thus it abstracts from wage dynamics. Let $W_t = 1$ for all t. The output is produced by labour and other fixed inputs. There is a one-period lag between labour employed and output, that is, $Q_{t+1} = \bar{F}(L_t)$. Firms are identical, perfectly competitive and they maximize $_tP_{t+1}.Q_{t+1} - L_t$ subject to the production function, where $_tP_{t+1}$ is the price level at $t+1$ expected as of t.[3] (The model is nonstochastic in the sense that the primitives of the economy – technology and preference parameters – are given and known to all agents.) Static expectations imply that $_tP_{t+1} = P_t$. This leads to an upward-sloping aggregate supply function of the form:

$$Q_{t+1} = F(P_t), \; F' > 0. \tag{6.1}$$

There are two assets in the economy, money and equities. The total endowment of each asset is given.

Household budget constraint

Consider a two-household economy and let household 1 be thriftier than household 2. A household's budget constraint at time t reads as

$$c_{ht} + p_{zt}Z_{ht+1} + \frac{M_{ht+1}}{P_t} \leq y_{ht} + p_{zt}Z_{ht} + \frac{M_{ht}}{P_t}, \quad h = 1, 2,$$

where, at t, $c_{ht} \equiv$ the real consumption of household h, $Z_{ht} \equiv$ its initial holding of the number of equity certificates, $M_{ht} \equiv$ its initial holding of money, $y_{ht} \equiv$ its real income, and $p_{zt} \equiv$ the real price of equity. Thus a household allocates the sum of its current income and wealth to current consumption and the next period's holding of wealth.

A household's income consists of labour earnings and dividend payments. It is assumed that there is no income effect on demand for leisure and that the preference for leisure is alike for both households. Hence it is reasonable to suppose that, at the going wage rate, both households work the same number of hours. Thus the labour earnings of household h are equal to $L_t/(2P_t)$ in real terms.

The dividend income equals $r_t Z_{ht}$, where r_t is the real dividend per equity. For notational simplicity, we normalize the total endowment of equity certificates to one. Let $r_t = Q_t - L_t/P_t =$ the total profit or profit per equity in real terms; then $y_{ht} = L_t/(2P_t) + r_t Z_{ht}$.

Asset demand functions

Given that there are three markets that clear, we may focus on any two of them. I choose the two asset markets. In general, the quantity demanded of any asset would be governed by the substitution effect (that is, rates of return on competing assets), the income effect and the wealth effect. But as it turns out, the income effect is not crucial in generating oscillations in this model and hence is ignored here for simplicity. (The model in the following section allows for income effects.) Denoting the rate of return on equity by ρ_{zt}, I specify:

Money demand functions:

$$\frac{M_{ht+1}}{P_t} = \upsilon + \eta(\rho_{zt})\left(p_{zt}Z_{ht} + \frac{M_{ht}}{P_t} \right), \quad 0 < \eta(.) < 1; \; \eta' < 0 \tag{6.2}$$

Equity demand functions:

$$P_{zt}Z_{1t+1} = \varphi + \alpha\beta(\rho_{zt})P_{zt}Z_{1t}, \ \varphi > 0, \ \alpha > 1, \ 0 < \alpha\beta < 1, \ \beta' > 0 \quad (6.3a)$$

$$P_{zt}Z_{2t+1} = \varphi + \beta(\rho_{zt})P_{zt}Z_{2t}.^{4} \quad (6.3b)$$

Several remarks on these demand functions are in order:

(a) Apart from the income effect being ignored for simplicity, the money demand function is standard. It increases with wealth and decreases with the rate of return on equity. Expectations being static, $_tP_{t+1} = P_t$. Thus the (gross) return on holding money is one and hence ignored in the asset demand functions.

(b) Turning to the equity demand functions, the parameter α (> 1) for household 1 captures that household 1 is thriftier. This is where household heterogeneity in preference comes in. Of course, preference heterogeneity can be present in the money demand function as well. But as will be seen, it is the change in the distribution of equity, not that of money holding, which interacts with the commodity market to cause oscillation. Hence I choose to represent heterogeneity in the equity demand function only.

(c) Given that the distribution of money holding is not crucial, its role is isolated by eliminating the real balance effect from the equity demand function. Consequently, the evolution of the distribution of money is essentially determined by equation (6.2). It does not affect the evolution of other variables in the system.

(d) The positive sign of the constant φ can be interpreted as a proxy for the income effect which is treated as exogenous here.

(e) Finally, expectations being static, there are no expected capital gains or losses, and thus $\rho_{zt} = 1 + r_t/p_{zt} = 1 + (Q_t - L_t/P_t)/p_{zt}$.

Instantaneous equilibrium
Instantaneous equilibrium is characterized by the clearing of money and equity markets:

$$\frac{\overline{M}}{P_t} \equiv m_t = 2\upsilon + \eta(\rho_{zt})\left(P_{zt} + \frac{\overline{M}}{P_t}\right) \quad (6.4)$$

$$1 = \frac{2\varphi}{P_{zt}} + \beta(\rho_{zt})(\alpha Z_{1t} + Z_{2t}), \quad (6.5)$$

where equations (6.2) and (6.3) are aggregated over the households and $\bar{M}$ is the total money stock in the economy. Recall that the total supply of equities is normalized to unity so that $Z_{1t} + Z_{2t} = 1$. Equations (6.4) and (6.5) determine two endogenous variables, P_t and p_{zt}, and implicitly define:

$$P_t = P\left(\underset{-}{Z_{1t}}, \underset{?}{Q_t}\right) \tag{6.6}$$

$$p_{zt} = P_z\left(\underset{?}{Z_{1t}}, \underset{+}{Q_t}\right).^5 \tag{6.7}$$

The signs of the partials, $\partial P_t / \partial Z_{1t}$ and $\partial p_{zt} / \partial Q_t$, will be central to understanding why oscillations may arise.

The sign of $\partial P_t / \partial Z_{1t}$ essentially contains the underconsumption argument. An increase in Z_{1t}, *ceteris paribus*, means a more unequal distribution of wealth and income (in the neighbourhood of the steady state). Since the rich are thriftier and have a lower propensity to consume, it implies a fall in the aggregate demand and in the price level. Thus $\partial P_t / \partial Z_{1t} < 0$. The fall in the aggregate demand would imply a decrease in the future output via (6.1).

An increase in Q_t increases current dividends, and under static expectations, it raises expected dividends and rate of return on equity. The real demand for equity thus increases, leading to an increase in the real price of equities. Hence $\partial p_{zt} / \partial Q_t > 0$.

Dynamics of the system
There are essentially three state variables in the system: Z_{1t}, Q_t and M_{1t}. First, if we substitute (6.5) into (6.3a), then, in view of (6.7), we may write

$$Z_{1t+1} = \frac{\varphi}{p_{zt}} + \left(1 - \frac{2\varphi}{p_{zt}}\right)\frac{\alpha Z_{1t}}{(\alpha - 1)Z_{1t} + 1} \equiv f_1\left(\underset{?}{Z_{1t}}, \underset{+}{Q_t}\right). \tag{6.8}$$

Next, substituting (6.6) into (6.1), the dynamics of the aggregate output can be written in the implicit form:

$$Q_{t+1} = f_2\left(\underset{-}{Z_{1t}}, \underset{?}{Q_t}\right). \tag{6.9}$$

Equations (6.8) and (6.9) are central to the dynamics of the system and determine the paths of Z_{1t} and Q_t. There are two initial conditions: Z_{10} and Q_0 are given.

As said earlier, since the money demand functions are assumed to be the same across households and the real balance effect is suppressed in the equity demand functions, the total stock of money, and not its distribution, affects the dynamics of Z_{1t} and Q_t.[6]

Steady state
In the steady state, equations (6.8) and (6.9) reduce to

$$Z_1^* = f_1\left(Z_1^*, Q^*\right); \quad Q^* = f_2\left(Z_1^*, Q^*\right), \qquad \text{(6.8*), (6.9*)}$$

which determine Z_1^* and Q^*.[7] The steady state values are marked by asterisks. The steady state versions of (6.6) and (6.7) then solve for P^* and p_z^*.

An expected implication is that in the steady state the thriftier household holds more equity and money, and obtains higher income. This is seen by obtaining (6.3a*) and (6.3b*) below from (6.3a) and (6.3b),

$$[1-\alpha\beta(.)]Z_1^* = \frac{\varphi}{p_z^*}; \quad [1-\beta(.)]Z_2^* = \frac{\varphi}{p_z^*} \qquad \text{(6.3a*), (6.3b*)}$$

and dividing (6.3a*) by (6.3b*) to get

$$Z_1^* = \frac{1-\beta(.)}{1-\alpha\beta(.)} Z_2^* > Z_2^* \ (\text{since } \alpha > 1). \qquad \text{(6.10)}$$

Thus household 1 holds more equity. Holding more equities implies more dividend income and hence higher income. It also implies more holding of money due to the wealth effect in the money demand function. We may then call household 1 'rich' and household 2 'poor'.

Local dynamics and the presence of oscillations
The local dynamics of the system are governed by the linearized version of (6.8) and (6.9) around the steady state:

$$\begin{bmatrix} Z_{1t+1} & -Z_1^* \\ Q_{t+1} & -Q^* \end{bmatrix} = \begin{bmatrix} f_{1Z} & f_{1Q} \\ f_{2Z} & f_{2Q} \end{bmatrix} \begin{bmatrix} Z_{1t} & -Z_1^* \\ Q_t & -Q^* \end{bmatrix}, \qquad \text{(6.11)}$$

where

$$f_{1Z} = \frac{\alpha\left(1 - 2\varphi / p_z^*\right)}{\left[(\alpha-1)Z_1^* + 1\right]^2} + \frac{\varphi\left[(\alpha+1)Z_1^* - 1\right]}{(\alpha-1)Z_1^* + 1}\frac{dp_{zt}}{dZ_{1t}} \gtreqless 0$$

$$f_{1Q} = \frac{\varphi\left[(\alpha+1)Z_1^* - 1\right]}{(\alpha-1)Z_1^* + 1}\frac{dp_{zt}}{dQ_t} > 0$$

$$f_{2Z} = F'\left(P^*\right)\frac{dP_t}{dZ_{1t}} < 0$$

$$f_{2Q} = F'\left(P^*\right)\frac{dP_t}{dQ_t} \gtreqless 0.$$

It is immediately seen that the cross effects, f_{1Q} and f_{2Z}, are opposite in sign, and parameter configurations can exist such that the oscillation condition, $4f_{1Q}$ $f_{2Z} + (f_{1Z}f_{2Q})^2 < 0$ is met. f_{2Z} being negative is a statement of the underconsumption argument that an increase in inequality has a negative impact on aggregate output. f_{1Q} being positive means that an increase in output has a positive impact on inequality. It is to be noted that the impact of a change in output on inequality is the missing component in the underconsumption theory. Ignoring

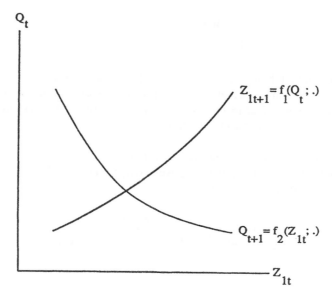

Figure 6.1   Asymmetric cross effects in the static expectations model

the own effects, these asymmetric cross effects or the dynamic reaction functions – which are the key behind oscillatory dynamics – are shown in Figure 6.1.

The rationale behind oscillatory dynamics therefore lies in why $f_{1Q} > 0$ and $f_{2Z} < 0$. An increase in the current output increases the current and the expected (real) return from equity and hence increases the demand for equity by both the rich and the poor. The price of equity increases. But it tends to reduce the quantity of equity demanded by both. The net impact on the allocation of equities is thus determined by the magnitudes of the initial demand shifts. Since the rich household has a higher propensity to accumulate equity than the poor, the initial shift in demand by the rich is greater, and therefore, the rich household ends up being the net purchaser of equity from the poor. Hence f_{1Q} is positive. The economics of $f_{2Z} < 0$ is more straightforward. We have already seen that greater economic inequality causes the price level to fall. This in turn tends to reduce future output through the aggregate supply function (6.1).

An example

I now present an example in which local oscillation arises. Let the production function be such that the elasticity of labour demand with respect to the real wage is constant, equal to μ, that is, let

$$Q_{t+1} = \begin{cases} 0 & \text{if } L_t = 0 \\ A + \dfrac{B}{1-1/\mu} L_t^{1-1/\mu} & \text{if } L_t > 0. \end{cases}$$

The implied labour demand function is: $L_t = (BP_t)^{\mu}$ and the aggregate supply function is:

$$Q_{t+1} = \begin{cases} 0 & \text{if } L_t = 0 \\ A + \dfrac{B^{\mu}}{1-1/\mu} P_t^{\mu-1} & \text{if } L_t > 0. \end{cases}$$

Let $\beta(.)$ and $\eta(.)$ functions be specified as

$$\beta(.) = \beta_z \left(\frac{1 + r_t / p_{zt}}{k_z + 1 + r_t / p_{zt}} \right)^{a_z} ; \quad \eta(.) = \eta_m \left(1 + r_t / p_{zt} \right)^{-a_m},$$

where $0 < \beta_z, \eta_m \leq 1$; $k_z > 0$; $a_z, a_m > 0$. These restrictions preserve the correct signs of $\beta'(.)$ and $\eta'(.)$ and moreover ensure that $\beta(.)$ and $\eta(.)$ are both less than unity.

If we choose the parametric values $A = 10$, $B = 1$, $\mu = 0.60$, $\alpha = 12$, $\beta_z = 0.20$, $\eta_m = 1$, $a_z = 2$, $a_m = 0.01$, $k_z = 5$, $\upsilon = 5.099$, $\varphi = 0.046$ and $\bar{M} = 527.86$, it turns out that in the steady state, $r^* = 7.5$, $Z_1^* = 0.95$, $Z_2^* = 0.05$, $P^* = p_z^* = 1$, $Q^* = 8.50$, and most importantly, the roots of the dynamic system (6.11) are complex conjugates, $-0.45 \pm (0.67)i$, whose modulus is less than one. Hence the system exhibits damped oscillation following a shock.

III   A rational expectations model with price rigidity

The model of this section departs from the previous model in several ways. First, there is nominal (product) price rigidity together with an increasing supply curve of labour instead of wage rigidity and infinite elasticity of labour supply. Moreover, the price rigidity is partial; in other words, price is not totally rigid over time. One rationale for using price rigidity rather than wage rigidity is the argument that the former is consistent with the empirical observation that real wages may be procyclical, while the latter is not (see McCallum, 1989, p. 197). Of course, there are competing micro models of price rigidity (or wage rigidity, – various contract theories, menu cost argument and so on – all of which are micro-based to some extent and explain some notion of rigidity. However, none of them is free from some valid criticism (see Blanchard and Fisher, 1989, ch. 9). Hence the criterion for choosing a particular notion of rigidity should, it seems, rest on the ease or simplicity with which such a notion can be integrated into the model or issues at hand. One model that seems to meet this criterion and hence is used below is due to Rotemberg (1982, 1987).

Second, the model assumes a monopolistically competitive product market structure. Third, there is no lag in production. Fourth, the model is stochastic; there are stochastic components in the production function, tastes and monetary endowment. Since my objective all along is to emphasize the internal mechanism, stochastic processes are kept deliberately simple. Each stochastic term is assumed to be i.i.d. (although allowing for AR processes is straightforward). In each period, demand and supply decisions are made after the realization of the stochastic terms. Fifth and last, expectations are rational.

The objective is to show the existence of an oscillatory time path of adjustment of the expected output. The models in the previous chapters were all real and hence real shocks were simulated to generate time paths. Money being present in the current model, I present simulation results for a (temporary) monetary shock.

Market structure and consumer behaviour

Consider a monopolistically competitive market structure in which firms produce differentiated products or varieties and consumer preferences over these varieties are represented by a sub-utility function:

$$u_{ht} = \left[\int_{j=0}^{1} c_{hjt}^{(\theta-1)/\theta} dj \right]^{\theta/(\theta-1)} , \quad \theta > 1, \tag{6.12}$$

where the varieties range from $j = 0$ to 1 in a continuous space and θ is the elasticity of substitution between any pair of them (see Svensson, 1986). If we define a general price index:

$$P_t = \left[\int_{j=0}^{1} P_{jt}^{1-\theta} dj \right]^{1/(1-\theta)} , \tag{6.13}$$

then the demand for variety j by household h is solved as

$$c_{hjt} = \left(\frac{P_{jt}}{P_t} \right)^{-\theta} c_{ht}, \tag{6.14}$$

where c_{ht} is its total real expenditure on all varieties.

The supply side
Given (6.14), the demand curve facing firm j in a two-household economy is given by

$$c_{jt} = \left(\frac{P_{jt}}{P_t} \right)^{-\theta} c_t, \tag{6.14a}$$

where

$$c_t = \sum_{h=1}^{2} c_{ht}$$

is the aggregate consumption in real terms. Any particular firm j is assumed to treat P_t and c_t parametrically.

Let the production function relating output to labour employed be expressed in its inverse form:

$$L_t = B_t g(Q_t), \quad g' > 0, \tag{6.15}$$

where B_t is the stochastic productivity term which is i.i.d with $EB_t = B > 0$. The optimal pricing rule is given by the familiar condition, $MR = MC$, that is,

$$\frac{\theta-1}{\theta} P_{jt}^* = W_t B_t g'(Q_t), \tag{6.16}$$

where W_t is the nominal wage rate at time t and P_{jt}^* the optimal price.

Following Rotemberg, price rigidity is introduced by supposing that the firms incur some private cost, say b, of changing prices from the previous period. The actual price set by firm j at t, P_{jt}, is obtained by minimizing $(P_{jt} - P_{jt}^*)^2 + b(P_{jt} - P_{jt-1})^2$, $b > 0$. The second term in this objective function is crucial in generating price sluggishness.[8] This leads to P_{jt} being equal to a weighted average of P_{jt}^* and P_{jt-1}:

$$P_{jt} = \frac{1}{1+b} P_{jt}^* + \frac{b}{1+b} P_{jt-1}. \tag{6.17}$$

Henceforth I suppress the index j since all firms have the same technology and face symmetric demand curves for their products.

Substituting (6.16) into (6.17), and denoting the real wage, W_t/P_t, by w_t, we get

$$\frac{\theta w_t B_t g'(Q_t)}{(\theta-1)(1+b)} + \frac{b}{1+b} \cdot \frac{P_{t-1}}{P_t} = 1. \tag{6.18}$$

As in the previous model, it is presumed that there are no income or wealth effects in the labour supply functions and these functions are the same for both households: $L_{hst} = \ell(w_t)/2$, $\ell' > 0$. Thus the aggregate labour supply function is: $L_{st} = \ell(w_t)$. In equilibrium, the demand for labour equals the supply of labour, i.e., $B_t g(Q_t) = \ell(w_t)$, which implicitly defines

$$w_t = \omega(Q_t, B_t), \quad \omega_Q > 0. \tag{6.19}$$

An implication of (6.19) is that real profit, $r_t = Q_t - \omega(Q_t, B_t) B_t g(Q_t) \equiv r(Q_t, B_t)$ is not necessarily an increasing function of output. Because an increase in output not only increases the amount of labour required but also the equilibrium wage rate. $\partial r_t/\partial Q_t = 1 - \xi\sigma_g - 1/\theta - \xi\sigma_g/\sigma_\ell$, where ξ is the share of labour ($w_t L_t/Q_t$) and σ_g and σ_ℓ are respectively the elasticity of $g(.)$ and $\ell(.)$ functions. Clearly, $\partial r_t/\partial Q_t < 1$.

Substituting (6.19) into (6.18) yields a 'dynamic' aggregate supply function of the following form:

$$Q_t = \overline{Q}_s \left(1 - \frac{b}{1+b} \cdot \frac{P_t - 1}{P_t}; B_t, b, \theta \right) \equiv Q_s \left(\frac{P_t}{P_{t-1}}, B_t; b, \theta \right), \quad (6.20)$$

which is an increasing function of the rate of inflation, P_t/P_{t-1}, unless the marginal costs are decreasing at a sufficiently rapid rate.[9]

Asset demand functions
Asset demand functions are similar to those in the previous section except that (a) there are stochastic components; (b) income effects are present in the money and equity demand functions; and (c) with rational expectations, the expected gross return on money, ρ_{mt}, is not necessarily equal to unity and hence it enters the demand functions explicitly.

Money demand functions:

$$\frac{M_{ht+1}}{P_t} = \upsilon_{ht} + h_m y_{ht} + \eta \left(\underset{-}{\rho_{zt}}, \underset{+}{\rho_{mt}} \right) \left(p_{zt} Z_{ht} + \frac{M_{ht} + \varepsilon_{ht}}{P_t} \right), \quad h_m > 0, \quad (6.21)$$

Equity demand functions:

$$p_{zt} Z_{1t+1} = \gamma_{1t} + h_z y_{1t} + \alpha \beta \left(\underset{+}{\rho_{zt}}, \underset{-}{\rho_{mt}} \right) p_{zt} Z_{1t}, \quad h_z > 0, \quad (6.22a)$$

$$p_{zt} Z_{2t+1} = \gamma_{2t} + h_z y_{2t} + \beta \left(\underset{+}{\rho_{zt}}, \underset{-}{\rho_{mt}} \right) p_{zt} Z_{2t}. \quad (6.22b)$$

y_{ht} is the income earned by household h, equal to $g(.)/2 + r_t Z_{ht}$. r_t is the real dividend per share, equal to $r(Q_t, B_t)$ defined earlier, since the total supply of equities is normalized to unity. ρ_{zt} and ρ_{mt} are respectively equal to $({}_t r_{t+1} + {}_t p_{zt+1})/p_{zt}$ and $\rho_{mt} = P_t/{}_t P_{t+1}$. ε_{ht}'s are the monetary endowment shocks, and υ_{ht} and γ_{ht} are the preference shocks. All the shocks are i.i.d with $E\varepsilon_{ht} = 0$, $E\upsilon_{ht} = \upsilon$ and $E\gamma_{ht} = \gamma$.[10,11]

As in the previous model, the difference in thriftiness is restricted to the wealth effect on demand for equities. By design, the money demand functions are aggregable. Hence it is the dynamics of the total stock of money, not its distribution, that matter in determining the dynamics of prices, output and distribution of equities. More generally, of course, difference in thriftiness can be present in the money demand function and in the income effect in both equity and money demand functions. Moreover, the proportion of income allocated to next period's holding of money and equity, h_m and h_z, will depend on asset returns. Perhaps the most transparent implication of these generalities is that the presumption of oscillation is likely to increase to the extent that the difference in thriftiness – or heterogeneity – manifests in the income effect also. However, the inclusion of these generalities will much further complicate an already complex model; hence they are avoided.

It is assumed further that in the asset demand functions own substitution effects outweigh the cross substitution effects, that is, $\sigma_{\beta z}\sigma_{\eta m} > \sigma_{\eta z}\sigma_{\beta m}$ where σ's are the respective elasticities in absolute terms of $\eta(.)$ and $\beta(.)$ functions with respect to the expected returns on money and equity.

Asset market-clearing conditions
Summing money demand and equity demand functions over the households the asset market clearing conditions are:

$$\frac{\overline{M} + \varepsilon_t}{P_t} \equiv m_t = \sum \upsilon_{ht} + h_m Q_t + \eta(\rho_{zt}, \rho_{mt})\left[p_{zt} + \frac{\overline{M} + \varepsilon_t}{P_t}\right] \quad (6.23)$$

$$1 = \frac{\sum \gamma_{ht} + h_z Q_t}{p_{zt}} + \beta(\rho_{zt}, \rho_{mt})[(\alpha - 1)Z_{1t} + 1]. \quad (6.24)$$

Equations (6.23) and (6.24) implicitly determine P_t and p_{zt} as functions of Z_{1t}, Q_t, $_tP_{t+1}$ and $_tp_{zt+1}$.

Dynamics of the system
Solving $\beta(.)$ from (6.24) and substituting it in (6.22a) yields

$$Z_{1t+1} = \frac{\gamma_{1t}}{p_{zt}} + h_z \frac{y_1(Z_{1t}, Q_t)}{p_{zt}} + \left(1 - \frac{\sum \gamma_{ht} + h_z Q_t}{p_{zt}}\right)\frac{\alpha Z_{1t}}{(\alpha - 1)Z_{1t} + 1}$$

$$= Z_1(Z_{1t}, p_{zt}, Q_t, \gamma_{1t}, \gamma_{2t}). \quad (6.25)$$

If we write the aggregate supply function (6.20) as

$$Q_{t+1} = Q_s\left(\frac{P_{t+1}}{P_t}; A_{t+1}, b, \theta\right), \quad (6.20')$$

equations (6.20'), (6.23), (6.24) and (6.25) constitute four stochastic expectational difference equations in four variables Q_t, P_t, p_{zt} and Z_{1t}. If we trace the system from $t = 0$ onwards, then there are two initial value conditions: Z_{10} and P_{-1}. The lagged value P_{-1} appears because of the lagged effect in the pricing equation (6.17).

Conceptually, the model is solved in three steps. First, the dynamics of Q_t, P_t, P_{zt}, and Z_{1t} are solved given the sequences $\{{}_tP_{t+1}\}$ and $\{{}_tP_{zt+1}\}$ and the evolution of the stochastic terms: A_t, υ_{ht}, γ_{ht} and ε_t. Second, conditional expectations are applied to P_t and p_{zt}, which are then equated to ${}_tP_{t+1}$ and ${}_tP_{zt+1}$ to solve for ${}_tP_{t+1}$ and ${}_tP_{zt+1}$. Finally, these solutions are ploughed back into the original solutions of Q_t, P_t, p_{zt} and Z_{1t}.

Steady state
Steady state is defined as the stationary solution of (6.20'), (6.23), (6.24) and (6.25) with the random components taking their expected values. In the steady state, the price level is constant, that is, $P_t/P_{t-1} = 1$, and $B_t = B$. The steady state output is determined by (6.20') only: $Q^* = Q_s(1,B;b,\theta)$. L^*, r^* and w^* are then determined uniquely.

The gross returns are equal to $p_z^* = 1 + r^*/p_z^*$, $\rho_m^* = 1$, $\eta^* = \eta(1 + r^*/p_z^*, 1)$ and $\beta^* = \beta(1 + r^*/p_z^*, 1)$. Equations (6.23) and (6.24) reduce to

$$m^* = 2\upsilon + h_m Q^* + \eta^*\left(p_z^* + m^*\right) \tag{6.23*}$$

$$1 = \frac{2\gamma + h_z Q^*}{p_z^*} + \beta^*\left[(\alpha - 1)Z_1^* + 1\right]. \tag{6.24*}$$

The steady state version of (6.25) is equivalent to that of (6.22a), which is

$$\left(1 - \alpha\beta^*\right)Z_1^* = \frac{\gamma + h_z y_1^*}{p_z^*} = \frac{\gamma + h_z w^* L^*/2 + h_z r^* Z_1^*}{p_z^*}$$

or $\quad \left(1 - \alpha\beta^* - \frac{h_z r^*}{p_z^*}\right)Z_1^* = \frac{\gamma + h_z w^* L^*/2}{p_z^*}. \tag{6.22a*}$

Equations (6.23*), (6.24*) and (6.22a*) determine P^*, p_z^* and Z_1^*. Moreover, in view of (6.22b)

$$\left(1 - \beta^* - \frac{h_z r^*}{p_z^*}\right)Z_2^* = \frac{\gamma + h_z w^* L^*/2}{p_z^*}. \tag{6.22b*}$$

Dividing (6.22a*) and (6.22b*) and using $Z_1^* + Z_2^* = 1$,

$$Z_1^* = \frac{1}{2} + \frac{(\alpha - 1)\beta^* / 2}{2 - 2h_z r^* / p_z^* - \beta^* - \alpha\beta^*}.$$

Thus $Z_1^* > 1/2$ and hence $Z_2^* = 1 - Z_1^* < 1/2$. Household 1, the thriftier, holds more equity in the long run. It is then implied that household 1 holds more money and obtains higher income in the steady state as well.[12]

Local dynamics
We will be concerned with the local dynamics of the system expected as of the initial period 0, that is, the paths of $_0Q_t$, $_0P_t$, $_0P_{zt}$ and $_0Z_{1t}$. Let '~' mark the deviation of the conditional expectation of a variable from its steady state, for example, $\tilde{Q}_t = {_0}Q_t - Q^*$.

The local dynamics of $\tilde{Q}_t$, $\tilde{P}_t$, $\tilde{p}_{zt}$ and $\tilde{Z}_{1t}$ are governed by linearizing the system around the steady state, taking expectations conditional on information available at $t = 0$ and equating market expectations with individual expectations. This is tantamount to equating Q_t with $\tilde{Q}_t$, $_{t-1}P_t$ and P_t with $\tilde{P}_t$, $_{t-1}p_{zt}$ and p_{zt} with $\tilde{p}_{zt}$ and Z_{1t} with $\tilde{Z}_{1t}$ in the linearized version of these equations. Implicit inversions yield

$$\mathbf{J}_1 = \Omega\mathbf{J}_0 + \Theta u_0$$
$$\mathbf{J}_{t+1} = \Omega\mathbf{J}_t, \ t \geq 1, \tag{6.26}$$

where $\mathbf{J}_t \equiv [\tilde{Q}_t, \tilde{P}_t, \tilde{p}_{zt}, \tilde{Z}_{1t}]'$, and $\mathbf{u}_0 \equiv [A_0, c_{10}, c_{20}, \gamma_{10}, \gamma_{20}, \varepsilon_0]'$ is the vector of initial shocks at $t = 0$. The matrix Ω is a 4×4 matrix which describes the propagation or the internal mechanism, and Θ is a 4×6 matrix which represents the initial, direct impact of shocks on the endogenous variables in period 1.

It is easy to obtain the analytical expressions of the elements of Θ, but not so easy to obtain those of Ω. The derivation of the elements of Ω is given in Appendix 6.2.

Presence of oscillations
Clearly, the dynamics of this model are far more complicated than that of the previous model which had static expectations (zero foresight) and no income effect. For one thing, it is a 4×4 system as compared to the 2×2 system in the previous model. Furthermore, it can be seen in Appendix 6.2 that 15 out of 16 elements of Ω are nonzero in general. Thus the dynamics of the variables are quite nested with one another.[13]

However, complicated as it is, the seeds of oscillatory internal mechanism lie in the opposite cross effects, implicit in the matrix Ω, between the aggregate output and the distribution of equity, that is, in the opposite signs of $\partial Z_{1t+1}/\partial Q_t$ and $\partial Q_{t+1}/\partial Z_{1t}$. But interestingly and importantly, the individual signs are *opposite* compared to the previous model. While in the previous model, $\partial Z_{1t+1}/\partial Q_t > 0$ and $\partial Q_{t+1}/\partial Z_{1t} < 0$, in this model $\partial Z_{1t+1}/\partial Q_t = \Omega_{41} < 0$ and $\partial Q_{t+1}/\partial Z_{1t} = \Omega_{14} > 0$. Accordingly, the economic explanation or the mechanism of oscillations here is radically different. In particular, the underconsumption argument itself gets reversed; it is not true that greater inequality tends to lower aggregate output. The asymmetric cross effects are depicted in Figure 6.2.

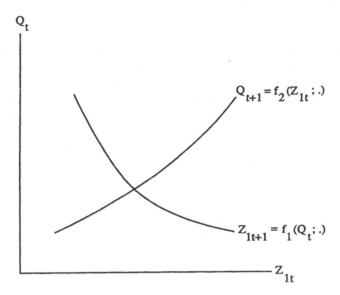

Figure 6.2   Asymmetric cross effects in the rational expectations model

At given p_{zt}, P_t and Z_{1t}, an increase in Q_t affects Z_{1t+1}, directly and indirectly. As Q_t increases, the income of household 1 may increase or decrease as $\partial y_{1t}/\partial Q_t = 1/2 + (Z_{1t} - 1/2)\partial r_t/\partial Q_t \gtrless 0$. By the income effect, this may increase or decrease its holding of equity in the next period, Z_{1t+1}. This is the direct impact. Also, as Q_t increases, the total demand for equities by both households together increases unambiguously by the income effect. However, the total endowment of equity certificates being constant, it forces them in equilibrium to allocate a smaller fraction of their already existing equity holdings to acquire next period's equity, that is, $\beta(.)$ is smaller (see equation (6.24)). This has a negative impact through the wealth effect on next period's equity holding. Compared to household 2, household 1 – the thriftier – allocates a larger fraction of its existing equity holding to next period's equity holding. This is the indirect impact. For household 1, then, the negative indirect impact on next period's equity holding either reinforces the direct negative impact, or, since it is large, outweighs the direct positive impact. The net impact of Q_t on expected Z_{1t+1} is thus unambiguously negative. Unlike in the previous model, the income effect on the demand for equities is critical here because the marginal impact of Q_t on Z_{1t+1} is exerted through this effect.

The positive impact of Z_{1t} on Q_{t+1} is more complicated and hinges on two things: rational expectations and that own substitution effects outweigh the cross substitution effects in the asset demand functions. Given rational expectations, an increase in Z_{1t} – at any given p_{zt}, P_t and Q_t – leads rational households to expect that p_{zt+1} and P_{t+1} cannot both decrease or increase because this is inconsistent with the money market clearing equation (6.23).[14] There are two possibilities: (a) p_{zt+1} increases and P_{t+1} decreases; or (b) vice versa. Turning to the equity market clearing, an increase in Z_{1t} (with an equal decrease in Z_{2t}) leads to an excess demand for equities, as household 1 is thriftier. The question is: at given p_{zt}, P_t and Q_t, which of possibilities (a) and (b) would lower the total (expected) excess demand for equities and hence clear the equity market in the expectational sense? Households rationally expect that (a) would imply a net increase in the demand for equities, because, as own substitution effects outweigh the cross substitution effects, the magnitude of an increase in $\beta(.)$ due to an increase in $_t p_{zt+1}$ would be greater than the magnitude of a decrease in $\beta(.)$ due to an equal decrease in $_t P_{t+1}$. Possibility (a) is thus inconsistent with the equity market clearing. That leaves out (b). In other words, households expect that $_t p_{zt+1}$ would decrease and P_{t+1} would increase. Firms perceive this too, and an increase in the expected P_{t+1} tends to increase expected Q_{t+1} via the aggregate supply function. Hence $\partial Q_{t+1}/\partial Z_{1t} > 0$.

An example

Let the production function be Cobb-Douglas: $g(Q_t) = BQ_t^a$, the labour supply function be $\ell(w_t) = w_t$ and the $\eta(.)$ and $\beta(.)$ function be

$$\eta(.) = \beta_m \, p_{zt}^{-a_m} p_m^{b_m}; \qquad \beta(.) = \beta_z \left(\frac{p_{zt}}{k_z + p_{zt}} \right)^{a_z} \left(\mu_z + \frac{1}{p_m} \right)^{b_z},$$

where $\beta_m \le 1$, $a_m > 0$, $b_m > 0$, $\beta_z \le 1$, $k_z > 0$, $-1 \le \mu_z \le 0$, $a_z > 0$, $b_z > 0$ and $a_z b_m > b_z a_m$. These restrictions are such as to ensure the correct signs of derivatives, $0 < \eta(.), \beta(.) < 1$ (at least along the steady state) and that $\sigma_{\eta m}\sigma_{\beta z} > \sigma_{\eta z}\sigma_{\beta m}$.

The heterogeneity parameter, α, was taken equal to 9. Other parametric values were: $B = 1$, $\theta = 6$, $a = 1.17$; $b = 5$; $\upsilon = -0.03$, $h_m = 0.5$, $\beta_m = 0.9$, $a_m = 0.2$, $b_m = 1.9$; $\gamma = -0.21$, $h_z = 0.85$, $k_z = 1$, $\beta_z = 0.3$, $a_z = 1.9$, $b_z = 0.2$, $\mu_z = -0.4$ and $\bar{M} = 8.8$. The steady state can be solved as $Q^* = 0.78$, $L^* = 0.74$, $r^* = 0.22$, $Z_1^* = 0.96$, $Z_2^* = 0.04$ and $p_z^* = P^* = 1$. Given the steady state values and the analytical expressions of the elements of Ω (in Appendix 6.2), the roots of the system turn out as 1.16, 1.11 and $0.476 \pm 0.496i$.

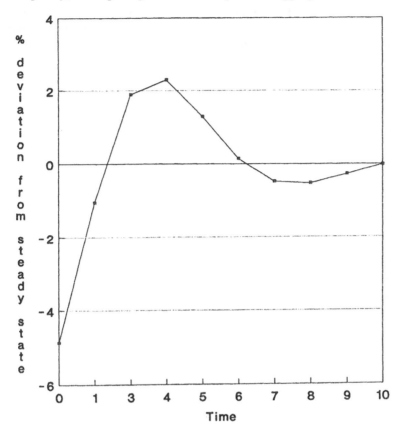

Figure 6.3A   Income share of household 1: temporary increase in money stock by 1 per cent

There are two initial value conditions and exactly two roots whose moduli are less than unity. Hence under this parametric configuration a unique rational expectations path exists that converges to the steady state. Moreover, the stable roots being complex conjugates, the dynamic system exhibits local oscillation in its adjustment path toward the steady state.

This model was simulated for a temporary monetary shock of +1 per cent. The resultant time paths of the expected income share of household 1 (which is equivalent to the Gini ratio in a two-household case) and the expected output are graphed in Figures 6.3A–B. (Recall that the distribution of such a monetary shock would affect the distribution of wealth, but not the total output, prices or income distribution.) The temporary monetary shock at $t = 0$ has a more than proportionate positive impact on output and negative impact on income inequality initially. Upon the expiration of the shock, oscillation begins in period 1.

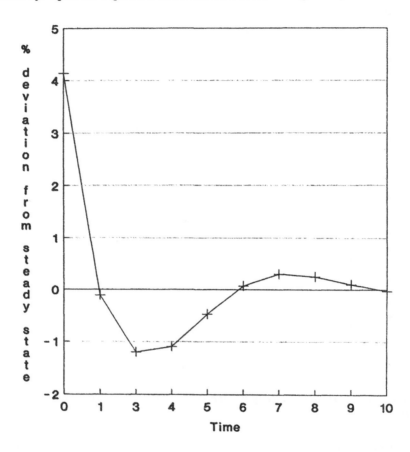

Figure 6.3B   Aggregate output: temporary increase in money stock by 1 per cent

IV   Concluding remarks

In the previous three chapters heterogeneity and inequality worked their ways essentially through the supply side of the economy, but in this chapter it is shown how they can work through the aggregate demand to produce oscillatory dynamics. I have developed two Keynesian models of the business cycle: one with absolute nominal wage rigidity and static expectations or no foresight, and the other with sluggish product price adjustment (but no wage rigidity) and rational expectations. A critical role is placed on the equity market as a channel through which inequality and aggregate output interact with each other via the aggregate demand – or equivalently, via the change in the product price. Oscillations in aggregate output can arise both in the absence and the presence of rational expectations. However, it is quite interesting that the nature of the asymmetric cross effects between inequality and aggregate output serving as the mechanism behind oscillations is opposite between the two models. In the static expectations model, inequality has a negative impact on output and output has a positive impact on inequality, whereas in the rational expectations model inequality has a positive impact on output and output has a negative impact on inequality.

Appendix 6.1   The partial derivatives of $P(.)$ and $p_z(.)$ functions in section II

Let μ denote the elasticity of labour demand with respect to the real wage, and $\sigma_{\beta\rho}$ and $\sigma_{\eta\rho}$ respectively the elasticity of $\beta(.)$ and $\eta(.)$ with respect to ρ_z, in absolute terms. Log-differentiating the money and equity market clearing conditions respectively and ignoring the asterisks for notational simplicity (here and in Appendix 6.2), we obtain

$$\left[-\frac{p_z+2\upsilon}{(m+p_z)(m-2\upsilon)}+\frac{\sigma_{\eta\rho}(L/P)(1-\mu)}{r+p_z}\right]\hat{P}_t-\left(\frac{\sigma_{\eta\rho}r}{r+p_z}+\frac{p_z}{m+p_z}\right)\hat{p}_{zt}$$

$$=-\left(\frac{\sigma_{\eta\rho}}{r+p_z}\right)dQ_t \qquad (6.A1)$$

$$-\left(1-\frac{2\varphi}{p_z}\right)\frac{\sigma_{\beta\rho}(L/P)(1-\mu)}{r+p_z}\hat{P}_t+\left[\frac{2\varphi}{p_z}+\left(1-\frac{2\varphi}{p_z}\right)\frac{\sigma_{\beta\rho}r}{r+p_z}\right]\hat{p}_{zt}$$

$$=\left[\frac{\alpha-1}{(\alpha-1)Z_1+1}\right]dZ_{1t}+\left[\left(1-\frac{2\varphi}{p_z}\right)\frac{\sigma_{\beta\rho}}{r+p_z}\right]dQ_t, \qquad (6.A2)$$

where '∧' denotes the log-derivative and the derivatives are evaluated at the steady state.

The determinant of the system (6.A1) and 6.A2) equals

$$D = -\frac{p_z + 2\upsilon}{m+p_z}\left[\frac{2\varphi}{p_z} + \sigma_{\beta\rho}\left(1 - \frac{2\varphi}{p_z}\right)\frac{r}{r+p_z}\right] - \frac{(1-\mu)(m-2\upsilon)(L/P)}{r+p_z}\left[\sigma_{\beta\rho}\left(1 - \frac{2\varphi}{p_z}\right)\frac{p_z}{m+p_z} - \frac{2\varphi}{p_z}\sigma_{\eta\rho}\right].$$

Consider the second term in D. In general, $1 - \mu$ can be positive, zero or negative, and depending on the magnitudes of $\sigma_{\beta\rho}$ and $\sigma_{\eta\rho}$ relative to each other, the expression in the square bracket inside the second term can be positive, zero or negative. Thus the sign of the second term in D is ambiguous. The sign of the first term is, however, negative unambiguously. Thus it is likely that D is negative and I assume so.

Solving (6.A1) and (6.A2), we get

$$\frac{\hat{P}_t}{dZ_{1t}} = \frac{m-2\upsilon}{D}\left[\frac{\alpha-1}{(\alpha-1)Z_1+1}\right]\left(\frac{\sigma_{\eta\rho}r}{r+p_z} + \frac{p_z}{m+p_z}\right) < 0 \quad \left(\begin{array}{l}\text{as the money market equilibrium}\\\text{implies that } m - 2\upsilon > 0\end{array}\right)$$

$$\frac{\hat{P}_t}{dQ_t} = \frac{m-2\upsilon}{(r+p_z)D}\left[\left(1 - \frac{2\varphi}{p_z}\right)\frac{\sigma_{\beta\rho}p_z}{m+p_z} - \frac{2\varphi\sigma_{\eta\rho}}{p_z}\right] \gtreqless 0$$

$$\frac{\hat{p}_{zt}}{dZ_{1t}} = \frac{\alpha-1}{D\left[(\alpha-1)Z_1+1\right]}\left[-\frac{p_z+2\upsilon}{m+p_z} + \frac{(m-2\upsilon)\sigma_{\eta\rho}(L/P)(1-\mu)}{r+p_z}\right] \gtreqless 0$$

$$\frac{\hat{p}_{zt}}{dQ_t} = -\frac{p_z+2\upsilon}{D(m+p_z)}\left(1 - \frac{2\varphi}{p_z}\right)\frac{\sigma_{\beta\rho}}{r+p_z} > 0 \quad \left(\begin{array}{l}\text{as the money market equilibrium}\\\text{implies that } p_z + 2\upsilon > 0\end{array}\right)$$

Appendix 6.2   Elements of matrix Ω in section III

Since $Q_{t+1} = Q_s(P_{t+1}/P_t, \cdot)$, and the elements of the first row of Ω are essentially determined by the partial of $Q(.)$ with respect to P_{t+1}/P_t, say Q_s', as well as the elements of the second row of Ω we have:

$$\Omega_{11} = \left(\frac{1}{P}\right)Q_s'\Omega_{21}; \quad \Omega_{12} = \left(\frac{1}{P}\right)Q_s'(\Omega_{22}-1); \quad \Omega_{13} = \left(\frac{1}{P}\right)Q_s'\Omega_{23}$$

and $\Omega_{14} = \left(\frac{1}{P}\right)Q_s'\Omega_{24}.$

We next differentiate the market clearing conditions (6.23) and (6.24) to obtain

$$\left(\sigma_{\eta m}+\frac{\sigma_{\eta z}\sigma_{rP}r}{r+p_z}\right)\hat{P}_{t+1}+\left(\frac{\sigma_{\eta z}p_z}{r+p_z}\right)\hat{p}_{zt+1}=\left(\frac{h_m}{m-2\upsilon-h_mQ}\right)\tilde{Q}_t$$

$$+\left(\frac{m}{m-2\upsilon-h_mQ}+\sigma_{\eta m}-\frac{m}{m+p_z}+\frac{\sigma_{\eta z}\sigma_{rP}r}{r+p_z}\right)\hat{P}_t+\left(\sigma_{\eta z}+\frac{p_z}{m+p_z}\right)\hat{p}_{zt}-\frac{(1-\eta)\varepsilon_t}{P}, \qquad (6.A3)$$

$$\left(\sigma_{\beta m}+\frac{\sigma_{\beta z}\sigma_{rP}r}{r+p_z}\right)\hat{P}_{t+1}+\left(\frac{\sigma_{\beta z}p_z}{r+p_z}\right)\hat{p}_{zt+1}=-\left(\frac{h_z}{p_z\beta[(\alpha-1)Z_1+1]}\right)\tilde{Q}_t$$

$$+\left(\sigma_{\beta m}+\frac{\sigma_{\beta z}\sigma_{rP}r}{r+p_z}\right)\hat{P}_t+\left(\frac{2\gamma+h_zQ}{p_z\beta[(\alpha-1)Z_1+1]}+\sigma_{\beta z}\right)\hat{p}_{zt}-\left(\frac{\alpha-1}{(\alpha-1)Z_1+1}\right)\tilde{Z}_{1t}, \qquad (6.A4)$$

where '^' denotes the proportionate deviation of the conditional expectations from the respective steady state value, for example, $\hat{p}_{zt}\equiv\tilde{p}_{zt}/p_z$, and σ_{rP} is the elasticity of r_t with respect to P_t/P_{t-1} – equal to the product of the elasticity of r_t with respect to Q_t and the elasticity of the aggregate supply function $Q_s(.)$. (In (6.A3), I have added the differential with respect to ε_t as the model is simulated for a temporary monetary shock.)

Equations (6.A3) and (6.A4) solve $\hat{P}_{t+1}$ and $\hat{p}_{zt+1}$ as functions of $\tilde{Q}_t$, $\hat{P}_t$, $\hat{p}_{zt}$ and $\tilde{Z}_{1t}$. The partials of these functions define the elements of the second and third row of Ω:

$$\Omega_{21}=-\left(\frac{P}{\Delta}\right)\left(\frac{p_z}{r+p_z}\right)\left(\frac{\sigma_{\eta z}h_z}{p_z\beta[(\alpha-1)Z_1+1]}+\frac{\sigma_{\beta z}h_m}{m-2\upsilon-h_mQ}\right)>0$$

$$\Omega_{22}=1-\frac{1}{\Delta}\left(\frac{\sigma_{\beta z}p_z}{r+p_z}\right)\left(\frac{m}{m-2\upsilon-h_mQ}-\frac{m}{m+p_z}\right)>1$$

$$\Omega_{23}=\frac{P}{\Delta(r+p_z)}\left(\frac{2\gamma+h_zQ}{p_z\beta[(\alpha-1)Z_1+1]}\sigma_{\eta z}-\frac{\sigma_{\beta z}p_z}{m+p_z}\right)\gtreqless0$$

$$\Omega_{24}=-\left(\frac{P}{\Delta}\right)\left(\frac{(\alpha-1)p_z}{(\alpha-1)Z_1+1}\right)\left(\frac{\sigma_{\eta z}p_z}{r+p_z}\right)>0$$

$$\Omega_{31}=\frac{p_z}{\Delta}\left[\frac{h_m}{m-2\upsilon-h_mQ}\left(\sigma_{\beta m}+\frac{\sigma_{\beta z}\sigma_{rP}r}{r+p_z}\right)+\frac{h_z}{p_z\beta[(\alpha-1)Z_1+1]}\left(\sigma_{\eta m}+\frac{\sigma_{\eta z}\sigma_{rP}r}{r+p_z}\right)\right]<0$$

$$\Omega_{32} = \frac{p_z}{P\Delta}\left(\sigma_{\beta m} + \frac{\sigma_{\beta z}\sigma_{r}p^r}{r+p_z}\right)\left(\frac{m}{m-2\upsilon-h_m Q} - \frac{m}{m+p_z}\right) < 0$$

$$\Omega_{33} = 1 + \frac{p_z}{r} + \left(\frac{1}{\Delta}\right)\left[\frac{p_z}{m+p_z}\left(\sigma_{\beta m} + \frac{\sigma_{\beta z}\sigma_{r}p^r}{r+p_z}\right) - \frac{2\gamma+h_z Q}{p_z\beta[(\alpha-1)Z_1+1]}\left(\sigma_{\eta m} + \frac{\sigma_{\eta z}\sigma_{r}p^r}{r+p_z}\right)\right]$$

$$\Omega_{34} = \left(\frac{1}{\Delta}\right)\frac{(\alpha-1)p_z}{(\alpha-1)Z_1+1}\left(\sigma_{\eta m} + \frac{\sigma_{\eta z}\sigma_{r}p^r}{r+p_z}\right) < 0,$$

where $\Delta \equiv (\sigma_{\eta z}\sigma_{\beta m} - \sigma_{\eta m}\sigma_{\beta z})p_z/(r+p_z) < 0$ given the assumption that $\sigma_{\eta m}\sigma_{\beta z} > \sigma_{\eta z}\sigma_{\beta m}$.

The elements of the last row of Ω are obtained by differentiating equation (6.25) only as it is in the reduced-form already.

$$\Omega_{41} = \left(\frac{h_z}{p_z}\right)\left(\frac{1}{2} + \left(Z_1 - \frac{1}{2}\right)\frac{\partial r_t}{\partial Q_t} - \frac{\alpha Z_1}{(\alpha-1)Z_1+1}\right) < 0, \text{ since } \frac{\partial r_t}{\partial Q_t} < 1 \text{ and } \frac{\alpha Z_1}{(\alpha-1)Z_1+1} > \frac{1}{2}$$

$$\Omega_{42} = 0$$

$$\Omega_{43} = \left(\frac{\gamma}{p_z^2}\right)\frac{(\alpha+1)Z_1-1}{(\alpha-1)Z_1+1} + \left(\frac{h_z}{p_z^2}\right)\left(\frac{\alpha Q Z_1}{(\alpha-1)Z_1+1} - y_1\right) \gtreqless 0$$

$$\Omega_{44} = \frac{h_z r}{p_z} + \frac{\alpha\beta}{(\alpha-1)Z_1+1} > 0.$$

Notes

1. In simpler frameworks, the asset demand functions are derived from explicit household optimization in Chapter 7.
2. A list of such models as well as a general discussion of the methodological issue of micro foundations in macro models are outlined in Chapter 2.
3. There is another constraint that ought to be satisfied, namely that $P_t Q_t - L_t \geq 0$. This is because there is no loan market in the model and thus current revenues must cover the total labour cost. This constraint will be binding only if the current output is sufficiently small. However, throughout the chapter, I will be concerned with local dynamics around the steady state and hence, as long as the steady state output is sufficiently large, this constraint will not be binding and thus can be ignored.
4. Substituting the money demand and equity demand functions in the household budget constraint, the implied consumption functions are:

$$c_{1t} = -(\upsilon+\varphi) + y_{1t} + [1-\alpha\beta(.)-\eta]p_{zt}Z_{1t} + (1-\eta)\frac{M_{1t}}{P_t}$$

$$c_{2t} = -(\upsilon+\varphi) + y_{2t} + [1-\beta(.)-\eta]p_{zt}Z_{2t} + (1-\eta)\frac{M_{2t}}{P_t}.$$

5. The partial derivatives of $P(.)$ and $p_z(.)$ functions and their signs are formally derived in Appendix 6.1.
6. Substituting (6.4) into (6.2), the dynamics of M_{1t} are given by

$$M_{1t+1} = P_t \left\{ \upsilon + \left(\frac{\overline{M}}{P_t} - 2\upsilon \right) \left(\frac{M_{1t}/P_t + p_{zt}Z_{1t}}{\overline{M}/P_t + p_{zt}} \right) \right\}.$$

This would affect the dynamics of money and wealth distribution, but not the dynamics of aggregate output or employment.

7. As shown below, f_{1Z} and f_{2Q} are ambiguous in sign. But it is reasonable to suppose – and likely, because of the ambiguity of signs – that both are less than unity. It is also shown below that $f_{1Q} > 0$ and $f_{2Z} < 0$. In particular, $f_{1Z} < 1$ and $f_{2Q} > 0$ together imply that equation (6.8*) defines a positive locus between Z_1^* and Q^*. Similarly, $f_{2Q} < 1$ and $f_{2Z} < 0$ together imply that equation (6.9*) implicitly defines a negative locus between Z_1^* and Q^*. Thus the solutions of Z_1^* and Q^* and, by implication, the solutions of other variables in the steady state are unique.

8. Rotemburg's pricing objective function is more general, but $b(P_{jt} - P_{jt-1})^2$ is the most critical term.

9. One implication of (6.20) is that if the monetary authority moves from a regime of lower money growth to another with a higher money growth, it can increase the long-run output. Hence the natural rate hypothesis does not hold. This is, however, true in the model only in a limited sense in that by moving to higher and higher money growth regimes, the monetary authority can increase the aggregate output only up to a limit. Because as P_t/P_{t-1} increases indefinitely, the term $1 - [b/(1+b)]P_{t-1}/P_t$ approaches 1 in (6.20) and Q_t approaches $\overline{Q}_s(1, B, b, \theta)$, where $B = E(B_t)$. It may be mentioned also that the well-known staggered contract model of Taylor (1980) also does not satisfy the natural rate hypothesis (McCallum, 1989, p.197). (For an exposition of Taylor's ideas, see Hall and Taylor, 1986.) In any event, there is no empirical evidence that decisively supports or rejects the natural rate hypothesis.

10. The implicit assumption is that the ranges of ε_{ht}, υ_{ht} and γ_{ht} are not large enough to imply negative quantities near the steady state.

11. As in the previous section, the consumption function can be derived by substituting the asset demand functions in the household budget constraint and solving for c_{ht}. My specifications imply that while a household's total expenditure on all goods, c_{ht}, is random, its allocation among individual products is not.

12. Furthermore, the above solution function of Z_1^* yields a negative relationship between Z_1^* and p_z^*, say $Z_1^* = g_1(p_z^*)$. Equation (6.24*) implies a positive relationship between Z_1^* and p_z^*, say $Z_1^* = g_2(p_z^*)$, unless γ is negative and sufficiently large. Equations $Z_1^* = g_1(p_z^*)$ and $Z_1^* = g_2(p_z^*)$ uniquely solve Z_1^* and p_z^*. Equation (6.23*) then solves for m^*. Given $\overline{M}$ and m^*, P^* is solved as $P^* = \overline{M} m^*$.

13. This is another right moment to stress the enormous costs associated with more micro-foundation in terms of deriving the asset demand functions from first principles. If asset demand functions were derived from first principles, we would have had at least four more endogenous variables – the shadow prices of money and equity accumulations by each household – and, as a result, an 8×8 system.

14. *Ceteris paribus*, an increase in $_tP_{zt+1}$ or $_tP_{t+1}$ would lower the demand for money.

PART II

INEQUALITY
AND FINANCIAL
MARKETS

7 Inequality, demand for stocks and demand for money

I Introduction

In an economic world without imperfections or frictions and where financial markets operate very smoothly, the real and financial sectors can be viewed separately. But such a world is unreal. Imperfections and rigidities are facts and that is why real and financial sectors are intertwined in real economies. If the objective is to better understand the real side of an economy, the financial side of it ought to be well understood.

This idea is, of course, not new. The importance of money in macro activity and business cycles is quite well-known. The role of non-monetary financial sectors – which I shall call the 'financial system' – in macro activity is well-known but it has had a chequered history in terms of emphasis. (See Gertler, 1988, for an excellent review of this literature.) The role of the financial system is recognized in the *General Theory* but not fully developed. A Keynesian theory of business cycles based on the balance sheet of firms and instability of the financial system is due to a number of contributions by Minsky (for example, 1975, 1982, 1986). Many other scholars have elaborated on Minsky's seminal work; see, for example, Taylor and O'Connell (1985) and Semmler (1989). A fundamental contribution was also made by Gurley and Shaw (1955), who emphasized financial intermediaries in the supply side of credit and their importance in real activities. Later on, however, research on the implications of the financial system for real activity was pushed back due to various reasons: the rigour and preciseness of the Modigliani–Miller Theorem implying that financial structures may not matter; the emphasis of the role of money owing to the work of Friedman and Schwartz (1963) and the subsequent preoccupation of macroeconomists with it; and the new practice/standard of macro model-building from first principles beginning in the 1970s. However, a revival of interest in the real implications of the financial system has occurred since the 1980s, because of new empirical studies linking the performance of the financial system with output fluctuations (for example, Eckstein and Sinai, 1986) as well as theoretical advancements in the economics of information.[1] Various types of asymmetric information between potential lenders and borrowers form the basis of the existence of financial intermediaries and many imperfections observed in the financial markets.[2] There are also models of business fluctuation in the presence of asymmetric information and capital market imperfections.[3]

My general hypothesis is that not only has the financial system implications for business cycles but, in particular, economic inequality contributes towards the business cycle *through* the financial system. It must be noted that the existing models of output (or investment) variation incorporating financial markets and asymmetric information do accommodate distributional changes. But these are mostly distributional changes in wealth between borrowers (or entrepreneurs) and lenders or between workers and capitalists (as in Woodford, 1989). They do not generally address the size (personal) distribution of wealth and income – which is the kind of distribution being considered in this monograph. Furthermore, the financial system in the existing models refers to an abstract market for real loans. They do not incorporate specific financial markets, such as the stock market or the banking sector, with some of their particular features.[4]

There is no denying that it is much easier to point the finger at these deficiencies than to rectify all of them simultaneously in a general equilibrium model. Generalizations can easily lead to loss of tractability. In Part II, which consists of Chapters 7 and 8, I attempt to analyse, based on explicit optimization of household behaviour, the impact of distributional changes on some aspects of some of the financial markets, and my objective is to generate sharp, empirically testable hypotheses. In the process, I totally overlook output variation.

Specifically, this chapter studies the implications of household inequality for the stock and the money markets. Clearly, these markets do not exhaust all important financial markets, but none the less they are important. The stock market performance serves in a capitalist economy as a barometer of market psychology or confidence which can have a significant impact on consumer and business spending. It can also influence the overall performance of the financial sector of an economy as an important input in the aggregate production process. Turning to the money market, there is no need to elaborate its importance in macro analysis, thanks to the seminal works of Professor Milton Friedman.

In what follows, in order to focus on the impact of economic inequality on these markets as clearly as possible, I examine each market separately and at the same time abstract from the production side of the economy. In essence I study the impact of an increase in household inequality on demand for stocks and demand for money, *all other things remaining unchanged*. In particular, this fills in, to some extent, the deficiency in Chapter 6 that the demand functions for stocks and money were directly postulated rather than derived from first principles.[5]

II Hypotheses
What are the hypotheses in the existing literature regarding the impact of economic inequality on the stock market and the money market? There is little

or nothing on economic inequality and the stock market. However, if previous chapters are any guide, they are suggestive that in an economy with heterogeneous households in terms of time preference, an increase in economic inequality will be associated with an increase in the demand for stocks, because the rich would have a higher propensity to accumulate assets than the poor, so that a redistribution towards greater inequality will result in more aggregate demand for stocks and a higher stock price. This is the hypothesis pursued here.

Something can be inferred from the existing theories of demand for money, however. Theories of money demand for transactions and precautionary motives point toward scale economies in holding money (see Laidler, 1985, p. 153). This should then imply that a more unequal distribution of income will lead to a decrease in the aggregate demand for money. However, a recent study by Cover and Hooks (1991) finds just the opposite for the US. Using postwar data and controlling for other factors, they find that income inequality has a positive impact on the real demand for M1 money. How, then, does one explain this? It is interesting that the finding of Cover and Hooks, while contrary to the existing theories of demand for money, is consistent with the heterogeneous time preference model for the same reason that the rich would have a higher propensity to accumulate assets than the poor. Similar to the demand for stocks, I pursue the hypothesis that an increase in inequality leads to an increase in the total demand for money.

True, once you think of demand for assets in terms of a heterogeneous time preference framework, these hypotheses probably appear direct and simple. But they are by no means trivial. To make this point, let me draw an analogy from international trade theory. A central theorem in international trade called the Heckscher–Ohlin theorem states that a relatively labour- (or capital-) abundant country would tend to export relatively labour- (or capital-) intensive goods. Clearly, this is quite intuitive and simple. Ask any undergraduate who has taken a course in international economics. But does it mean the theorem is trivial? No. Ask a graduate student who has drilled through a graduate course in trade theory. If you state the assumptions of the theorem carefully and completely, the list will easily pass eight or nine, and importantly, the theorem – which is so intuitive – can fail to hold if some of the assumptions are violated. The situation is somewhat similar here.

III   A general equilibrium model of the stock market

Consider an economy with one commodity which is produced and consumed, and one asset – equity certificates or shares. There are two households (or two types of households).[6]

Output is a function of labour and capital. Both factors are fully employed. Each household possesses ½ unit of labour, so the total labour endowment equals 1. The total capital endowment is also given, normalized to 1. Thus total output is given and it is effectively an exchange economy. Let w and r denote the fixed unit reward to labour and capital.[7]

Capital is owned through equity certificates which are traded. The market for these certificates is the stock market. To focus on distributional changes it is assumed that the total endowment of such certificates is given to this economy, normalized to unity. Let z_{ht} denote the holding of equity certificates by household h during period t. Thus

$$z_{1t} + z_{2t} = 1. \tag{7.1}$$

It is assumed that preferences differ across households and the rate of time preference is variable. Following Lucas and Stokey (1984) and Benhabib, Jafarey and Nishimura (1988), I assume an *aggregator function* of the form: $u_{ht} = V_h(c_{ht}, u_{ht+1})$, where u_{ht} is the 'utility' or value function and c_{ht} is the current consumption. The $V_h(.)$ function fulfils

V.1. V_h is continuous and bounded;

V.2. V_h is strictly concave;

V.3. $V_h(0,0) = 0$;

V.4. $(c',m') < (c'',m'') \Rightarrow V_h(c',m') < V_h(c'',m'')$;

V.5. $|V_h(c',m') - V_h(c',m'')| \le \delta|m'-m''|$ for some $\delta \in (0,1)$;

V.6. $V_{hc} \equiv \partial V_{ht}/\partial c_{ht} > 0$, $V_{hu} \equiv \partial V_{ht}/\partial u_{ht+1} > 0$, V_{hcc} and V_{huu} (the second partials) < 0;

V.7. Future utility is a normal good, that is, $V_{hu}V_{hcc} - V_{hc}V_{hcu} < 0$;

V.8. Marginal impatience is increasing, that is, $V_{hcu}(1-V_{hu}) + V_{huu}V_{hc} < 0$, where the partial derivatives are evaluated at a constant stream of consumption.

Thus preferences are recursive and the discount factor V_{hu} is variable. Some examples of the aggregator function that satisfy these conditions are:

Example 1: $u_{ht} = a_{hc}\left(1 - e^{-c_h}\right) + a_{hu}\left(1 - e^{-m_h}\right)$, $a_{hc} > 0$, $0 < a_{hu} < 1$.

Example 2: $u_{ht} = a_{hc}\left(1 - \dfrac{1}{1+c_h}\right) + a_{hu}\left(1 - \dfrac{1}{1+m_h}\right)$, $a_{hc} > 0$, $0 < a_{hu} < 1$.

Another example that satisfies all but V.2 and V.6 is

Example 3: $u_{ht} = (m_h - 1)e^{-a_{hc}\phi(c_h)}$, $\phi' > 0 > \phi''$ (Epstein and Hynes, 1983).

It is assumed that household 1 is more patient than household 2. Accordingly, at any constant stream of consumption c, the discount factor of household 1 is greater than that of household 2, that is, $\beta_1(c) \equiv V_{1u}(c, u_1(c..)) > \beta_2(c) \equiv V_{2u}(c, u_2(c..))$.[8] This is depicted in Figure 7.1.

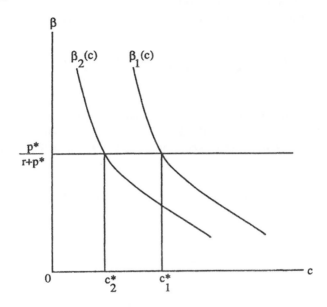

Figure 7.1   Patience curves

At the initial time, say 0, the decision problem of household h ($h = 1, 2$) is to

$$\text{Maximize } u_{h0},$$
$$c_{ht}, z_{ht}$$

subject to

$$c_{ht} + p_t z_{ht+1} = \frac{w}{2} + rz_{ht} + p_t z_{ht} \tag{7.2}$$

$$u_{ht} = V_h\left(c_{ht}, u_{ht+1}\right) \qquad (7.3)$$

$$z_{h0} = \bar{z}_{h0}, \text{ given,} \qquad (7.4)$$

where p_t is the real stock price. Note that in view of the asset market clearing condition (7.1), equation (7.2) implies that the total consumption, $c_{1t} + c_{2t}$, equals the total income $w + r \equiv c$, which is fixed.

The Euler equations associated with this optimization problem are:

$$\frac{p_t}{r + p_{t+1}} = V_{hc}\left(c_{ht+1}, u_{ht+2}\right) \frac{V_{hu}\left(c_{ht}, u_{ht+1}\right)}{V_{hc}\left(c_{ht}, u_{ht+1}\right)}, \quad h = 1, 2. \qquad (7.5)$$

Since it is a competitive economy, equation (7.5) can also be derived as necessary conditions of Pareto optimality. But the approach followed here is more general as it can be used even when distortions are present in the model.

The steady state
Equations (7.1), (7.2), (7.3) and (7.5) imply that in the steady state

$$z_1^* + z_2^* = 1 \qquad (7.1^*)$$

$$c_h^* = \frac{w}{2} + r z_h^* \qquad (7.2^*)$$

$$u_h^* = V_h\left(c_h^*, u_h^*\right) \qquad (7.3^*)$$

$$\frac{p^*}{r + p^*} = V_{1u}\left(c_1^*, u_1^*\right) = V_{2u}\left(c_2^*, u_2^*\right). \qquad (7.5^*)$$

Equation (7.1*), (7.2*), (7.3*) and (7.5*) constitute seven equations in seven variables: $c_1^*, u_1^*, z_1^*, c_2^*, u_2^*, z_2^*$ and p^*. Equation (7.5*) in particular implies that along the steady state the equilibrium rates of patience are equalized, that is, $V_{1u} = V_{2u}$. It is then clear from Figure 7.1 that c_1^* exceeds c_2^*. Next, equation (7.2*) implies that z_1^* exceeds z_2^*. Thus the more patient household holds more equity, earns higher income and consumes more in the long run.[9]

Local dynamics
Noting that $c_{1t} + c_{2t} \equiv c$ is given and eliminating one equation in (7.2) by virtue of the market clearing condition (7.1), equations (7.2), (7.3) and (7.5) describe

a system of five second-order difference equations with five variables $z_{1t}, p_t, u_{1t}, u_{2t}$ and c_{1t}.

The system of second-order difference equations is readily converted into a system of first-order difference equations by the transformation, $y_{ht} = u_{ht+1}$:

$$c_{1t} + p_t z_{1t+1} = \frac{w}{2} + (r + p_t) z_{1t} \qquad (7.2a)$$

$$y_{1t} = V_1(c_{1t+1}, y_{1t+1}); \quad y_{2t} = V_2(c - c_{1t+1}, y_{2t+1}) \quad (7.3a), (7.3b)$$

$$\frac{p_t}{r + p_{t+1}} = V_{1c}(c_{1t+1}, y_{1t+1}) \frac{V_{1u}(c_{1t}, y_{1t})}{V_{1c}(c_{1t}, y_{1t})} \qquad (7.5a)$$

$$\frac{p_t}{r + p_{t+1}} = V_{2c}(c - c_{1t+1}, y_{2t+1}) \frac{V_{2u}(c - c_{1t}, y_{2t})}{V_{2c}(c - c_{1t}, y_{2t})}. \qquad (7.5b)$$

Totally differentiating these equations and evaluating the derivatives at the steady state, we obtain

$$\mathbf{J}_t = \mathbf{N} \mathbf{J}_{t+1},$$

where

$$\mathbf{J}_t \equiv [\tilde{z}_{1t}, \tilde{p}_t, \tilde{y}_{1t}, \tilde{y}_{2t}, \tilde{c}_{1t}]'$$

is the matrix of deviations from the respective steady state values.[10]

In Appendix 7.1 it is proved that all five roots of $\mathbf{N}$ are positive and only one of them, say v_1, has modulus exceeding one. Since there is effectively one initial condition, $z_{10} = \bar{z}_{10}$, it follows that the solution of the perfect foresight path is unique, and locally, it is given by

$$\mathbf{J}_t = (1, R_2, R_3, R_4, R_5)' (\bar{z}_{10} - z_1^*) v_1^{-t}, \qquad (7.6)$$

where $(1, R_2, R_3, R_4, R_5)$ is the normalized eigenvector of v_1.

Hypothesis of a positive relationship between inequality and demand for stocks

Since $z_1^* > z_2^*$, an increase in z_{1t} over time represents an increase in wealth and income inequality. The total demand for stocks in real terms at each t is equal to the total supply of stocks or equity certificates in real terms and the latter equals p_t as the total number of equity certificates is constant and normalized to unity. Thus a positive relationship between inequality and demand for stocks is equivalent to a positive relationship between p_t and z_{1t}, that is, $dp_t/dz_{1t} > 0$.

From the solution expressions above and the definition of $\mathbf{J}_t$, it is clear that the sign of dp_t/dz_{1t} is the same as that of R_2. So the sign of R_2 is critical. It is shown in Appendix 7.2 that R_2 has same sign as $\chi_2 - \chi_1$ where

$$\chi_h \equiv \frac{\left[V_{hc}V_{huu} + \left(1 - V_{hu}\right)V_{hcu}\right]V_{hc}}{\left[V_{hu}V_{hcc} - V_{hc}V_{hcu}\right]\left(1 - V_{hu}\right)} = -\frac{\left(c_h / \beta_h\right)\beta_{hc}}{\left(\dfrac{c_{hc}}{V_{hu}/V_{hc}}\right)\partial\left(V_{hu}/V_{hc}\right)/\partial c_{ht}}.$$

Thus

$$\frac{dp_t}{dz_{1t}} > 0 \text{ if and only if } \chi_2 - \chi_1 > 0. \tag{7.7}$$

Note that χ_h involves second partials of the $V_h(.)$ function and the sign of $\chi_2 - \chi_1$ is dictated by how χ_h changes with respect to the patience parameter. Hence condition (7.7) is basically a third-order condition, which is hard to interpret. But it could be seen as an 'elasticity ratio condition'. The numerator of χ_h equals the elasticity of the discount factor with respect to a constant stream of consumption and hence concerns the curvature of the patience curve in Figure 7.1; its denominator is the elasticity of the marginal valuation of current consumption in terms of future value with respect to current consumption, which concerns the curvature of the aggregator function. Thus χ_h equals the ratio of two elasticity terms. Household 2 being more impatient, it follows that $\chi_2 - \chi_1$ is positive if and only if the elasticity ratio is an increasing function of impatience.

It is obvious that the elasticity ratio condition (7.7) may not be met by all aggregator functions. However, as it turns out, it *is* met by at least some classes of aggregator functions, which include those given as examples earlier.

Example 1: The elasticity condition is met if $a_{1c} = a_{2c} = a_c$. It is easy to show that a higher value of a_u means less impatience. Thus $a_{1u} > a_{2u}$. It is seen that

$$V_{hc} = a_c e^{-c_h}; \quad V_{hu} = a_{hu}e^{-u_h}; \quad V_{hcc} = -a_c e^{-c_h}; \quad V_{huu} = -a_{hu}e^{-u_h}; \quad V_{hcu} = 0.$$

Hence

$$\chi_h = \frac{a_c e^{-c_h}}{1 - V_{hu}}.$$

In general, along the steady state, $V_{1u} = V_{2u}$, and $c_1^* > c_2^*$ since the more patient household consumes more. Thus $\chi_2 > \chi_1$ and hence R_2 is positive.

Example 2: Here also, the elasticity condition is met if $a_{1c} = a_{2c} = a_c$. Higher a_u means less impatience and so $a_{1u} > a_{2u}$. We have

$$V_{hc} = \frac{a_c}{(1+c_h)^2}; \quad V_{hu} = \frac{a_u}{(1+u_h)^2}; \quad V_{hcc} = -\frac{2a_c}{(1+c_h)^3}; \quad V_{huu} = -\frac{2a_u}{(1+u_h)^3};$$

$$V_{hcu} = 0.$$

Thus

$$\chi_h = \frac{a_c}{(1-V_{hu})(1+c_h)(1+u_h)}.$$

Along the steady state, $V_{1u} = V_{2u}$ amounts to $a_{1u}/(1+u_1)^2 = a_{2u}/(1+u_2)^2$. Thus $u_1 > u_2$ as $a_{1u} > a_{2u}$. This together with $c_1^* > c_2^*$ implies that $\chi_2 > \chi_1$ and $R_2 > 0$.

Example 3: In this aggregator function, greater impatience is indicated by higher a_c, that is, $a_{1c} < a_{2c}$. The elasticity condition is satisfied if, for example, $\phi = \ln(c_{ht})$ or if it is a constant-absolute-risk-aversion utility function. First, we obtain

$$V_{hc} = -(u_h - 1)a_{hc}\phi'(.)e^{-a_{hc}\phi(.)}; \quad V_{hu} = e^{-a_{hc}\phi(.)};$$

$$V_{hcc} = -(u_h - 1)a_{hc}e^{-a_{hc}\phi(.)}\left(\phi''(.) - a_{hc}(\phi'(.))^2\right);$$

$$V_{huu} = 0; \quad V_{hcu} = -a_{hc}\phi'(.)e^{-a_{hc}\phi(.)}.$$

Therefore

$$\chi_h = -\frac{a_{hc}\left(\phi'\left(.\right)\right)^2}{\left(1-V_{hu}\right)\phi''(.)}.$$

If $\phi(.) \equiv \ln(c_{ht})$, then $(\phi'(.))^2/\phi''(.) = -1$. Thus $\chi_2 > \chi_1$ if and only if $a_{1c} < a_{2c}$. The latter inequality is true as household 2 is more impatient. R_2 is thus positive. If $\phi(.)$ satisfies constant absolute risk aversion, it follows that $-(\phi'(.))^2/\phi''(.)$ is a decreasing function of consumption. Since $c_1^* > c_2^*$, the term $(\phi'(.))^2/\phi''(.)$ is smaller for household 1 than for household 2. This together with $a_{1c} < a_{2c}$ implies that $\chi_2 > \chi_1$.

Hence the upshot is the hypothesis that, *ceteris paribus*, an increase in inequality leads to an increase in the total demand for stocks and an increase in the stock price.

IV   A general equilibrium model of the money market

There are several approaches to the demand for money from the viewpoint of (a) its major determinants, such as the old quantity theory, Cambridge theory, Keynesian theory and Friedman's new quantity theory, and (b) the basic motivations to hold money, such as money in the utility function, cash-in-advance or Clower constraint, transactions cost and so on. These examples do not exhaust all the approaches, and (a) and (b) are not mutually exclusive. However, there is no single approach which is generally considered superior to the rest. Each has its merits as well as its fair share of valid criticisms. In what follows, I use the simplest approach that one could think of in an intertemporal context, namely, money in the utility function. The standard argument behind money in the utility function rests on special services which the holding of money provides to an agent.

Consider, as before, a full employment economy with heterogeneous households.

The model

In order to focus on the money market, let all other asset markets, including that of equity, be suppressed. The total output or income is given. Since there is no trade in equity, the income of each household is given, say equal to y_h for household h. Thus, unlike in the previous model, the income distribution is exogenous. Let households be ranked in decreasing order of income, that is, $y_1 \geq y_2 \geq ... \geq y_H$, where H is the total number of households.

The total monetary endowment to the economy is given, equal to $\bar{M}$. But the distribution of money holding endogenously evolves over time.

A household's instantaneous utility function is given by $u(c_{ht}, M_{ht+1}/P_t) = f[\psi(c_{ht}, M_{ht+1}/P_t)]$, where M_{ht+1} is the amount of cash carried through period

t – which equals a household's initial endowment of cash in period $t+1$ – and P_t the price level in period t. It is assumed that $f' > 0$, $\psi(.)$ is a homogeneous and $u(.)$ a strictly concave function in both arguments. The function $\psi(.)$ being homogeneous, we can define

$$\frac{u_{hmt}}{u_{hct}} = g\left(\frac{M_{ht+1}/P_t}{c_{ht}}\right), \tag{7.8}$$

where u_{hc} and u_{hm} are the respective partials. It is further assumed that $g' < 0$.

Although, similar to the previous model, there is one good and one asset here, the model is more complicated as there are two arguments in the instantaneous utility function. Hence I use a more restricted intertemporal utility function. First, instead of a general aggregator function, I assume, following Uzawa (1968) and Obstfeld (1982), that the discount factor, say β, is a nondecreasing function of the instantaneous utility, u_{ht}. Second, as in the first model in Chapter 5, β is a stepwise rather than a smoothly increasing function of u_{ht}. In other words, the $\beta(.)$ function here is similar to the $\beta(.)$ function depicted in Figure 5.1.

The household optimization problem is to

$$\underset{c_{ht}, M_{ht}}{\text{Maximize}} \sum_{t=0}^{\infty} \left\{ \prod_{s=0}^{t} \beta \left[u\left(c_{hs}, \frac{M_{hs+1}}{P_s} \right) \right] \right\} u\left(c_{ht}, \frac{M_{ht+1}}{P_t} \right)$$

subject to

$$c_{ht} + \frac{M_{ht+1}}{P_t} \le y_h + \frac{M_{ht}}{P_t}, \tag{7.9}$$

$$M_{h0} = \overline{M}_{h0}, \text{ given,}$$

where Π denotes the product function.

We will be concerned with steady state and local dynamics around the steady state. Assuming, similar to the first model in Chapter 5, that along the steady state the equilibrium discount factor of each household is in the interior of the flat regions of the $\beta(.)$ function, the Euler equation can be stated as

$$\frac{P_t}{P_{t+1}} \beta_h u_c\left(c_{ht+1}, \frac{M_{ht+2}}{P_{t+1}} \right) = u_c\left(c_{ht}, \frac{M_{ht+1}}{P_t} \right) - u_m\left(c_{ht}, \frac{M_{ht+1}}{P_t} \right). \tag{7.10}$$

Moreover, in each period, the money market clears, that is,

$$\sum_{h=1}^{H} M_{ht} = \overline{M}. \qquad (7.11)$$

Equations (7.9), (7.10) and (7.11) govern the dynamics of this system.[11] They constitute $2H + 1$ equations with $2H + 1$ endogenous variables: c_{ht} and M_{ht} for H households and P_t.

Steady State
In the steady state, $P_t = P^*$, $c_{ht} = c_h^*$, $M_{ht} = M_h^*$ for all t, and accordingly, equations (7.9) and (7.10) reduce to

$$c_h^* = y_h; \quad (1-\beta_h)u_c\left(c_h^*, n_h^*\right) = u_m\left(c_h^*, n_h^*\right), \qquad (7.9^*), (7.10^*)$$

where $n_h^* \equiv M_h^*/P^*$. For notational simplicity, I avoid asterisks in marking the steady state discount factors. Substituting (7.9^*) in (7.10^*), rearranging (7.10^*) and recalling that u_m/u_c is defined as the function $g(.)$,

$$\beta_h = 1 - g\left(n_h^* / y_h\right). \qquad (7.12)$$

Equation (7.12) and the $\beta(u_{ht})$ function determine n_h^* and β_h.

The determination of n_h^* and β_h is illustrated in Figure 7.2. In the steady state $\beta_h = \beta\ (u_h(y_h, n_h)) \equiv \hat{\beta}(n_n; y_h)$. Then $\hat{\beta}(.)$ is an increasing step function of n_h. Let $1 - g(n_h/y_h) \equiv \hat{g}(n_h; y_h)$; then $\hat{g}(.)$ is a continuously increasing function of n_h as $g' < 0$. If $\hat{\beta}(.)$ and $\hat{g}(.)$ functions intersect once, then n_h^* is determined at the intersection. Otherwise, as shown in Figure 7.2, it is determined at the farthest intersection to the right, since a household maximizes the discounted sum of utility along the steady state, equal to $u(c_h, n_h)/[1 - \hat{\beta}(n_h; y_h)]$ – which is an increasing function of n_h.

An increase in y_h shifts the $\hat{\beta}(.)$ function up and $\hat{g}(.)$ function to the right, so that n_h^* is greater and β_h may be the same or greater. Thus, compared to a given household, a higher-income household holds more money and is more or equally patient. Since $y_1 \geq y_2 \geq ... \geq y_h$, it follows that $\beta_1 \geq \beta_2 \geq ... \geq \beta_H$ and $n_1^* \geq n_2^* \geq ... \geq n_H^*$. If the range (y_1, y_H) is not too small, then the chain of inequalities in β_h holds with strict inequality for some h and $h + 1$, implying that y_h and β_h are positively correlated.

The total real demand for money in the steady state is equal to

$$L^* = \sum_{h=1}^{H} n_h^*$$

and the price level equals $P^* = \bar{M}/L^*$. It is now straightforward to establish that a permanent increase in income inequality in terms of a mean preserving spread leads to an increase in the total demand for money in the steady state.

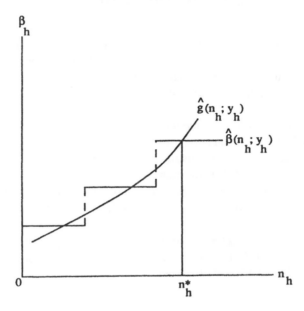

Figure 7.2   Determination of n_h^* and β_h^*

Define $\phi(\beta_h) \equiv g^{-1}(1 - \beta_h)$. Since $g' < 0$, it follows that $\phi' > 0$. y_h and β_h^* being positively correlated and $\phi' > 0$ imply that ϕ_h and y_h are positively correlated. Thus Cov $(\phi_h, y_h) > 0$, or,

$$\frac{1}{H}\sum_h \phi_h y_h - \bar{\phi}\bar{y} > 0, \tag{7.13}$$

where $\bar{\phi}$ and $\bar{y}$ are the respective means.

Consider now a mean preserving spread of income distribution by defining $\hat{y}_h = \gamma y_h + \theta$ and letting γ increase with the restriction that $d\theta/d\gamma = -\bar{y}$. In view of (7.12) and definition of the $\phi(.)$ function, the total demand for money in the steady state equals

$$L^* = \sum_h n_h^* = y_h g^{-1}(1-\beta_h) = \hat{y}_h \phi_h = \sum_h (\gamma y_h + \theta) \phi_h.$$

Thus

$$\frac{dL^*}{d\gamma} = \sum_h (y_h - \bar{y}) \phi_h = \sum_h y_h \phi_h - H\bar{y}\bar{\phi}.$$

Inequality (7.13) then implies that $dL^*/d\gamma$ is positive. The intuition is that high-income households, being more patient, maintain a higher proportion of money holding to consumption. Hence a redistribution toward greater inequality results in a net increase in the total demand for money in the steady state.

Short-run effects in a two-household economy

I now consider the short-run or out-of-the-steady-state effects of permanent and temporary changes in income distribution on the total demand for money. In general, the derivation of short-run impacts is more complicated than that of long-run impacts because explicit (local) solution of the dynamics of the system is needed. In this case it is deceptively complex even for a two-household economy.

We see this by making the transformations: $N_{ht} \equiv M_{ht+1}$ and $n_{ht} \equiv N_{ht}/P_t$, so that equations (7.9), (7.10) and (7.11) are expressed as first-order difference equations (7.14), (7.15) and (7.16) below.

$$c_{ht+1} + n_{ht+1} = y_h + \frac{P_t}{P_{t+1}} n_{ht} \tag{7.14}$$

$$\frac{P_t}{P_{t+1}} \beta_h u_c(c_{ht+1}, n_{ht+1}) = u_c(c_{ht}, n_{ht}) - u_m(c_{ht}, n_{ht}) \tag{7.15}$$

$$\frac{P_t}{P_{t+1}} \sum n_{ht} = \bar{M}. \tag{7.16}$$

The initial conditions are $P_{-1} n_{h(-1)} \equiv \bar{M}_{h0}$. Even for $H = 2$, these are five equations in five variables, $c_{1t}, c_{2t}, n_{1t}, n_{2t}$ and P_t, and the variables are too nested to yield anything definite unless specific functional forms are assumed.

Consider a two-household economy and assume the commonly used log-linear utility function. Let $u_{ht} = a + \ln(c_{ht}) + \ln(n_{ht})$, where the coefficients of the last two terms are normalized to unity for convenience.

It turns out that it is much simpler to express the system in terms of nominal variables. Let $C_{ht} = P_t c_{ht}$. Recall that $N_{ht} = P_t n_{ht}$. Using (7.16), equations (7.14) and (7.15) then reduce to

$$C_{1t+1} + N_{1t+1} = \rho_1\left(C_{1t+1} + C_{2t+1}\right) + N_{1t} \qquad (7.17)$$

$$\frac{\beta_1}{C_{1t+1}} = \frac{1}{C_{1t}} - \frac{1}{N_{1t}} \qquad (7.18)$$

$$\frac{\beta_2}{C_{2t+1}} = \frac{1}{C_{2t}} - \frac{1}{\bar{M} - N_{1t}}, \qquad (7.19)$$

where ρ_1 is the income share of household 1.[12] Equations (7.17)–(7.19) solve for C_{1t}, C_{2t} and N_{1t}. It is presumed that $y_1 - y_2$ is sufficiently large so that in the steady state $\beta_1 > \beta_2$. There is one initial condition: $N_{1(-1)} = \bar{M}_{10}$.

Totally differentiating (7.17)–(7.19), the local dynamics are expressed as

$$\mathbf{J}_{t+1} = \mathbf{M}\mathbf{J}_t, \qquad (7.20)$$

where $\mathbf{J}_t = [\tilde{C}_{1t}, \tilde{C}_{2t}, \tilde{N}_{1t}]'$ is the vector of deviations from respective steady states, and

$$\mathbf{M} = \begin{bmatrix} \dfrac{1}{\beta_1} & 0 & -\xi_1 \\[2ex] 0 & \dfrac{1}{\beta_2} & \xi_2 \\[2ex] \dfrac{\rho_2}{\beta_1} & \dfrac{\rho_1}{\beta_2} & 1+\xi \end{bmatrix}, \quad \xi_h = \frac{\left(1-\beta_h\right)^2}{\beta_h}, \quad \xi = \rho_2\xi_1 + \rho_1\xi_2.$$

It is shown in Appendix 7.3 that $\mathbf{M}$ has exactly one root, λ_3, whose modulus is less than one and it is positive. Hence the system (7.17)–(7.19) has a unique monotonic perfect foresight path.

The total real demand for money is inversely proportional to the price level since $(M_{1t} + M_{2t})/P_t = \bar{M}P_t$, where $\bar{M}$ is constant. Hence the path of P_t reflects that of the real demand for money.

Permanent distributional shock
In the case of a permanent shock, the path of P_t is solved as

$$P_t - P^* = \frac{\bar{M}_{10} - M_1^*}{y_1 + y_2}\vartheta\lambda_3^{t+1}, \qquad (7.21)$$

where

$$\vartheta = \frac{\xi_1}{1/\beta_1 - \lambda_3} - \frac{\xi_2}{1/\beta_2 - \lambda_3} \quad \text{(see Appendix 7.3)}.$$

Using the definition of ξ_h and that $\beta_1 > \beta_2$, it can be shown easily that ϑ is negative. Equation (7.21) says that if the initial holding of cash by the more patient household is greater than its steady state holding of cash, the price level falls over time; this is because, as the more patient household attempts to get rid of its cash and the less patient household does the opposite, the total nominal spending on goods falls since the more patient a household is, the lower is its propensity to spend. At $t = 0$,

$$P_0 - P^* = \frac{M_{10} - M_1^*}{y_1 + y_2} \vartheta \lambda_3. \tag{7.22}$$

From (7.22), the short-run impact of a permanent change in the income distribution is given by

$$dP_0 = dP^* - \frac{\lambda_3 \vartheta}{y_1 + y_2} dM_1^*, \tag{7.23}$$

assuming that the economy is initially in a steady state. Hence we require the expressions for changes in P^* and M_1^* as income distribution changes. In the steady state, equations (7.17)–(7.19) reduce to

$$C_1^* = \rho_1 \left(C_1^* + C_2^* \right); \quad \frac{1 - \beta_1}{C_1^*} = \frac{1}{M_1^*}; \quad \frac{1 - \beta_2}{C_2^*} = \frac{1}{M - M_1^*},$$

and using these equations and that $C_h^* = P^* y_h$, it is easy to obtain

$$\frac{dM_1^*}{d(y_1 / y_2)} = \frac{1 - \beta_2}{1 - \beta_1 + (y_1 / y_2)(1 - \beta_2)} > 0 \tag{7.24}$$

$$\frac{dP^*}{d(y_1 / y_2)} = -\left(\frac{\beta_1 - \beta_2}{y_1 + y_2} \right) \frac{dM_1^*}{d(y_1 / y_2)} < 0. \tag{7.25}$$

Thus, consistent with our earlier result that a permanent increase in income inequality leads to an increase in total (real) demand for money in the steady state, the price level in the steady state falls and the more patient household ends up holding more cash. Substituting (7.24) and (7.25) in (7.23),

$$\frac{dP_0}{d(y_1 / y_2)} = \left[-(\beta_1 - \beta_2) - \lambda_3 \vartheta\right] \frac{dM_1^* / d(y_1 / y_2)}{y_1 + y_2}. \qquad (7.26)$$

The first term, $-(\beta_1 - \beta_2)$, captures the short-run impact of an increase in inequality on the price level through its long-term impact on the price level; this is negative as $dP^*/d(y_1/y_2) < 0$. The second term, $-\lambda_3 \vartheta$, is the short-term impact through the long-term impact on the distribution of (nominal) money holding. It is positive, because as the rich household gets richer and the poor poorer, the former attempts to accumulate cash and spend less and the latter does the opposite, and consequently the net impact on aggregate nominal spending and hence on the price level is positive, since the poor has a greater propensity to consume. However, relative to the first effect, the second effect is of second-order magnitude and, as a result, the sign of the first effect dominates and $dP_0/d(y_1/y_2) < 0$.[13]

As noted earlier, the total real demand for money at any t is inversely proportional to the price level. Hence an increase in income inequality increases the total demand for money in the short run as well.

The time paths of the price level and the total demand for money due to a permanent increase in income inequality are illustrated in Figures 7.3A–B. It is interesting that there is an overshooting of the price level and the total demand for money in the short run. As an increase in income inequality leads to an increase in M_1^*, $\bar{M}_{10} - M_1^*$ is negative initially. Thus equation (7.21) implies that, after the initial shock, P_t must follow a monotonically increasing path. This, together with the implication that, compared to the old steady state, the price level is lower at $t = 0$ as well as in the new steady state, implies that the magnitude of the short-run decrease in the price level must be larger than that of its long-run decrease. The dynamics of the total demand for money are a mirror reflection of that of the price level.

Overshooting occurs due to the combination of a couple of factors. First, after the unanticipated distributional shock towards greater inequality, the new desired (long-run) stock of money of the rich increases and that of the poor decreases. Toward this end, the rich initially demand more money and the poor less. Since the rich have a higher propensity to accumulate money than the poor, the aggregate demand for money tends to increase in the short run. Second, during the course of adjustment to the new steady state, the rich tend to spend less and the poor tend to spend more on goods relative to their cash

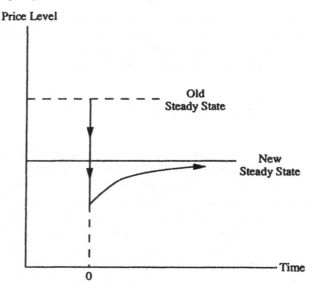

Figure 7.3A   Dynamics of the price level

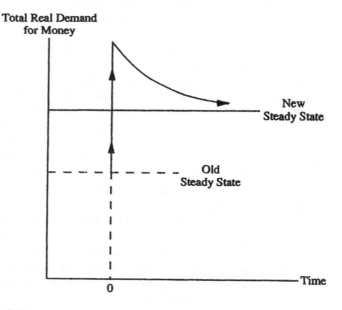

Figure 7.3B   Dynamics of the total real demand for money

holding, and because of the difference in the rate of time preference, in the aggregate there is relatively more demand for goods and less demand for money, which tends to increase the price level. The increase in the price level reduces the demand for money in real terms. In summary, then, rational agents expect a *decreasing path* of demand for money in real terms *over time* leading to a *greater* long-run demand for money. Hence the optimal response in terms of the initial or short-run demand for money is an overshooting.

Temporary distributional shock
In Appendix 7.3, the impact of a temporary increase in income inequality at $t = 0$ (denoted by $d\rho_{10}$) on P_0 is solved as

$$P_0 - P^* = kP^* \left[1 - \frac{(1-\beta_2)^2(1-\lambda_3\beta_1)}{(1-\beta_1)^2(1-\lambda_3\beta_2)} \right] d\rho_{10},$$

where k is a positive constant. Defining a function, $F(\beta;\lambda_3) \equiv (1-\beta)^2/(1-\lambda_3\beta)$, it is seen that $F_\beta < 0$. Since $\beta_1 > \beta_2$, it then follows that $(1-\beta_2)^2/(1-\lambda_3\beta_2) > (1-\beta_1)^2/(1-\lambda_3\beta_1)$. Hence the coefficient of $d\rho_{10}$ is negative. Thus a temporary increase in income inequality also lowers the price level and increases the real demand for money in the short run.

V Concluding remarks
The main objective of this chapter was to derive empirically testable hypotheses concerning the impact of economic inequality on the demand for stocks and money, namely, *ceteris paribus,* an increase in wealth and income inequality leads to an increase in the total demand for stocks and money. In order to do so, I have developed simple models of an exchange economy which allow for heterogeneous time preference across households. Given that different households have different patience schedules, the hypotheses are quite intuitive. However, the complexity of the 'proofs' proves that it is anything but trivial. Furthermore, in particular, the overshooting in the real demand for money following a distributional shock towards greater inequality is an interesting result, which is neither direct nor intuitive.

The analytical complexity arising due to heterogeneity virtually rules out inclusion of more than one asset market at a time. In principle, however, it is straightforward to incorporate other asset markets, but then simulations would have to substitute for analytical results. The hypotheses basically result from income or wealth effects. As long as assets are normal goods there should be a strong presumption that they will continue to hold in a multi-asset setting.

In particular, the stock market analysis can be interpreted as that of any other asset as long as the ownership of the asset amounts to ownership of productive factors and the asset is tradable, for example, market for land. Finally, the analysis has obvious implications for asset pricing in general: greater inequality leads to higher asset prices. To avoid misunderstanding, however, I must stress that this does not mean that other factors are claimed to be insignificant or less significant in affecting asset demand and asset pricing. The point is that distributional changes may also matter at the margin.

Appendix 7.1   Elements of matrix *N* and its roots

In Appendices 7.1 and 7.2, asterisks are omitted to simplify notations. By direct calculation, the elements of the matrix **N** are:

$$N_{11} = \frac{p}{r+p};\ N_{12} = 0;\ N_{13} = \frac{N_{53}}{r+p};\ N_{14} = \frac{N_{54}}{r+p};\ N_{15} = \frac{N_{55}}{r+p};$$

$$N_{21} = 0;\ N_{22} = N_{11};$$

$$N_{23} = pk_1\left(\frac{V_{2cc}}{V_{2c}} - \frac{V_{2cu}}{V_{2u}}\right);\ N_{24} = pk_2\left(\frac{V_{1cc}}{V_{1c}} - \frac{V_{1cu}}{V_{1u}}\right);\ N_{25} = \frac{V_{1c}}{V_{1u}}N_{23} - \frac{V_{2c}}{V_{2u}}N_{24};$$

$$N_{31} = 0;\ N_{32} = 0;\ N_{33} = V_{1u};\ N_{34} = 0;\ N_{35} = V_{1c};$$

$$N_{41} = 0;\ N_{42} = 0;\ N_{43} = 0;\ N_{44} = V_{2u};\ N_{45} = -V_{2c};$$

$$N_{51} = 0;\ N_{52} = 0;\ N_{53} = k_1;\ N_{54} = -k_2;\ N_{55} = \alpha,\ \text{where}$$

$$k_h = \frac{V_{hcu}(1 - V_{hu}) + V_{hc}V_{huu}}{V_{hc}D} > 0;\quad D = \frac{V_{1cc}}{V_{1c}} + \frac{V_{2cc}}{V_{2c}} - \frac{V_{1cu} + V_{2cu}}{V_{hu}} < 0;$$

$$\alpha = \frac{1}{D}\left(\frac{V_{1cc}}{V_{1c}} + \frac{V_{2cc}}{V_{2c}} - V_{1cu} - V_{2cu} + \frac{V_{1c}}{V_{1u}}V_{1uu} + \frac{V_{2c}}{V_{2u}}V_{2uu}\right) > 1.$$

Given these elements of the **N** matrix, the characteristic equation of **N** is:

$$(N_{11} - v)^2 (V_{hu} - v)\big[(V_{hu} - v)(\alpha - v) - k_1V_{1c} - k_2V_{2c}\big] = 0. \quad (7.\text{A1})$$

Clearly, three of the five roots are N_{11}, N_{11} and V_{hu}. These are positive and less than one. The remaining two roots are the solutions of the quadratic equation

$$\left(V_{hu}-v\right)(\alpha-v)-k_1 V_{1c}-k_2 V_{2c}=0.$$

The solutions are equal to

$$v_1, v_2 = \frac{\alpha+V_{hu} \pm\left(\left(\alpha+V_{hu}\right)^2-4\left(\alpha V_{hu}-k_1 V_{1c}-k_2 V_{2c}\right)\right)^{1/2}}{2}$$

$$= \frac{\alpha+V_{hu} \pm\left(\left(\alpha-V_{hu}\right)^2+4\left(k_1 V_{1c}+k_2 V_{2c}\right)\right)^{1/2}}{2}.$$

From the definitions, $\alpha V_{hu}-k_1 V_{1c}-k_2 V_{2c}$ is positive, which implies that both roots are positive. Moreover,

$$v_1 > \frac{\alpha+V_{hu}+\left(\alpha-V_{hu}\right)}{2}=\alpha>1; \quad v_2 < \frac{\alpha+V_{hu}-\left(\alpha-V_{hu}\right)}{2}=V_{hu}<1.$$

Hence all five roots of matrix **N** are positive and only one of them, v_1, exceeds one.

Appendix 7.2 Proof that R_2 has same sign as $\chi_2-\chi_1$

R_2, R_3, R_4 and R_5 are solved from the system:

$$\begin{bmatrix} 0 & N_{13} & N_{14} & N_{15} \\ N_{22}-v_1 & N_{23} & N_{24} & N_{25} \\ 0 & N_{33}-v_1 & N_{34} & N_{35} \\ 0 & 0 & N_{44}-v_1 & N_{45} \end{bmatrix} \begin{bmatrix} R_2 \\ R_3 \\ R_4 \\ R_5 \end{bmatrix} = \begin{bmatrix} v_1-N_{11} \\ 0 \\ 0 \\ 0 \end{bmatrix}$$

Applying Cramer's rule,

$$R_2 = -\left(\frac{1}{\Delta}\right)\left(v_1-N_{11}\right)\left(V_{hu}-v_1\right)\left[N_{23}N_{35}+N_{24}N_{45}-N_{25}\left(V_{hu}-v_1\right)\right],$$

$$= -\frac{1}{V_{hu}\Delta}\underset{+}{\left(v_1-N_{11}\right)}\underset{-}{\left(V_{hu}-v_1\right)}\underset{+}{pv_1}\underset{?}{\left(V_{1c}N_{23}-V_{2c}N_{24}\right)}, \text{ where}$$

$$\Delta \equiv \frac{\left(V_{hu}-v_1\right)^2}{r+p}\left[k_1 V_{1c}+k_2 V_{2c}-\alpha\left(V_{hu}-v_1\right)\right]>0.$$

Hence the sign of R_2 is the sign of

$$V_{1c}N_{23}-V_{2c}N_{24}=\frac{1}{V_{1c}V_{2c}V_{hu}D}\left\{\left[V_{1c}V_{1uu}+\left(1-V_{hu}\right)V_{1cu}\right]\left[V_{hu}V_{2cc}-V_{2c}V_{2cu}\right]\right.$$

$$V_{1c}-\left[V_{2c}V_{2uu}+\left(1-V_{hu}\right)V_{2cu}\right]\left[V_{hu}V_{1cc}-V_{1c}V_{1cu}\right]V_{2c}\Big\},$$

which has the same sign as $\chi_2-\chi_1$, where

$$\chi_h\equiv\frac{\left[V_{hc}V_{huu}+\left(1-V_{hu}\right)V_{hcu}\right]V_{hc}}{\left[V_{hu}V_{hcc}-V_{hc}V_{hcu}\right]\left(1-V_{hu}\right)}.$$

χ_h can be expressed in terms of the ratio of two elasticities:

$$\chi_h=-\frac{\left(c_h/\beta_h\right)\beta_{hc}}{\left(\dfrac{c_h}{V_{hu}/V_{hc}}\right)\partial\left(V_{hu}/V_{hc}\right)/\partial c_{ht}}.$$

Appendix 7.3   The model of the demand for money
Let λ_1, λ_2 and λ_3 be the roots of matrix **M**. Then

(a) $\qquad\qquad\lambda_1+\lambda_2+\lambda_3=$ sum of the diagonal elements of **M**

$$=\frac{1}{\beta_1}+\frac{1}{\beta_2}+1+\xi>3.$$

It turns out that $|\mathbf{M}| = 1/(\beta_1\beta_2) > 0$; thus

(b) $\qquad\qquad\qquad\qquad\lambda_1\lambda_2\lambda_3>0.$

Consider the matrix $\mathbf{M}-\mathbf{I}$. It is straightforward to obtain that $|\mathbf{M}-\mathbf{I}| = -\rho_1\xi_2(1/\beta_1-1)-\rho_2\xi_1(1/\beta_2-1)<0$. Thus, the roots of $\mathbf{M}-\mathbf{I}$ being equal to λ_1-1, λ_2-1 and λ_3-1,

(c) $$(\lambda_1 - 1)(\lambda_2 - 1)(\lambda_3 - 1) < 0.$$

Now suppose all three roots of $\mathbf{M}$ are real. Then all three roots of $\mathbf{M} - \mathbf{I}$ are real, and (c) implies that either (i) $\lambda_1 - 1$, $\lambda_2 - 1$ and $\lambda_3 - 1$ are all negative, or (ii) two of these are positive and the third negative. However, (i) implies that $\lambda_1 + \lambda_2 + \lambda_3 < 3$, which is inconsistent with (a). Thus (ii) must be true, that is, $\lambda_1 > 1$, $\lambda_2 > 1$ and $\lambda_3 < 1$. Furthermore, λ_1 and λ_2 being positive, (b) implies that λ_3 is positive. Thus there is exactly one root, λ_3, whose modulus is less than one and it is positive.

Suppose two roots of $\mathbf{M}$ are complex conjugates, say λ_1 and λ_2. Then $\lambda_1 - 1$ and $\lambda_2 - 1$ are also complex conjugates. (c) then implies that $\lambda_3 - 1 < 0$, that is, $\lambda_3 < 1$. λ_1 and λ_2 being complex conjugates also implies, in view of (b), that $\lambda_3 > 0$. Thus $0 < \lambda_3 < 1$. All that remains to be shown is that $|\lambda_1| = |\lambda_2| > 1$. Let $\lambda_1, \lambda_2 = \alpha \pm \delta i$. Then $\lambda_1 + \lambda_2 + \lambda_3 = 2\alpha + \lambda_3$. Since $\lambda_3 < 1$, it follows from (a) that $\alpha > 1$. But $\alpha > 1$ implies that $|\lambda_1| = |\lambda_2| > 1$, as needed.

Hence the matrix $\mathbf{M}$ has one stable root, λ_3. Moreover, the eigenvector associated with λ_3 is equal to $[a_m \xi_1/(1/\beta_1) - \lambda_3), -a_m \xi_2/(1/\beta_2 - \lambda_3), a_m]'$, where a_m is the undetermined coefficient.

Permanent distributional shock

For a permanent shock, $\tilde{N}_{1t} = a_m \lambda_3^t$ for $t \geq -1$, $\tilde{C}_{1t} = [a_m \xi_1/(1/\beta_1 - \lambda_3)]\lambda_3^t$ for $t \geq 0$ and $\tilde{C}_{2t} = -[a_m \xi_2/(1/\beta_2 - \lambda_3)]\lambda_3^t$ for $t \geq 0$. For $t = -1$, $\tilde{N}_{1t} = N_{1(-1)} - N_1^* = \bar{M}_{10} - M^* = a_m/\lambda_3$. Thus $a_m = (\bar{M}_{10} - M_1^*)\lambda_3$. The solutions of C_{1t} and C_{2t} are then

$$C_{1t} - C_1^* = \frac{\left(\bar{M}_{10} - M_1^*\right)\xi_1}{1/\beta_1 - \lambda_3}\lambda_3^{t+1}; \quad C_{2t} - C_2^* = -\frac{\left(\bar{M}_{10} - M_1^*\right)\xi_2}{1/\beta_2 - \lambda_3}\lambda_3^{t+1}.$$

Since $C_{1t} + C_{2t} = (y_1 + y_2)P_t$,

$$P_t - P^* = \frac{1}{y_1 + y_2}\left(C_{1t} - C_1^* + C_{2t} - C_2^*\right) = \frac{\bar{M}_{10} - M_1^*}{y_1 + y_2}\left(\frac{\xi_1}{1/\beta_1 - \lambda_3} - \frac{\xi_2}{1/\beta_2 - \lambda_3}\right)\lambda_3^{t+1}.$$

Temporary distributional shock

The solutions of the undetermined coefficient a_m and the initial jumps are more complicated in the case of a temporary shock. The first two equations in (7.20) are not affected by a temporary increase in income inequality, say $d\rho_{10}$. Thus

$$C_{11} - C_1^* = \frac{1}{\beta_1}\left(C_{10} - C_1^*\right) - \xi_1\left(M_{11} - \overline{M}_1^*\right) \tag{7.A2}$$

$$C_{21} - C_2^* = -\frac{1}{\beta_2}\left(C_{20} - C_2^*\right) + \xi_2\left(M_{11} - \overline{M}_1^*\right). \tag{7.A3}$$

But the third equation in (7.20) is affected by $d\rho_{10}$ and accordingly, for $t = 0$,

$$C_{10} - C_1^* + M_{11} - M_1^* = \rho_1\left(C_{10} - C_1^* + C_{20} - C_2^*\right) + yP^* d\rho_{10}, \tag{7.A4}$$

as $y_1P_0 = \rho_1(C_{10} + C_{20})$ from the commodity market clearing, and $\overline{M}_{10} - M_1^* = 0$.
   The general solutions of $\tilde{C}_{1t}$ and $\tilde{C}_{2t}$ for $t \geq 1$ and $\tilde{N}_{1t}$ for $t \geq 0$ are given by λ_3 and the associated eigenvector. For $t = 1$,

$$C_{11} - C_1^* = \frac{a_m\xi_1\lambda_3}{1/\beta_1 - \lambda_3}; \quad C_{21} - C_2^* = -\frac{a_m\xi_2\lambda_3}{1/\beta_2 - \lambda_3}, \tag{7.A5), (7.A6}$$

and for $t = 0, \tilde{N}_{10} =$

$$M_{11} - M_1^* = a_m. \tag{7.A7}$$

   Equations (7.A2)–(7.A7) solve for six variables, $C_{10} - C_{10}^*, C_{20} - C_2^*, C_{11} - C_1^*, C_{21} - C_2^*, M_{11} - M_1^*$ and a_m in terms of $d\rho_{10}$. The price level at $t = 0$ is solved from the following equation implied by the commodity market clearing:

$$C_{10} - C_1^* + C_{20} - C_2^* = y\left(P_0 - P^*\right). \tag{7.A8}$$

By substitutions, equations (7.A2)–(7.A8) yield

$$P_0 - P^* = kP^*\left[1 - \frac{(1-\beta_2)^2(1-\lambda_3\beta_1)}{(1-\beta_1)^2(1-\lambda_3\beta_2)}\right]d\rho_{10},$$

where

$$k \equiv \rho_2 + \frac{1}{\xi_1\beta_1 + \xi_1\lambda_3/(1-\lambda_3\beta_1)} + \frac{\rho_1\beta_2\xi_2(1-\lambda_3\beta_1)}{\beta_1\xi_1(1-\lambda_3\beta_2)} > 0.$$

Notes

1. The role of credit, as opposed to money, in macro analysis has been emphasized by Friedman (1983).
2. See, for example, Jaffee and Russell (1976), Stiglitz and Weiss (1981), Townsend (1983), Gale and Hellwig (1985), Mankiw (1986) and deMeza and Webb (1987). For a recent collection of empirical work on financial markets and crises, see Hubbard (1991).
3. Farmer (1984), Scheinkman and Weiss (1986), Blinder (1987), Bernanke and Gertler (1989) and Woodford (1989), among many others.
4. Bernanke and Gertler (1987) is an exception.
5. Recall that in Chapter 6 household inequality did not affect the money market directly. But that was by design; it could have done so had a parameter such as α been introduced in the money demand function.
6. A more-general general-equilibrium model of the stock market but with a single representative agent is contained in the well-known work of Brock and Turnovsky (1981).
7. The model is essentially a synthesis of the section 'A Two-agent Exchange Economy: Stability', in Lucas and Stokey (1984) and Lucas's (1978) asset-pricing model.
8. In Examples 1 and 2, this is implied if $a_{1u} > a_{2u}$, and in Example 3, it is ensured by $a_{1c} < a_{2c}$.
9. The uniqueness of the steady state can be established as follows. Equations (7.5*) imply that $V_{hu} < 1$ in the steady state. Equations (7.3*) then imply that u_h^* is an increasing function of c_h^*, say, $u_h^* \equiv \upsilon_h(c_h^*)$. Thus $V_{hu} = V_{hu}(c_h^*, \upsilon_h(c_h^*)) \equiv \tilde{V}_{hu}(c_h^*)$ is such that, in view of the assumption V.8, $\tilde{V}_{hu}' < 0$. Recall that $c_1^* + c_2^* = c$, a constant. Given $\tilde{V}_{hu}(.)$, the equation $V_{1u} = V_{2u}$ can be expressed as $\tilde{V}_{1u}(c_1^*) - \tilde{V}_{2u}(c - c_1^*) \equiv \Gamma(c_1^*) = 0$ such that $\Gamma' < 0$. The function $\Gamma(.)$ being strictly monotonic, it follows that the solution of c_1^* from $\Gamma(c_1^*) = 0$ is unique. Given c_1^*, the other steady-state values are uniquely solved.
10. It turns out that it is easier to compute analytically the elements of N rather than to express the system as $J_{t+1} = MJ_t$ and compute the elements of $M = N^{-1}$.
11. As long as u_c and u_m are positive, the household budget constraint (7.9) is satisfied with equality.
12. For household 1, equation (7.14) can be written as $C_{1t+1} + N_{1t+1} = y_1 P_{t+1} + N_{1t}$. The clearance of the money market is equivalent to that of the commodity market and the latter can be stated as $C_{1t} + C_{2t} = (y_1 + y_2)P_t$. Thus $y_1 P_{t+1} = \rho_1(C_{1t+1} + C_{2t+1})$. Substituting this in the earlier equation gives (7.17). Equations (7.18) and (7.19) are straightforward to derive.
13. Let $\beta_1 - \beta_2 + \lambda_3 \vartheta = \beta_1 - \beta_2 + \lambda_3(1-\beta_1)^2/(1-\lambda_3\beta_1) - \lambda_3(1-\beta_2)^2/(1-\lambda_3\beta_2) \equiv \Gamma$. Define $G(\beta;\lambda_3) \equiv \beta + \lambda_3(1-\beta)^2/(1-\lambda_3\beta)$. Since $\beta_1 > \beta_2$, Γ is positive if G_β is positive. By direct differentiation, $G_\beta = (1-\lambda_3)^2/(1-\lambda_3\beta)^2 > 0$. Hence $\Gamma > 0$ and $dP_0/d(y_1/y_2) < 0$.

8   Inequality and the stability of the banking sector

I   Introduction

Banking is a key sector, the stability of which is a prerequisite for the sound growth and development of any economy. However, stability of the banking sector cannot be taken for granted as the business of banking rides – as Diamond and Dybvig (1983) have aptly put it – on 'the transformation of illiquid assets into liquid liabilities' and hence involves risk by banking firms and the confidence of the public, probably more than any other sector of an economy. Lately, the phenomenal increase in the incidence of bank failures in the US has raised this issue among policy-makers as well as the general public. Why has this happened? Popular explanations include deregulation resulting in fierce competition among banks, a depressed oil or real-estate market and so on, that have led many banks to invest heavily in risky assets. These factors seem reasonable and probably explain well the extent of bank failure observed recently in the US.

The episode, however, raises the question of factors in general – not just the woes of particular asset markets that the banks may be investing in – which may contribute to the likelihood that a bank will fail. In line with previous chapters, this chapter argues that distributional changes may have implications for the stability of the banking sector. More precisely, it advances a hypothesis that *increased disparities in savings (presumably due to increased disparities in income) in a market economy would lead to a higher proportion of risky to riskless assets in a bank's portfolio*, thereby contributing to commercial bank failure. I call this Hypothesis M – the main hypothesis. I show that Hypothesis M is built on two more basic hypotheses which are related but largely independent of each other:

Hypothesis A: Increase in savings disparities beyond a certain threshold leads to a larger ratio of time to demand deposits (T/D ratio briefly).

Hypothesis B: A larger T/D ratio implies a larger share of risky projects in a bank's asset portfolio.

II   Hypothesis A

Consider a simple model of household savings behaviour, somewhat similar to those typically used in the literature on bank runs, as in Diamond and Dybvig (1983) and Waldo (1985) for example.

150

Assumption 1: Households live for two periods. In the beginning of period 1, a household receives an endowment, w_h. Different households receive different endowments. Let $(\underline{w}_h, \overline{w}_h)$ be the support of w_h. Their preferences are alike.

Assumption 2: Households face random assessment, x, at the end of period 1 (as in Waldo).

There are two critical assumptions imposed on the distribution of x.

Assumption 3a: x has a finite support, say $(\underline{x}, \overline{x})$.

Assumption 3b: The density function $g(x)$ is the same across the households, that is, independent of w_h. (The implications of relaxing this assumption are discussed later.)

Assumption 4: The households consume only at the end of period 2.

It is thus a savings model. The scenario is equivalent to imagining three periods. Endowments are received in period 1, assessments are made in period 2 and households consume in period 3.

At the beginning of period 1, the endowments are put into commercial banks in the form of one-period 'demand deposit', s_{1h}, or two-period 'time deposit', s_{2h}, or both. Thus

$$s_{1h} + s_{2h} = w_h. \tag{8.1}$$

Demand and time deposits respectively pay gross interest rates, r_1 and r_2 per period.

Since the assessment is random, it may fall short of or exceed the total yield on demand deposits, equal to $s_{1h}r_1$. In the former case, the excess amount can be put into a one-period deposit paying an interest rate r'.[1] In the latter case,

Assumption 5: A household can withdraw from time deposit but the interest rate paid on the amount of early withdrawal is zero.

This is the penalty for early withdrawal. More generally, it could be any rate below r_1 or r' without changing any results. Also, the penalty may not be just monetary; it could include the cost of inconvenience.

Assumption 5 rules out the corner solution of all deposits being held in time deposits as a necessary outcome. To rule out the other corner solution of zero time deposit as a necessary outcome, it is assumed that

Assumption 6: $r_2 > \max(r_1, r')$.

In order to concentrate on the savings allocation of households,

Assumption 7: Households are not allowed to borrow from each other or from the commercial banks.

Assumption 8: If the assessment x net of total yield on demand deposits exceeds the amount of time deposit, the deficit is covered by working for an outside agent. Leisure and terminal consumption are perfect substitutes of each other. (This happens when low-endowment households face the prospect of negative terminal consumption, more precisely when $w_h r_1 < \bar{x}$)

Given the above structure, the expression for a household's (terminal) consumption inclusive of leisure equals

$$
c = \begin{cases} c_1 = \left[s_{1h}r_1 - x\right]r' + s_{2h}r_2^2 + L & \text{if } x \leq s_{1h}r_1 \\ c_2 = \left[s_{2h} - (x - s_{1h}r_1)\right]r_2^2 + L & \text{if } x \geq s_{1h}r_1, \end{cases}
$$

where L is the total leisure in terms of terminal consumption. Using the budget constraint (8.1), these expressions can be written as

$$
c = \begin{cases} c_1 = -s_{1h}\delta_1 - xr' + w_h r_2^2 + L & \text{if } x \leq s_{1h}r_1 \\ c_2 = (w_h - x)r_2^2 + s_{1h}\delta_2 + L & \text{if } x \geq s_{1h}r_1, \end{cases} \tag{8.2}
$$

where $\delta_1 = r_2^2 - r_1 r' > 0$ and $\delta_2 = (r_1 - 1)r_2^2 > 0$. δ_1 and δ_2 are the opportunity costs, in terms of the terminal consumption, of the first-period demand deposit in the event of no early withdrawal and in the event of early withdrawal respectively.

Finally, it is assumed that

Assumption 9: Households are risk neutral or risk averse. If risk averse, the measure of absolute risk aversion is nonincreasing.

Hypothesis A under risk neutrality
Hypothesis A is seen most clearly in the risk neutrality case. Suppressing the h subscript, the household problem can be stated as

$$
\text{Maximize } y = \int_{\underline{s_1}}^{s_1 r_1} c_1 dG(x) + \int_{s_1 r_1}^{\bar{x}} c_2 dG(x) \tag{8.3}
$$

subject to $0 \leq s_1 \leq w$ and (8.2). $G(x)$ is the cumulative distribution function of $g(x)$. Substituting (8.2) into (8.3), and differentiating

$$\frac{dy}{ds_1} = -\delta_1 \int_{\underline{x}}^{s_1 r_1} dG(x) + \delta_2 \int_{s_1 r_1}^{\bar{x}} dG(x)$$

and

$$\frac{d^2 y}{ds_1^2} = -(\delta_1 + \delta_2) r_1 g(s_1 r_1) < 0.$$

Let $\tilde{s}_1$ solve for $dy/ds_1 = 0$. $\tilde{s}_1$ is clearly independent of w. If $\tilde{s}_1 < w$, the optimal s_1, say s_1^*, equals $\tilde{s}_1$, independent of w; this is an interior solution. Otherwise, a corner solution is implied at $s_1^* = w$. s_1^* as a function of w is depicted as the kinked line OAB in Figure 8.1A. Any household with endowment below or equal to w_a keeps all its savings in the form of demand deposits and those with endowment above w_a keep a fixed amount in the form of demand deposit and the rest in the form of time deposit.

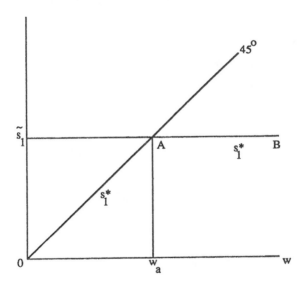

Figure 8.1A   Demand deposit under risk neutrality

It is clear from Figure 8.1A that any redistribution of endowment among households to the left of w_a or among those to the right of w_a does not affect the total amount of demand or time deposit. But transfers from low-endowment households to the left of w_a to high-endowment households to the right of w_a lead to a one-to-one decrease in demand deposit and hence a one-to-one increase in time deposit, since the low-endowment households do not participate in the time deposit market and the high-endowment households keep every extra dollar of savings in the form of time deposits. This supports Hypothesis A.

It is assumed in the preceding analysis that the distribution of assessments is independent of endowment (Assumption 3b). In reality, assessments which largely arise out of necessities (such as basic medical bills) may well approximate this assumption. However, other assessments, associated typically with durable goods, luxuries (status!) and so on, may vary with endowment. It may be reasonable to suppose that the expected assessment is an increasing function of endowment. To capture this, define $x \equiv z + \theta$, where z is random with support $(\underline{z},\ \bar{z})$ and θ is a positive term independent of z. Expected assessment is then equal to $E(x) = E(z) + \theta$. An increase in θ implies an increase in expected assessment. Let $\theta = \theta(w)$, $\theta' > 0$. It is straightforward to derive that $\tilde{s}_1$ is no longer independent of w. dy/ds_1 equals

$$\frac{dy}{ds_1} = -\delta_1 \int_{\underline{z}}^{s_1 r_1 - \theta(w)} dG(z) + \delta_2 \int_{s_1 r_1 - \theta(w)}^{\bar{z}} dG(z).$$

Setting $dy/ds_1 = 0$,

$$\frac{d\tilde{s}_1}{dw} = \frac{\theta'(w)}{r_1} > 0$$

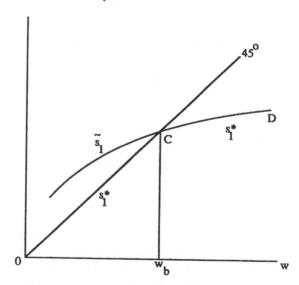

Figure 8.1B   Demand deposit under risk neutrality (assessments dependent on endowment)

and hence $d\bar{s}_1^2/dw^2 \gtreqless 0$ according as $\theta'' \gtreqless 0$. It is now immediate that Hypothesis A holds as long as θ'' is zero or negative, that is, expected assessments are proportional to or a strictly concave function of endowment. The case of $\theta'' < 0$ is depicted in Figure 8.1B. The s_1^* function is indicated by the kinked curve *OCD*. Any redistribution of endowment from a point to the left of w_b to a point to the right of w_b would result in a decrease in total demand deposit and hence an increase in total time deposit since households to the left of w_b keep every dollar in demand deposit and households to the right of w_b keep less than a dollar out of an extra dollar of total savings.

Hypothesis A under nonincreasing absolute risk aversion
Returning to Assumption 3b, and denoting the nonlinear utility function by $u(c)$, $u' > 0 > u''$, the household problem is to

$$\text{Maximize } z = \int_{s_1}^{s_1 r_1} u(c_1)dG(x) + \int_{s_1 r_1}^{\bar{x}} u(c_2)dG(x)$$

subject again to $0 \le s_1 \le w$ and (8.2).

To begin with, consider any household for which there is an interior solution for s_1. For this household, s_1^* is determined by

$$\frac{dz}{ds_1} = -\delta_1 \int_{\underline{x}}^{s_1 r_1} u'(c_1)dG(x) + \delta_2 \int_{s_1 r_1}^{\bar{x}} u'(c_2)dG(x) = 0. \qquad (8.4)$$

The second order condition, $d^2z/ds_1^2 < 0$, is ensured by risk aversion. The utility function being nonlinear, s_1^* is generally dependent on w. Totally differentiating (8.4),

$$\frac{ds_1^*}{dw} = -\frac{r_2^2 K}{dz^2/ds_1^2}, \quad \text{where}$$

$$K \equiv -\delta_1 \int_{\underline{x}}^{s_1 r_1} u''(c_1)dG(x) + \delta_2 \int_{s_1 r_1}^{\bar{x}} u''(c_2)dG(x).$$

In the special case of constant absolute risk aversion, $K = (u''/u')dz/ds_1 = 0$, in view of the first-order condition (8.4). Thus the implication of a savings distribution is analogous to the risk neutrality case.

In case of decreasing absolute risk aversion, hypothesis A holds even more strongly. In this case, as shown in Appendix 8.1, K turns out to be negative. Thus $ds_1^*/dw < 0$. Thus, interestingly, *for those households for whom there is an interior solution for s_1^* demand deposits are an inferior good* – in contrast to it being a neutral good under risk neutrality or constant absolute risk aversion. This stems from two factors: (a) risk is a decreasing function of endowment, so that as endowment increases, the household tends to take greater advantage of the chance of keeping more in time deposit and less in demand deposit, and (b) the assumption that households do not consume in period 1 at all.

Starting from any particular endowment level for which there is an interior solution, if the endowment is continuously reduced, the difference between endowment and s_1^* will decrease continuously and there will be a critical level of endowment, say w_c, at and below which s_1^* equals the endowment. Households with endowment w_c or less keep all their savings in the form of demand deposits. Starting from w_c, if endowment is increased continuously, s_1^* would asymptotically approach $\underline{x}/r_1$, the minimum possible assessment. This says that it is never optimal to save for one period an amount which would not cover the minimum assessment (unless of course the endowment is too low as a binding constraint). Formally, this is seen by evaluating dz/ds_1 at $s_1 = \underline{x}/r_1$ – which equals

$$\delta_2 \int_{s_1 r_1}^{\bar{x}} u'(c_2) dG(x) > 0.$$

Thus, a marginal increase in s_1 at $\underline{x}/r_1$ increases expected utility.

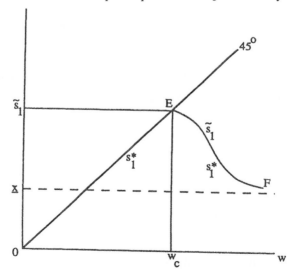

Figure 8.2   Demand deposit under decreasing absolute risk aversion

s_1^* as a function of w in the decreasing absolute risk aversion case is depicted as the kinked curve *OEF* in Figure 8.2. w_c is the solution of the equation $dz/ds_1|_{s_1=w} = 0$. As in the previous case, any redistribution within the lower end of endowment distribution (below w_c) does not affect the total amount of demand or time deposits. A more unequal redistribution within the higher end of endowment distribution will leave unchanged, decrease or possibly increase the total amount of demand deposits as long as the redistribution takes place within the linear, strictly concave or strictly convex range of s_1^*. However, a more drastic redistribution of endowment from low-endowment households to the left of w_c to high-endowment households to the right of w_c will have *a double-barrel negative effect* on demand deposit and hence *a double-barrel positive effect* on time deposit. This is because both the low-endowment households and the high-endowment households will keep less in the demand deposit. Thus Hypothesis A comes out even stronger.

Supply schedule of time deposit
I now derive the household supply schedule of time deposit at given r_1, which will be needed later, and regard a change in endowment distribution as a parametric shift.[2] The demand for deposits by households is viewed here as the 'supply' of inputs to a banking firm.

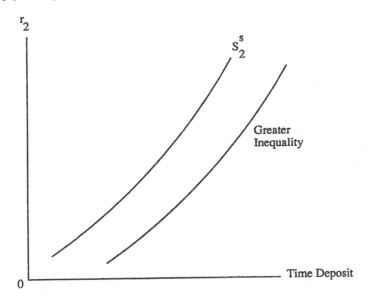

Figure 8.3A   Supply curve of time deposit under risk neutrality

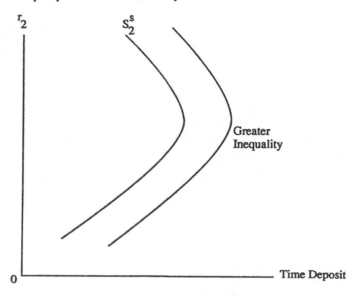

Figure 8.3B   Supply curve of time deposit under nonincreasing absolute risk aversion

In the risk neutrality case, it is straightforward to derive from $dy/ds_1 = 0$ that $ds_1^*/dr_2 < 0$. Hence, those who supply time deposits will supply more (hence supply demand deposits less) as r_2 increases. $ds_1^*/dr_2 < 0$ also implies that the point w_a in Figure 8.1A moves to the left; as a result, some households who did not participate in the time deposit market do so now. Hence the time deposit supply curve is unambiguously positively sloped. Under risk aversion, however, ds_1^*/dr_2 is ambiguous in sign (even under constant absolute risk aversion). Thus, the time deposit supply curve may have a portion which is negatively sloped.

These possibilities are illustrated in Figures 8.3A–B. In each case, however, a sufficiently strong redistribution from low- to high-endowment households shifts the supply curve, S_2^s, to the right.

III   Hypotheses B and M
We now turn to the banking behaviour. Hypothesis B concerns the impact of the liability portfolio of a bank on its asset portfolio. The Modigliani–Miller theorem reminds us that there will be no impact if banks have access to a perfect capital market. Hence the necessary condition for generating Hypothesis B is to assume some form of imperfection in capital market. This is spelled out in Assumption 13 below, among other assumptions.

Assumption 10: Commercial banking is a competitive industry and all banks are alike.

Assumption 11: Like households, bankers live for two periods.

Assumption 12: At the beginning of period 1, banks face two types of investment projects: a liquid project and an illiquid project. The liquid project matures in one period with a sure gross return of ρ_1. The illiquid project matures in two periods with a random (two-period) gross return, ρ_2. The expected ρ_2 exceeds ρ_1^2.[3]

Similar to the borrowing constraint facing the households,

Assumption 13: Banks cannot borrow from each other or from outside in period 1. In case of a negative net worth due to a low realization of ρ_2, the banker works for an outside agent to cover the deficit. Leisure has the same unit as the terminal profit.

Assumption 13 captures in an extreme form the imperfection in the capital market facing the banks.

In this section, let s_1, s' and s_2 denote respectively a bank's demand for a one-period demand deposit at the beginning of period 1, that at the beginning of period 2, and the demand for a (two-period) time deposit at the beginning of period 1. Let i_1 and i_2 be a bank's investment at the beginning of period 1 in the liquid and in the illiquid project respectively. Assumption 13 then implies the following overall budget constraint facing a bank

$$i_1 + i_2 = s_1 + s_2 \tag{8.5}$$

as well as an end-of-period-one constraint:

$$s_1 r_1 \leq i_1 \rho_1.^4 \tag{8.6}$$

We may substitute (8.5) into (8.6) and eliminate i_1:

$$s_1 r_1 \leq \left(s_1 + s_2 - i_2\right)\rho_1. \tag{8.6'}$$

Assumption 14: A bank perceives the early withdrawal from time deposits as a random variable, v, with a given distribution.

Assumption 15: Banks are risk averse and the measure of the absolute risk aversion is nonincreasing.

Hypothesis B

The optimization problem facing a bank is solved backwards. At the end of period 1 the only choice variable is the demand for one-period demand deposits. The bank maximizes

$$\pi_2 = Eu\left[L_b + \left(i_1\rho_1 - s_1 r_1\right)\rho_1 + s'\left(\rho_1 - r'\right) + \left(i_2 - v\right)\rho_2 - \left(s_2 - v\right)r_2^2\right]. \quad (8.7)$$

The first term is the total leisure available to the banker. Because of the borrowing constraint (8.6), the second term is always nonnegative. This is the total yield on any excess investment in the liquid asset in the beginning of period 1. (It will, however, be shown below that in equilibrium this term is zero.) The third term is the net profit/loss made from demand deposits in period 2. (This term will also be shown to be zero in equilibrium.) The fourth term is the total return from investment in the illiquid asset. The last term is the cost of time deposits to the bank. Finally, the expectation operator is defined over the distribution of ρ_2 and v.

From (8.7), $d\pi_2/ds' = (\rho_1 - r')Eu'(.) \gtreqless 0$. The bank has a perfectly elastic demand schedule for s' at $r' = \rho_1$. Hence in market equilibrium, $r' = \rho_1$. (In view of the previous model of household behaviour, the supply of s' at r' is of course random depending on the realization of assessment across the households.)

The decision problem facing a bank at the beginning of period 1 can now be stated as

$$\underset{s_1, s_2, i_1, i_2}{\text{Maximize}}\ \bar{\pi} \equiv Eu(\pi) \equiv Eu\left\{L_b + \left[\left(s_1 + s_2 - i_2\right)\rho_1 - s_1 r_1\right]\rho_1 + \left(i_2 - v\right)\rho_2 - \left(s_2 - v\right)r_2^2\right\}$$

subject to (8.6'). Setting the Lagrangian

$$\mathcal{L} = Eu\left\{L_b + \left[\left(s_1 + s_2 - i_2\right)\rho_1 - s_1 r_1\right]\rho_1 + \left(i_2 - v\right)\rho_2 - \left(s_2 - v\right)r_2^2\right\}$$

$$+ \lambda\left[\left(s_1 + s_2 - i_2\right)\rho_1 - s_1 r_1\right],$$

we obtain $\partial\mathcal{L}/\partial s_1 = (\rho_1 - r_1)\left[\rho_1 Eu'(\pi) + \lambda\right] \gtreqless 0$. Hence the first period demand for demand deposits is also perfectly elastic at $r_1 = \rho_1$. In market equilibrium then, $r_1 = \rho_1$.

The first-order conditions with respect to s_2 and i_2 are:

$$\partial\mathcal{L}/\partial s_2 = \left(\rho_1^2 - r_2^2\right)Eu'(\pi) + \lambda\rho_1 = 0 \qquad (8.8a)$$

$$\partial \mathcal{L} / \partial i_2 = E\left[u'(\pi)\left(\rho_2 - \rho_1^2\right)\right] - \lambda \rho_1 = 0. \tag{8.8b}$$

Since $r_2 > r_1$ by assumption and $r_1 = \rho_1$, it follows that $r_2 > \rho_1$. Hence (8.8a) implies that λ must be positive and therefore (8.6') must be satisfied with equality. It is then immediate that $i_1 = s_1$ and $i_2 = s_2$, which proves Hypothesis B. A larger s_2/s_1 ratio in equilibrium would imply a larger i_2/i_1 ratio. It may be recapitulated that it is the capital market imperfection and the presumption that illiquid assets are risky which are critical in generating Hypothesis B.

This is a strong separation result: all demand deposits are allocated to short-term liquid investment and all time deposits are channelled into the longer-term illiquid investment. The result is due to the strong borrowing constraint assumption. A weaker borrowing constraint should imply that a major portion of demand deposits is allocated to the liquid investment and a major portion of the time deposits is allocated to the illiquid risky investment.

Hypothesis M
The bank behaviour and the household behaviour can now be integrated to generate Hypothesis M. Continuing with the bank behaviour, if we add (8.8a) and (8.8b) and use $r_1 = \rho_1$ and $i_2 = s_2$, the rule for optimal i_2 (or s_2) can be stated as:

$$E\left(u'\left[i_2\left(\rho_2 - r_2^2\right)\right]\left(\rho_2 - r_2^2\right)\right) = 0.^5 \tag{8.8c}$$

(8.8c) defines i_2 as a function of r_2. It can be derived (see Appendix 8.2) that under nonincreasing absolute risk aversion, $di_2/dr_2 < 0$, as expected. This function is illustrated in Figure 8.4. We may call it loosely the demand curve of time deposit or equivalently the demand for the risky asset, although it is not so in the usual sense of the term since the market equilibrium condition for the demand deposit is already implicit in it.

It is now straightforward to deduce the impact of an increase in savings disparity on i_2. As Figure 8.4 shows, a sufficiently strong increase in endowment disparity shifts the supply curve of time deposits, S_2^s, to the right. In equilibrium, r_2 falls. Consequently, there are more time deposits and investment in the illiquid risky project at the new equilibrium. (This holds even when the supply curve is backward-bending as long as it is steeper than the demand curve to ensure stability.) Total savings remaining unchanged by assumption, there are less demand deposits and less investment in the riskless asset. The proportion of risky to riskless investments is thus higher.

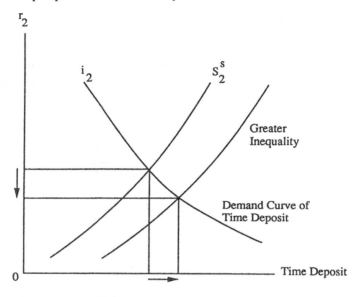

Figure 8.4   Equilibrium time deposit and the effect of greater inequality

IV   Probability of bank failure and measures of bank risk

An increase in the proportion of relatively risky to riskless asset holdings would not necessarily increase but would contribute to the probability of a bank failure. We may define the probability of bank failure as directly proportional to the probability of negative net worth. If N (> 0) denotes the initial bank endowment, profits equal $\pi = i_2(\rho_2 - r_2^2) + Nr_2^2$ and accordingly the probability of negative net worth equals

$$\Pr\left[i_2\left(\rho_2 - r_2^2\right) + Nr_2^2\right] < 0, \text{ or } \Pr\left[\rho_2 < r_2^2\left(1 - \frac{N}{i_2}\right)\right]. \tag{8.9}$$

Hence greater investment in risky assets increases the probability of negative net worth, but a change in r_2 has an ambiguous impact. In view of (8.9) and the result that an increase in inequality leads to an increase in i_2 and a decrease in r_2, it follows that an increase in inequality will unambiguously increase the probability of negative net worth if $N/i_2 > 1$. If $N/i_2 < 1$, the effect is ambiguous in general but positive if the magnitude of the decrease in r_2 is not large. This can happen if the demand curve for time deposits is convex and the banking sector is sufficiently large so that the equilibrium in the market for time deposits is at a relatively low value of r_2. It is interesting that in a regulatory regime with the interest rate ceiling at a rate well below the equilibrium rate, r_2 remains unchanged and hence an increase in inequality unambiguously enhances the likelihood of a bank failure.

The probability of bank failure is one of several definitions of 'bank risk' in the literature on banking; see, for example, Blair and Heggestad (1978) and Mitchell (1982), among others.[6] The impact of inequality on other measures of bank risk would, however, be similar.[7]

V   Concluding remarks
A change in the total volume of savings could possibly affect the ratio of time to demand deposits and hence the proportion of risky assets in the commercial bank portfolio. However, this 'size' effect was ruled out by construction in order to emphasize the impact of changes in the distribution of savings across households on the composition of savings and on the composition of banks' investment profile. The model of this chapter clearly abstracts from many intricacies of the banking sector and many other determinants of stability of the banking sector, such as the availability of insurance and different forms of regulation. Also it does not directly address the phenomenon of bank runs. The objective was quite specific: *ceteris paribus*, how does the distribution of savings affect a bank's portfolio of risky versus riskless assets and hence how may distributional changes in income contribute to commercial bank failure? The implications of changes in the distribution of savings can be linked to that in income, to the extent that savings and income are positively correlated.

The model developed in the chapter is a bench-mark model in that it generates Hypotheses A, B and M in an extreme form. But it seems to illustrate clearly the mechanisms which bring about these hypotheses. Quantitative impact of these hypotheses is of course an empirical matter.

Distributional changes in an economy can affect the stability of the banking sector in other ways that are not explored here. For example, a greater dispersion of wealth or income may change the distribution of borrowers towards more borrowers with less creditworthiness and hence greater risk for these individuals as well as for banks. Furthermore, the theory of risk-behaviour says that individuals with more wealth or income are likely to undertake high-return risky ventures. And the banks may find, and provide funds to, many of these individuals who demand loans for large, highly ambitious, risky projects and who are capable of satisfying collateral requirements.

The upshot is that although there is a host of factors that can affect the stability of the banking sector, distributional changes may be one of them.

Appendix 8.1   Proof that $K < 0$
Let the terminal consumption be equal to c' when $x = s_1 r_1$. Thus, if $x < s_1 r_1$, then $c_1 > c'$ and hence

$$R_a(c_1) < R_a(c'), \tag{8.A1}$$

where $R_a \equiv -u''/u' \equiv$ the measure of absolute risk aversion, is decreasing in c. Multiply both sides of (8.A1) by $\delta_1 u'(c_1)$. This gives $-\delta_1 u''(c_1) < R_a(c')\delta_1 u'(c_1)$, which implies

$$-\delta_1 \int_{\underline{x}}^{s_1 r_1} u''(c_1) dG(x) < R_a(c')\delta_1 \int_{\underline{x}}^{s_1 r_1} u'(c_1) dG(x). \tag{8.A2}$$

Similarly, if $x > s_1 r_1$, then $c_2 < c'$ and hence $R_a(c_2) > R_a(c')$. Multiplying both sides of this inequality by $-\delta_2 u'(c_2)$ gives $\delta_2 u''(c_2) < -R_a(c')\delta_2 u'(c_2)$. Integrated over $x \in (s_1 r_1, \bar{x})$,

$$\delta_2 \int_{s_1 r_1}^{\bar{x}} u''(c_2) dG(x) < -R_a(c')\delta_2 \int_{s_1 r_1}^{\bar{x}} u'(c_2) dG(x). \tag{8.A3}$$

Adding up (8.A2) and (8.A3), we have

$$K < R_a(c') \left(\delta_1 \int_{\underline{x}}^{s_1 r_1} u'(c_1) dG(x) - \delta_2 \int_{s_1 r_1}^{\bar{x}} u'(c_2) dG(x) \right). \tag{8.A4}$$

In view of the first-order condition (8.4), the right-hand side of (8.A4) is zero. Thus $K < 0$.

Appendix 8.2   Proof that $di_2/dr_2 < 0$ under nonincreasing absolute risk aversion

Totally differentiating (8.8c),

$$\frac{di_2}{dr_2} = 2r_2 \frac{Eu'(\pi) + i_2 E\left[u''(\pi)(\rho_2 - r_2^2)\right]}{E\left[u''(\pi)(\rho_2 - r_2^2)^2\right]}. \tag{8.A5}$$

The denominator and the first term of the numerator of (8.A5) are respectively positive and negative. It is proved below that $E[u''(\pi)(\rho_2 - r_2^2)]$ is positive.

Define $\pi = \pi_0$ at $\rho_2 = r_2^2$. When $\rho_2 \leq r_2^2$, $\pi \leq \pi_0$ and hence with nonincreasing risk absolute aversion, $R_a(\pi) \geq R_a(\pi_0)$. This inequality can be rewritten as

$$u''(\pi) \leq R_a(\pi_0)u'(\pi).$$

Multiplying both sides of the above inequality by $(\rho_2 - r_2^2)$, integrating totally over v and partially over ρ_2,

$$\int_{\alpha}^{r_2^2}\left(\int_v u''(\pi)(\rho_2 - r_2^2)d\phi(v)\right)d\psi(\rho_2) \geq R_a(\pi_0)\int_{\alpha}^{r_2^2}\left(\int_v u'(\pi)(\rho_2 - r_2^2)d\phi(v)\right)d\psi(\rho_2),$$

(8.A6)

where $\phi(v)$ and $\psi(\rho_2)$ are the respective cumulative distribution functions and α is the lower bound of ρ_2. Similar reasoning leads to

$$\int_{r_2^2}^{\beta}\left(\int_v u''(\pi)(\rho_2 - r_2^2)d\phi(v)\right)d\psi(\rho_2) \geq R_a(\pi_0)\int_{r_2^2}^{\beta}\left(\int_v u'(\pi)(\rho_2 - r_2^2)d\phi(v)\right)d\psi(\rho_2),$$

(8.A7)

where β is the upper bound of ρ_2.
  Adding up (8.A6) and (8.A7) yields

$$E\left[u''(\pi)(\rho_2 - r_2^2)\right] \geq R_a(\pi_0)E\left[u'(\pi)(\rho_2 - r_2^2)\right] = 0,$$

as $E[u'(\pi)(\rho_2 - r_2^2)] = 0$ according to (8.8c). Hence the numerator of the r.h.s of (8.A5) is unambiguously positive, and di_2/dr_2 is negative.

Notes

1. It will be shown that, in equilibrium, r' will be equal to r_1.
2. It will be shown that r_1 is constant in equilibrium.
3. A similar assumption is used in the banking model of Bernanke and Gertler (1987).
4. It is assumed here without loss of generality that the initial endowment of the bank is zero. However, the initial endowment is obviously an important element in the overall risk facing a bank and the probability of bank failure. See section IV.
5. For an interior solution, it is necessary that $E(\rho_2) > r_2^2$, i.e., $E(\rho_2) > \rho_1^2$ – which we assume (see *Assumption 12*).
6. A good discussion of various measures of bank risk is contained in Di Cagno (1990).
7. Consider, for instance, just the variance of banks' profits, equal to $i_2^2\sigma_\rho^2$ where σ_ρ^2 is the variance of ρ_2. It increases as i_2 increases. Consider the coefficient of variation in profits (as in Mitchell, 1982), equal to $\sigma_\rho^2/[\bar{\rho}+(N/i_2 - 1)r_2^2]$. It also increases as i_2 increases.

PART III

EMPIRICAL EVIDENCE

9 Preliminaries: available data and correlations

I Introduction

In Parts I and II, I have developed various theoretical models linking distributional changes to business cycles and financial activities. In Part III, my task is to shed empirical evidence on some of these links. In this chapter, I present some preliminaries, while more substantive empirical analysis is undertaken in Chapter 10. I begin with a discussion of the availability of data on distributional changes.

II Availability of data

A lot of data on wealth and income distribution are available across time as well as countries. However, what is required for short-run macro or business-cycle analysis are *continuous* time-series data. Unfortunately such data on distributional changes are generally hard to come by at present, except for a few countries and over a few time intervals. Most available data are unevenly and widely dispersed for most countries. Lack of systematic data collection on distributional changes is probably due to two reasons: first, equity issues are not generally regarded as important as efficiency or aggregate issues, such as changes in real GNP or employment; and second, there is a general lack of understanding that equity itself may be a significantly contributing factor to efficiency – which is precisely the subject matter of this monograph. It is, however, heartening that the state of data collection is improving. Apart from attempts by individual countries and researchers to collect and compile data on distributional changes, efforts are also being made by institutions and research organizations.[1]

In what follows, I discuss the data for the US and their sources, and for a few other countries. Also, in the Appendix I list all the data available to me in the consideration that because such data are not easily available – at least as easily as data on aggregate macro variables – other researchers may find them handy and may perhaps be in a position to expand them to larger and more comprehensive data sets in the future.

Wealth and income distribution data for the US
Incidentally, compared to other countries, the availability of data on distributional changes in the US is not so bad. But there is still much to be desired relative to the availability of regular macro time-series data on GNP, employment, money supply, interest rate, government spending and the like.

Let me begin with data on wealth distribution. It is a fact that a lot of empirical work has been done on wealth distribution and its implications for the macroeconomy in the course of American history. Well-known works include Smith and Franklin (1974), Soltow (1975), Williamson and Lindert (1980) and Williamson (1991), among others. But from the perspective of time-series modelling, the data on wealth distribution are glaringly deficient. They are available only for selected calendar years, units are typically different from one study to another and there is no particular data source on a regular basis – at least, not yet.[2] Table 9.A1 presents the wealth distribution data for the US since 1922.

The availability of data on income distribution is much better. *Historical Statistics of the U.S.: Colonial Times to 1970* (US Department of Commerce, 1975) contains annual data on income shares of the top 1 per cent and 5 per cent of the population over the periods 1913–48 and 1917–48 respectively (see Table 9.A2). Postwar data at annual frequency on income distribution are published regularly in *U.S. Census Population Studies P-60* (US Department of Commerce). Percentage shares of pretax incomes and Gini ratios across families are available from 1947; Gini ratios based on pretax incomes across households are available from 1967 (see Table 9.A3).[3]

Data for other countries

I am less familiar with principal data sources in other countries, but they surely exist – at least for some – and I am aware of the following publications:

Canada	*Survey of Consumer Finances*
Germany	*Transfer Survey*
Israel	*Family Expenditure Survey*
Japan	*Family Income and Expenditure Survey*, Bureau of Statistics, Office of the Prime Minister; *Cost of Living Survey of Farm Households*, Ministry of Agriculture, Forestry and Fisheries; *Survey of People's Living Conditions*, Ministry of Health and Welfare; *Survey of Consumer Finances*
Norway	*Norwegian Tax Files*
Sweden	*Swedish Income-Distribution–Living Survey*
United Kingdom	*Family Expenditure Survey*, annual publications, Department of Employment.[4]

Data on other countries which are available to me from some of these sources and elsewhere are presented in Tables 9.A4–9.A9. As in the case of US, the data on income distribution is much more readily available than those on wealth distribution.

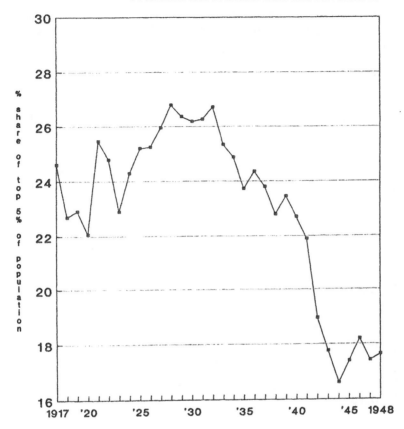

Source: See table 9.A2.

Figure 9.1   Trend in income inequality in the US, 1917–48

III   Some time-series plots

It should be obvious from the tables in the Appendix that there are not many time-series on wealth and income distribution with what may be considered a minimum 'reasonable' number of data points – except the income distribution data for the US (Tables 9.A2 and 9.A3), the UK (Tables 9.A4 and 9.A5), The Netherlands (Table 9.A7) and Japan 1899–1944 (Table 9.A8). The income share of top 5 per cent over 1917–48 and the Gini ratio across families for 1947–90 in the US are graphed in Figures 9.1 and 9.2 respectively. The Gini ratio in Britain over 1961–78 and the top decile's income as a percentage of median income in the UK over 1970–89 are graphed in Figures 9.3 and 9.4 respectively.

Figures 9.5 and 9.6 trace the coefficient of variation in income in The Netherlands over 1914–39 and 1950–72, and finally, Figure 9.7 depicts the same in Japan over 1899–1944.

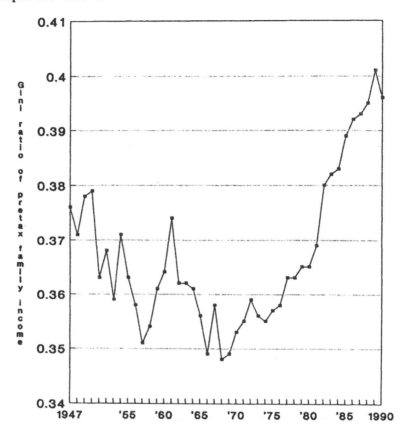

Source: See table 9.A3.

Figure 9.2   Trend in income inequality in the US, 1947–90

The time-series plots illustrate some similarities across countries. During the interwar years, roughly 1920–39, income inequality had an upward trend till the beginning of the Great Depression period, and a downward trend afterwards in both the US and The Netherlands. (There was no increasing or decreasing trend in income inequality in Japan during that period, although over 1899–1938 it had an increasing trend.) There are striking similarities in trend during the postwar years. In the second half of the postwar period, income inequalities in the US and the UK are growing persistently (compare Figures 9.2 and 9.4), and the correlation between the measures in the US and the UK over 1970–89 is 0.97. On the contrary, in the first half of the postwar period, income inequality had a declining trend in the US and The Netherlands. The same cannot be verified for the UK because of lack of data for the initial postwar years, but over 1961–73 the Gini ratio of income in Britain had a declining trend.

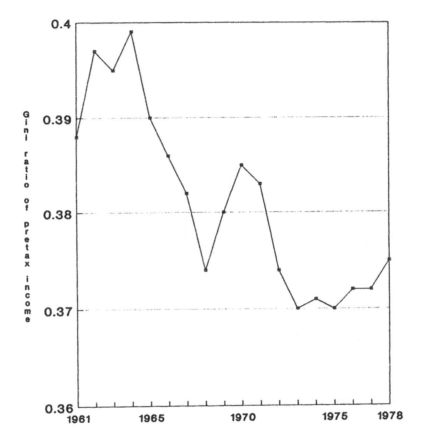

Source: See table 9.A4.

Figure 9.3   Trend in income inequality in the UK, 1961–78

The general pattern that emerges seems to be that at least for some industrialized countries including the US, inequities decreased over roughly the first

20 years following the Second World War but since then they have been on an increasing time trend.

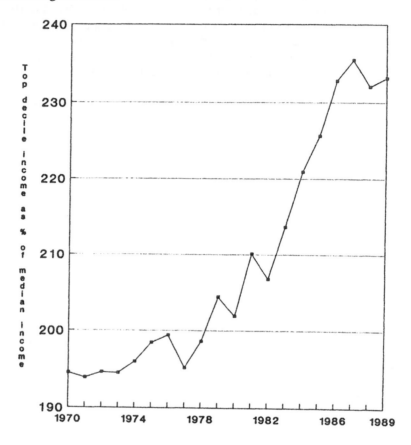

Source: See table 9.A5.

Figure 9.4   Trend in income inequality in the UK, 1970–89

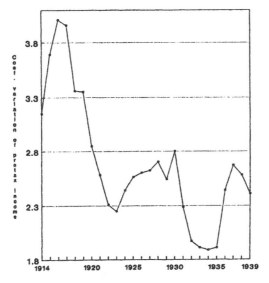

Source: See table 9.A7.

Figure 9.5   Trend in income inequality in The Netherlands, 1914–39

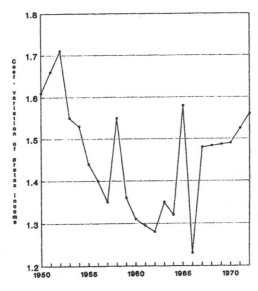

Source: See table 9.A7.

Figure 9.6   Trend in income inequality in The Netherlands, 1950–72

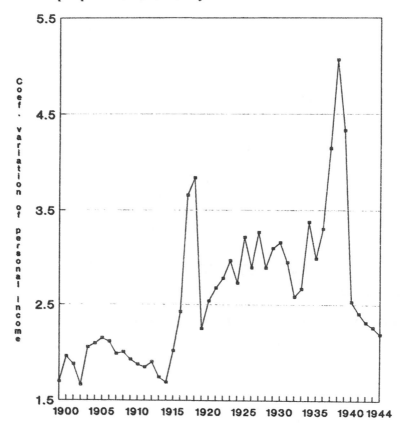

Source: See table 9.A8.

Figure 9.7   Trend in income inequality in Japan, 1899–1944

IV   Correlations

Data constraints do not permit any meaningful time-series analysis involving
wealth distribution. Hence the analysis in this chapter as well as in Chapter 10
will be restricted to income distribution.

I now present some relevant correlation coefficients. Naturally, the most
important one is that between inequality and real GNP/GDP. Chapters in Part
I show that the dynamic interactions between variables result from cross effects
on one another *given their own impacts from the past*. Thus what is more
revealing than just the simple correlation coefficient is the correlation between
residuals from own impacts from the past – or, in other words, between 'innovations' – which are calculated as residuals from univariate time-series modelling
(see Blanchard and Fisher, 1989, ch. 1).

These correlations between income inequality and GNP/GDP were estimated for the US, the UK and Japan over different sample periods. The results are presented in Table 9.1. In each case the time-series of the income inequality measure was nonstationary and an ARIMA(1,0,0) process fitted the data best. Needless to say, the time-series of the log of GNP/GDP was nonstationary; an ARIMA(1,0,0) process turned out to be best-fit, except for the US GNP during 1921–39, which was an ARIMA(1,1,0).[5, 6, 7]

Statistical significance should not be of primary concern at this stage of the analysis primarily because, in general, correlations are based on the slope coefficient of the corresponding simple regression, which could be subject to serious specification errors in the absence of other relevant regressors. It is, however, of independent interest that some correlations are statistically significant and all but one of them pertain to the US. Let us discuss the economic significance in terms of their sign and magnitude.

First, the contemporaneous correlation between innovations in GNP/GDP and income inequality is generally negative, except for UK 1971–89 and Japan 1899–1940, where it is positive. It is interesting that income inequality has been found to be negatively correlated with economic growth *across* countries by Persson and Tabellini (1991). What is seen here is that they may be generally (but not universally) negatively related *across time* as well. A related observation is that the contemporaneous correlation is stronger in the US compared to other countries.

Second, dynamic effects are governed by lagged correlations, and we find that the lagged effects in some cases are 'large' and are not necessarily smaller than contemporaneous correlations. This bears testimony to the hypothesis that distributional changes and aggregative activities may be highly dynamically interactive – at least more interactive than we may have anticipated *a priori*.

Third, there is also a pattern of asymmetry in the lagged correlations. In the postwar US, GNP and lagged inequality are positively correlated, while inequality and lagged GNP are negatively correlated. The above sign pattern also holds for Japan 1899–1940. This is also true for other countries if we concentrate on the correlations which are highest over the three lags, except for UK 1961–78. For example, in UK 1971–89 innovations in lagged inequality and GDP at 0-lag have the highest correlation coefficient, equal to 0.30, when inequality is lagged by three years. Compare this with the highest correlation between lagged GDP and inequality at 0-lag, equal to –0.12, when GDP is lagged by two years. The evidence for interwar US is to the contrary, of course, which means that the nature of dynamic interrelationship in the US may have changed from the interwar period to the postwar period. But this is not inconsistent with the general finding in Part I that there are several channels or mechanisms of interaction between inequality and aggregate output, and they may very well differ from one era to another.

Table 9.1   Contemporaneous and lagged correlation between real GNP/GDP and income inequality

---

US, 1948–1990

	Innovations in GNP at time						
	–3	–2	–1	0	1	2	3
Innovations in income inequality at time 0	–0.20	–0.03	–0.05	–0.51[*]	0.26[***]	0.02	0.04

Innovations in GNP: $\Delta \log (\text{GNP})_t$
Innovations in income inequality: ΔGINI_t

US, 1921–39

	Innovations in GNP at time						
	–3	–2	–1	0	1	2	3
Innovations in income inequality at time 0	0.14	0.21	–0.08	–0.24	0.07	0.10	–0.19

Innovations in GNP: $\Delta \log (\text{GNP})_t - 0.01 - (0.43) \, \Delta \log (\text{GNP})_{t-1}$
Innovations in income inequality: ΔIS_t, IS ≡ income share of top 5% of population

UK, 1971–89

	Innovations in GDP at time						
	–3	–2	–1	0	1	2	3
Innovations in income inequality at time 0	–0.11	0.07	–0.12	0.04	–0.01	0.12	0.30

Innovations in GDP: $\Delta \log (\text{GDP})_t$
Innovations in income inequality: ΔDIN_t, DIN ≡ top decile's income as % of the median income

UK, 1961–78

	Innovations in GDP at time						
	–3	–2	–1	0	1	2	3
Innovations in income inequality at time 0	0.10	–0.04	–0.04	–0.20	–0.09	0.22	0.10

Innovations in GDP: $\Delta \log (\text{GDP})_t$
Innovations in income inequality: ΔGINI_t

Japan, 1899–1940

	Innovations in GNP at time						
	–3	–2	–1	0	1	2	3
Innovations in income inequality at time 0	–0.12	–0.05	–0.04	0.14	0.32[**]	0.03	0.08

Innovations in GNP: $\Delta \log (\text{GNP})_t$
Innovations in income inequality: ΔCV_t, CV ≡ coefficient of variation

---

Notes: [*] = significant at 1%; [**] = significant at 5%; [***] = significant at 10%

V Concluding remarks

It must be stressed that continuous time-series data on wealth and income distribution are a relatively scarce commodity at the moment. It is hoped that more resources will be expended to collect more frequent and better quality data on a regular basis. Only then more definitive conclusions may be reached.

From whatever is available – mostly on income distribution – it appears that during the first half of the postwar years, income inequality was on a declining trend in some of the developed countries including the US, but during the latter half the trend has reversed; it is increasing in the US and the UK at least.

I have presented correlations between innovations in income inequality and real GNP/GDP. Correlations between innovations in inequality and other macro variables may be of some interest, but no compelling reason was felt for reporting and discussing them here, as this chapter is meant to be preliminary anyway. It is erroneous to infer any causality from the lagged correlations. Causal links are formally investigated in Chapter 10.

We have seen in the chapters in Part I that asymmetric lagged cross effects are central to oscillatory dynamics. In the present context, the lagged effects are reflected in the signs of the lagged correlations. Perhaps the most important finding of this chapter is that the observed asymmetric sign pattern of lagged correlations is consistent with the central hypothesis of this monograph that the interaction between distributional changes and aggregate output is itself a source of business fluctuation.[8]

Appendix 9.1

Table 9.A1   Trend in wealth inequality in the US

	Wealth share of top 0.5% of the population (in %)		Wealth share of top 0.5% of the population (in %)
1922	29.8	1956	25.0
1929	32.4	1958	21.7
1933	25.2	1962	22.2
1939	28.0	1965	23.7
1945	20.9	1969	21.8
1949	19.3	1972	21.9
1953	22.7	1976	14.3
1954	22.5	1983	26.9*

Note: * This number is obtained from Phillips (1990, Appendix B). It is the wealth share of the top 0.5 per cent of households (rather than of population).

Sources: Figures for 1922, 1929, 1933, 1939, 1945, 1949, 1953, 1954, 1956, 1958, 1965 from Williamson and Lindert (1980, p. 54); figures for 1962, 1969, 1972 and 1976 from *Statistical Abstracts of the U.S., 1985*, Department of Commerce.

	Wealth share of top 1% of the population (in %)
1958	26.9
1962	23.8
1965	29.2
1969	27.4
1972	27.7
1976	19.2

Sources: Figures for 1958, 1965 from Williamson and Lindert (1980, p. 54); figures for 1962, 1969, 1972 and 1976 from *Statistical Abstracts of the U.S., 1985*, Department of Commerce.

continued

Table 9.A1 continued

	Wealth share of top 1% of adults (in %)	Wealth share of top 1% of adults or families (in %)
1922	31.6	31.6
1929	36.3	36.3
1933	28.3	28.3
1939	30.6	30.6
1945	23.3	23.3
1949	20.8	20.8
1953	24.3	27.5
1954	24.0	n.a.
1956	26.0	26.0
1958	23.8	26.9
1962	22.0	27.4
1963	n.a	31.6
1965	23.4	29.2
1969	20.1	24.9
1972	20.7	n.a.
1983	n.a	34.3
1987	n.a	36.0

Note: n.a. = not available

Sources: Wealth share of adults from *Statistical Abstracts of the U.S., 1985;* Wealth share of adults or families from Batra (1988).

Table 9.A2   Trend in income inequality in the US, 1913–48

	Income share of population (in %)				
	top 1%	top 5%		top 1%	top 5%
1913	14.98	n.a.	1931	13.31	26.27
1914	13.07	n.a.	1932	13.25	26.71
1915	14.32	n.a.	1933	12.48	25.34
1916	15.58	n.a.	1934	12.48	24.88
1917	14.16	24.60	1935	12.05	23.73
1918	12.69	22.69	1936	13.14	24.35
1919	12.84	22.91	1937	12.84	23.80
1920	12.34	22.07	1938	11.45	22.80
1921	13.50	25.47	1939	11.80	23.45
1922	13.38	24.79	1940	11.89	22.71
1923	12.28	22.89	1941	11.39	21.89
1924	12.91	24.29	1942	10.06	18.94
1925	13.73	25.20	1943	9.38	17.75
1926	13.93	25.25	1944	8.58	16.62
1927	14.39	25.96	1945	8.81	17.39
1928	14.94	26.78	1946	8.98	18.20
1929	14.65	26.36	1947	8.49	17.41
1930	14.12	26.19	1948	8.38	17.63

Note: n.a. = not available

Source: Historical Statistics of the U.S., Colonial Times to 1970, Department of Commerce of the US, 1975.

Table 9.A3   Trend in income inequality in the US, 1947–90

	% distribution of aggregate income across families					across families	across households
	Lowest fifth	Second fifth	Third fifth	Fourth fifth	Highest fifth	Top 5%	Gini ratio	Gini ratio
1947	5.0	11.9	17.0	23.1	43.0	17.5	.376	n.a.
1948	4.9	12.1	17.3	23.2	42.4	17.1	.371	n.a.
1949	4.5	11.9	17.3	23.5	42.7	16.9	.378	n.a.
1950	4.5	12.0	17.4	23.4	42.7	17.3	.379	n.a.
1951	5.0	12.4	17.6	23.4	41.6	16.8	.363	n.a.
1952	4.9	12.3	17.4	23.4	41.9	17.4	.368	n.a.
1953	4.7	12.5	18.0	23.9	40.9	15.7	.359	n.a.
1954	4.5	12.1	17.7	23.9	41.8	16.3	.371	n.a.
1955	4.8	12.3	17.8	23.7	41.3	16.4	.363	n.a.
1956	5.0	12.5	17.9	23.7	41.0	16.1	.358	n.a.
1957	5.1	12.7	18.1	23.8	40.4	15.6	.351	n.a.
1958	5.0	12.5	18.0	23.9	40.6	15.4	.354	n.a.
1959	4.9	12.3	17.9	23.8	41.1	15.9	.361	n.a.
1960	4.8	12.2	17.8	24.0	41.3	15.9	.364	n.a.
1961	4.7	11.9	17.5	23.8	42.2	16.6	.374	n.a.
1962	5.0	12.1	17.6	24.0	41.3	15.7	.362	n.a.
1963	5.0	12.1	17.7	24.0	41.2	15.8	.362	n.a.
1964	5.1	12.0	17.7	24.0	41.2	15.9	.361	n.a.
1965	5.2	12.2	17.8	23.9	40.9	15.5	.356	n.a.
1966	5.6	12.4	17.8	23.8	40.5	15.6	.349	n.a.
1967	5.4	12.2	17.5	23.5	41.4	16.4	.358	.399
1968	5.7	12.4	17.7	23.7	40.5	15.6	.348	.388
1969	5.6	12.4	17.7	23.7	40.6	15.6	.349	.391
1970	5.5	12.2	17.6	23.8	40.9	15.6	.353	.394
1971	5.5	12.0	17.6	23.8	41.0	15.6	.355	.396
1972	5.5	11.9	17.5	23.9	41.4	15.9	.359	.401
1973	5.5	11.9	17.5	24.0	41.1	15.5	.356	.397
1974	5.6	12.0	17.5	24.0	41.0	15.4	.355	.395
1975	5.5	11.8	17.6	24.1	41.1	15.5	.357	.397
1976	5.5	11.8	17.6	24.1	41.1	15.6	.358	.398
1977	5.3	11.6	17.5	24.2	41.4	15.7	.363	.402
1978	5.3	11.6	17.5	24.1	41.5	15.6	.363	.402
1979	5.3	11.6	17.5	24.0	41.7	15.8	.365	.404
1980	5.2	11.5	17.5	24.3	41.5	15.3	.365	.403
1981	5.1	11.3	17.4	24.4	41.8	15.3	.369	.406
1982	4.8	11.2	17.1	24.2	42.7	15.9	.380	.412
1983	4.7	11.1	17.1	24.3	42.8	15.9	.382	.414
1984	4.7	11.0	17.0	24.3	42.9	16.0	.383	.415
1985	4.7	10.9	16.8	24.1	43.5	16.7	.389	.419
1986	4.6	10.8	16.8	24.0	43.7	17.0	.392	.425
1987	4.6	10.8	16.8	24.0	43.8	17.2	.393	.426
1988	4.6	10.7	16.7	24.0	44.0	17.2	.395	.427
1989	4.6	10.6	16.5	23.7	44.6	17.9	.401	.431
1990	n.a.	n.a.	n.a.	n.a.	n.a.	n.a.	.396	.428

Note: n.a. = not available

Sources: US Census. *Population Studies, P-60*, no. 162, February 1989, for 1947–66, no. 168, September 1990, for 1967–89, no. 174, August 1991, for 1990.

Table 9.A4   Trend in income inequality in the UK, 1949–82

					Share of pre-tax income					
	Top 1%	Top 5%	Top 10%	Top 20%	4th qntl	3rd qntl	2nd qntl	Bottom 20%	Bottom 10%	Gini ratio
1949	11.1	23.8	33.2	47.3	20.8	n.a.	n.a.	n.a.	n.a.	.411
1954	9.3	20.8	30.1	45.2	22.9	16.3	n.a.	n.a.	n.a.	.403
1959	8.4	19.9	29.4	44.5	23.3	16.6	10.3	5.3	n.a.	.398
1961	8.1	19.2	28.9	43.7	23.3	17.1	10.6	5.4	n.a.	.388
1962	8.3	19.5	29.2	44.4	23.5	16.8	10.4	5.1	n.a.	.397
1963	8.0	19.2	28.9	44.3	23.5	16.6	10.3	5.3	n.a.	.395
1964	8.2	19.5	29.1	44.6	23.5	16.6	10.1	5.2	n.a.	.399
1965	8.1	19.6	29.0	44.2	23.2	16.8	10.3	5.6	n.a.	.390
1966	7.7	18.8	28.5	43.7	23.5	16.5	10.7	5.6	2.2	.386
1967	7.4	18.4	28.0	43.2	23.7	16.8	10.8	5.6	2.2	.382
1968–9	7.1	17.8	27.1	42.5	23.9	17.0	10.9	5.7	2.3	.374
1969–70	7.0	17.8	27.2	42.7	24.0	17.0	10.8	5.5	2.2	.380
1970–1	6.6	17.7	27.5	43.4	24.1	16.4	10.5	5.6	2.5	.385
1971–2	6.5	17.5	27.3	43.2	24.2	16.6	10.4	5.6	2.3	.383
1972–3	6.4	17.2	26.9	42.7	24.1	16.7	10.7	5.8	n.a.	.374
1973–4	6.5	17.1	26.8	42.4	24.1	16.8	10.5	6.2	2.7	.370
1974–5	6.2	16.8	26.6	42.4	24.1	16.9	10.4	6.2	2.6	.371
1975–6	5.6	16.0	25.8	41.9	24.5	16.9	10.5	6.2	2.6	.366
1976–7	5.5	16.3	26.2	42.4	24.4	16.5	10.5	6.2	2.5	.372
1977–8	5.5	16.1	26.2	42.5	24.4	16.4	10.5	6.1	2.5	.371
1978–9	5.3	16.0	26.1	42.6	24.7	16.5	10.3	5.9	2.4	.375
1981–2	6.0	17.6	28.3	45.0	23.9	15.6	10.2	5.5	2.0	.400

Note: n.a. = not available

Source: Nolan (1987, Table 2.1).

Table 9.A5   Trend in income inequality in the UK, 1970–89

	Income of the top decile as % of median income		Income of the top decile as % of median income
1970	194.4	1980	201.9
1971	193.8	1981	210.1
1972	194.5	1982	206.7
1973	194.4	1983	213.6
1974	195.9	1984	220.9
1975	198.4	1985	225.6
1976	199.4	1986	232.7
1977	195.1	1987	235.4
1978	198.6	1988	232.0
1979	204.4	1989	233.1

Source: Family Expenditure Survey, annual publications, Department of Employment.

Table 9.A6   Trend in wealth inequality in Britain, 1923–72

| | % of total personal wealth | | | |
| | England and Wales | | Great Britain | |
	Top 1%	Top 5%	Top 1%	Top 5%
1923	61	82	n.a.	n.a.
1925	61	82	n.a.	n.a.
1927	60	81	n.a.	n.a.
1929	56	79	n.a.	n.a.
1930	58	79	n.a.	n.a.
1936	54	77	n.a.	n.a.
1938	55	77	n.a.	n.a.
1950	47	74	47	74
1952	43	70	43	70
1954	45	72	45	72
1956	45	71	44	71
1959	41	68	42	68
1960	34	59	34	60
1962	31	55	32	55
1964	35	59	35	59
1966	31	56	31	56
1968	34	58	34	59
1970	30	54	30	54
1972	32	56	32	57

Note: n.a. = not available

Source: Atkinson (1983, p. 168).

Table 9.A7   Trend in income inequality in The Netherlands, 1914–72

	% of taxable personal incomes per recipients decile										Coefficient of variation in taxable personal income
					Deciles						
	1	2	3	4	5	6	7	8	9	10	
1914	n.a.	n.a.	n.a.	n.a.	n.a.	n.a.	5.7	8.1	10.8	42.0	3.15
1915	n.a.	n.a.	n.a.	n.a.	n.a.	n.a.	5.5	7.5	10.2	47.6	3.69
1916	n.a.	n.a.	n.a.	n.a.	n.a.	n.a.	5.7	7.5	10.4	49.6	4.01
1917	n.a.	n.a.	n.a.	n.a.	n.a.	n.a.	6.1	8.1	11.1	48.4	3.96
1918	n.a.	n.a.	n.a.	n.a.	n.a.	4.7	7.0	8.7	12.1	44.3	3.36
1919	n.a.	n.a.	n.a.	n.a.	4.3	6.2	7.8	9.3	12.3	45.6	3.35
1920	n.a.	n.a.	n.a.	3.8	5.4	7.1	8.4	10.3	12.7	42.4	2.85
1921	n.a.	n.a.	n.a.	4.1	5.8	7.4	9.0	11.1	13.6	40.8	2.58
1922	n.a.	n.a.	n.a.	3.5	5.7	7.3	9.1	11.3	14.3	39.9	2.31
1923	n.a.	n.a.	n.a.	3.3	5.7	7.3	9.0	11.1	14.4	39.8	2.25
1924	n.a.	n.a.	n.a.	3.4	5.7	7.2	8.8	10.8	14.1	40.7	2.44
1925	n.a.	n.a.	n.a.	3.5	5.7	7.2	8.8	10.7	13.9	40.7	2.56
1926	n.a.	n.a.	n.a.	3.5	5.7	7.2	8.8	10.6	13.8	40.9	2.60
1927	n.a.	n.a.	n.a.	3.6	5.7	7.1	8.7	10.5	13.7	41.2	2.62
1928	n.a.	n.a.	n.a.	3.9	5.7	7.1	8.5	10.4	13.5	41.4	2.70
1929	n.a.	n.a.	n.a.	4.2	5.8	7.2	8.6	10.5	13.5	40.8	2.54
1930	n.a.	n.a.	n.a.	4.0	5.8	7.2	8.8	10.6	13.6	39.9	2.80
1931	n.a.	n.a.	n.a.	n.a.	5.3	7.0	8.7	11.1	14.3	39.0	2.29
1932	n.a.	n.a.	n.a.	n.a.	4.0	6.8	8.8	11.0	14.7	38.2	1.97
1933	n.a.	n.a.	n.a.	n.a.	n.a.	6.7	8.6	11.1	14.7	37.8	1.91
1934	n.a.	n.a.	n.a.	n.a.	n.a.	6.0	8.4	11.1	14.5	37.5	1.89
1935	n.a.	n.a.	n.a.	n.a.	n.a.	5.5	8.4	10.8	14.4	37.4	1.91
1936	n.a.	n.a.	n.a.	n.a.	n.a.	5.5	8.3	10.6	14.1	38.0	2.44
1937	n.a.	n.a.	n.a.	n.a.	n.a.	5.7	8.2	10.6	13.9	38.5	2.67
1938	n.a.	n.a.	n.a.	n.a.	n.a.	5.9	8.2	10.5	13.8	38.5	2.58
1939	n.a.	n.a.	n.a.	n.a.	n.a.	6.8	8.3	10.6	13.7	38.6	2.41
1946	n.a.	n.a.	6.5	6.5	6.6	6.6	10.0	10.7	14.6	38.2	n.a.
1950	1.8	2.8	4.5	4.7	8.0	8.0	9.5	11.1	14.3	34.7	1.61
1952	1.5	3.0	4.0	5.9	7.1	8.3	9.9	11.0	14.1	34.7	1.71
1953	1.5	3.0	3.8	6.0	6.9	8.7	9.6	11.3	14.2	34.5	1.55
1954	1.6	3.3	4.1	5.8	7.0	8.6	9.2	11.1	14.5	34.3	1.53
1955	1.7	3.0	4.3	5.3	7.8	7.8	10.2	11.2	14.4	33.1	1.44
1957	1.8	2.6	4.4	6.1	7.1	8.8	9.7	11.4	14.4	33.1	1.35
1958	1.8	2.5	4.3	6.0	7.2	8.4	9.8	11.2	14.2	33.4	1.55
1959	2.0	2.6	4.2	6.0	7.5	8.2	10.0	11.3	14.3	33.4	1.36
1960	1.7	2.7	4.1	5.8	7.5	8.8	9.8	11.5	14.3	33.2	1.31
1962	1.7	2.8	4.1	5.8	7.4	8.6	10.0	11.7	15.1	32.3	1.28
1963	1.2	2.9	4.1	5.6	7.2	8.6	9.9	11.5	15.3	33.2	1.35
1964	1.0	2.8	4.2	5.7	7.2	8.6	9.9	12.0	14.8	33.3	1.32
1965	0.8	1.8	3.8	5.6	7.1	8.5	9.8	11.9	14.6	35.4	1.58
1966	0.9	2.9	4.4	5.8	7.4	8.7	9.9	11.7	14.8	33.0	1.23
1967	1.1	3.1	4.6	5.9	7.3	8.7	9.9	11.6	14.8	32.6	1.48
1970	1.0	3.4	4.7	5.9	7.3	8.6	10.2	11.8	15.2	31.4	1.49
1972	0.7	3.1	4.7	6.1	7.5	8.9	10.2	12.0	14.8	31.5	1.56

Note: n.a. = not available

Source: Hartog and Veenbergen (1978, Tables 1 and 3).

Table 9.A8   Trend in income inequality in Japan, 1899–1944

	Coefficient of variation of personal income		Coefficient of variation of personal income
1899	1.6986	1922	2.7770
1900	1.9553	1923	2.9634
1901	1.8770	1924	2.7295
1902	1.6638	1925	3.2096
1903	2.0535	1926	2.8882
1904	2.0934	1927	3.2630
1905	2.1494	1928	2.8863
1906	2.1137	1929	3.0940
1907	1.9844	1930	3.1542
1908	2.0017	1931	2.9436
1909	1.9255	1932	2.5840
1910	1.8749	1933	2.6661
1911	1.8439	1934	3.3722
1912	1.8983	1935	2.9831
1913	1.7424	1936	3.2986
1914	1.6895	1937	4.1472
1915	2.0157	1938	5.0594
1916	2.4234	1939	4.3310
1917	3.6579	1940	2.5289
1918	3.8406	1941	2.4030
1919	3.2504	1942	2.3121
1920	2.5391	1943	2.2601
1921	2.6776	1944	2.1904

Source: Takahashi (1959, p. 23).

Table 9.A9   Trend in income inequality in Japan, 1962–74

Gini ratio across household income	
1962	.3759
1963	.3607
1964	.3528
1965	.3441
1966	n.a.
1967	.3523
1968	.3488
1969	.3539
1970	.3553
1971	.3521
1972	.3570
1973	.3496
1974	.3443

Note: n.a. = not available

Source: Mizoguchi and Takayama (1984, p. 12).

Notes

1. For example, there are databases at the World Bank on income inequality indices for various countries. See also Fields (1989). There is the LIS (*Luxembourg Income Study*) database which is very recent and which attempts to collect comparable data on income distribution across countries including Australia, Canada, Germany, Israel, Luxembourg, The Netherlands, Norway, Sweden, Switzerland, the UK and the US. See Smeeding, O'Higgins and Rainwater (1990) for a discussion of the LIS project and the database.
2. Tax returns to the Internal Revenue Service are being increasingly used to compute wealth distribution statistics.
3. Income distribution measures based on post-tax income are available only for some years (see *Statistical Abstracts of the U.S.*, 1985).
4. The sources in Canada, Germany, Israel, Norway, Sweden and the United Kingdom are listed in Smeeding, O'Higgins and Rainwater (1990, p. 5). The sources in Japan are discussed in Mizoguchi and Takayama (1984).
5. In principle, the univariate time-series model of the same variable over the same sample period could differ according to the frequency of the data. This is true at least for the postwar US real GNP. For example, in contrast to ARIMA(1, 0, 0), it is reported in Blanchard and Fisher (1989, ch. 1) that, at quarterly frequency, an ARIMA(1, 1, 2) fits this variable the best over 1947.I – 1987.II.
6. The data on US GNP (at 1982 prices) is collected from two sources: Romer (1989) for the years prior to 1930, and *Economic Report of the President* for later years. GDPs (at 1985 prices) of the UK in the postwar years are obtained from *International Financial Statistics* (annual). Historical data on Japan's GNP (at 1934–36 prices) are collected from Ohkawa and Shinohara (1979, Table A9).
7. The Netherlands is not reported because (a) for the postwar period there are some gaps in the income distribution data, although the GDP data is readily available; and (b) for the period 1914–1939 the data on GDP or GNP is not available to me.
8. It is worth noting that a similar sign pattern is observed between GNP and inventory investment (Blanchard and Fisher, 1989, ch. 1, Table 1.1), and this perhaps rationalizes business-cycle models based on changes in inventory behaviour. See, for example, Metzler (1941).

10 Linkage of income inequality to aggregate output, unemployment, demand for money and stock price: postwar US

I Introduction

In Chapter 9 we observed some patterns of correlation between income inequality and aggregate output in the US and other countries in various time periods. In this penultimate chapter, I present some empirical evidence – beyond simple correlations – for the postwar US economy, on the linkage of income inequality to (a) aggregate output and unemployment, and (b) financial markets. Just as in the theoretical analysis in Parts I and II, the following empirical analysis does not address all, or nearly all, real and financial markets that may be considered important in a macro economy. But it covers some of them.

In Chapter 2 I asked: 'What does it take to show theoretically that a particular factor contributes to business cycles?' Asking about the empirical link between inequality on one hand and aggregate output and unemployment on the other is equivalent to asking a similar question: 'What does it take to show *empirically* that a particular factor contributes to business cycles?'. This leads to the methodology of macroeconometrics research, a short historical review of which may be useful to keep things in the right perspective.

The history of what may be called 'modern' macroeconometrics goes back to Frisch (1933) and Kalecki (1935) before Keynes's *General Theory* but after his *Treatise on Money*. Each defined a dynamic system, but there was little statistical estimation. Frisch took 'reasonable' values for structural parameters, whereas crude estimation of some parameters was done by Kalecki (see Bodkin, Klein and Marwah, 1991, ch. 1). As we all know, macroeconometrics took a big leap forward with the Keynesian revolution. Prime examples of Keynesian macroeconometric models include, among others, Klein's interwar model, the Klein–Goldberger model, the Wharton model, the DRI model and the St Louis model for the US economy. Methodologically, these models are variants of simultaneous equation models, emphasizing contemporaneous relations. This is not to say that lagged or dynamic relations were totally ignored. Some of them entered naturally from physical definitions and others from directly specified behavioural assumptions. Forecasting was typically based on the assessments of likely future values of exogenous variables, and as Granger and Newbold (1986, p. 202) have remarked, these assessments were often done judgementally.

Parallel to the history of Keynesian macrotheory, the Keynesian macroeconometrics had its heyday until the 1970s. It was then overtaken by two different approaches to macroeconometrics – both being offshoots of the inability of Keynesian macroeconometrics to predict effectively macroeconomic behaviour in the seventies. These are: the rational expectations approach and the time-series approach. The rational expectations approach to macroeconometrics owes its intellectual debt mainly to the so-called 'Lucas critique'. It emphasized the estimation of individual, behavioural parameters along with other relations in the model in mutually consistent ways satisfying rational expectations. The time-series approach, coming from the discipline of statistics, is, in contrast, largely atheoretical. A well-known early comparative study of the time-series approach to macro forecasting is due to Cooper (1972), who showed that, out of 33 actual macro time-series data, in the majority of cases the naive univariate time-series models out-performed in forecasting all the other macro-econometric models (seven of them) that he considered.

Although one is theoretical and the other mostly atheoretical, they are not mutually inconsistent, however. A theoretical model with or without rational expectations, as long as it incorporates intertemporal trade-offs and adjustment costs over time, would imply a univariate, or a multivariate, time-series model (that is a vector auto regressive (VAR) system) in the reduced form. An example of a rational expectations model leading to a VAR system is due to Sargent (1978). Of course, the distinction is that a particular dynamic theoretical model will imply a particular univariate time-series or a VAR system, not an unrestricted VAR. A VAR system derived from the primitives of a theoretical model is referred to as a structural VAR or an SVAR system.

A dramatic turnaround in macroeconometric modelling occurred in the early 1980s with the work of Sims (1980a, 1980b). He described the restrictions imposed by any particular theory on the coefficients in an SVAR model as 'incredible' and went on to advocate 'unrestricted VAR' as a tool of macro-econometric system modelling and forecasting. In contrast to SVAR, the unrestricted VAR is more atheoretical and closer to the spirit of time-series analysis in statistics. However, it is noteworthy in passing that some unnecessary confusion has arisen by interpreting an unrestricted VAR or even a structural VAR that is not explicitly derived from theory as totally atheoretical. The source of confusion lies in the failure to realize that no model can ever be *totally* atheoretical: to write *any* behavioural equation with or without explicit theorization is tantamount to assuming some theory. Hence, it is a question of how much, not whether, to rely on well-defined theories – for which there may never be a unique answer. To brand one approach as theoretical and another atheoretical is confusing, wrong and unnecessary. The correct interpretation is that a typical (unrestricted) VAR is significantly less theoretical than a typical SVAR.

It is interesting that since the pioneering work of Sims, the pendulum has swung back in the direction of SVAR, with more emphasis on theory and structural interpretation. Important recent works in the evolution of VAR methodology include

Blanchard and Watson (1986), Bernanke (1986), Runkle (1987) and Blanchard and Quah (1989). In any event, some form of VAR methodology seems to be the current norm in modelling and evaluating interrelationships among macro variables as well as in macro forecasting. The VAR tool-kit includes causality tests and estimation of dynamic impulse response functions and variance decompositions.

In what follows, I use the VAR method to examine the empirical link between income inequality and aggregate output and unemployment. The VAR analysis below is not an SVAR to the extent that a specific dynamic theory is used to 'derive' the VAR system. Instead, it will be largely atheoretical and the reason is the following. As we have seen in Part I, there is not just one theory or model but many which link distributional changes to changes in output, and at this point it is not important whether one model is more promising than another. The pressing task and my objective here is to get a first-hand feel for the interrelationship implied by the data with as much independence from any particular theory as possible.

Furthermore, recall that in the essays in Part I I have examined the role of inequality in the internal mechanism of business cycles. As will be clear, the causality analysis essentially tests the internal mechanism of a dynamic system and hence is particularly relevant for my purpose.

Turning now to the empirical link between inequality and financial markets, I estimate the impact of inequality on the demand for money – or the money market – and the stock market. This corresponds to the theoretical models of money and stock markets in Chapter 7. Empirical analysis to test the hypotheses developed in Chapter 8 concerning the impact of distributional changes on banking behaviour is not attempted. This is because a typical banking firm operates in a significantly different environment compared to a typical firm in the manufacturing sector – for example, with respect to various forms of regulation. Thus it seems that standard econometric procedures should be accordingly modified or new procedures developed to capture adequately the special banking environments before the hypotheses are tested with the data. This is left to future research.

There is no need to elaborate that the money market – in particular, the demand for money – occupies a central place in the modern macro economic analysis. It is therefore important to investigate the impact of income inequality on the demand for money. Although a number of factors have been argued as determinants of the demand for money, a typical estimation of money demand includes as explanatory variables the lagged dependent variable, a scale variable (real GNP or consumption or sometimes aggregate wealth) and an opportunity cost variable, for example, a short-term or a long-term interest rate.[1] I add to this list a measure of income inequality. Throughout this chapter, the Gini ratio for income across families is used as the measure of overall income inequality.

It is surprising that relative to the enormous empirical literature on the demand for money, there does not exist much on demand for other assets in the aggregate, including that for stocks. Unlike aggregate stock price indices, continuous time-series data on aggregate stock quantity indices do not seem to be available. In what follows, I concentrate on the (real) stock price, rather than stock demand, as a 'function' of income inequality. In general, this leads to the issue of asset pricing. Again, there exists a vast theoretical and empirical literature on asset pricing, especially in the field of finance. Most of this literature is concerned with individual asset prices, their excess returns or risk premia and differences in asset prices.[2] There is also a more recent literature which attempts to explain the second moments of asset returns, for example, Roll (1988) and Shiller (1990). In empirical analysis, a common issue is the estimation of an asset's 'beta' or its covariance with the 'market portfolio' – which, in the context of the stock market, is typically taken to be the entire basket of stocks.

However, my objective is to investigate the impact of income inequality on the *average* stock price over time, not individual stock prices *vis-à-vis* one another. Accordingly, the modelling of the stock price in this chapter is different from a typical asset-pricing model.

II   Link between income inequality and aggregate output and unemployment: a VAR analysis

Inclusion of variables
Recall from Chapter 9 that the data on aggregate indices of income inequality are available only in annual frequencies. For the postwar period they are available since 1947 (see Table 9.A3). The number of data points is thus limited. This imposes a severe constraint on the number of relevant variables to be allowed in any VAR analysis that attempts to include income inequality. In addition to the Gini ratio, I include three other variables at a time: (a) real GNP or the (civilian) rate of unemployment; (b) M1 money stock; and (c) an interest rate: the six-month commercial paper rate as a short-term interest rate or the AAA-rated corporate bond rate as a long-term interest rate. Inclusion of a money-stock variable and an interest-rate variable is most common in VAR business-cycle models (see, for example, Sims (1980a), Friedman (1986) and Dominguez, Fair and Shapiro (1988)). The data sources are listed in Appendix 10.1.

The logs of real GNP and M1 as well as other variables as such, including the rate of unemployment, were found to be nonstationary over the postwar period.[3] Formally, the null hypothesis of a unit root could not be rejected by the Dickey–Fuller test at 5 per cent. But the first differences were found to be stationary. Also, pairwise co-integration tests indicated the absence of co-integration among these variables. Hence the first (log) differenced series are used to represent the respective variables. The following notations are used:

CGINI   first difference in the Gini ratio
GY   growth rate of real GNP
CUN   first difference in the civilian rate of unemployment
GM   growth rate of M1 money stock
CRS   first difference in the six-month commercial paper rate as a short
         term interest rate
CRL   first difference in the AAA-rated corporate bond rate as a long term
         interest rate.

Causality tests
Causality tests carry the notion of information content in the time-series of one variable (or more) in predicting the one-period forward forecast of another variable. Standard causality tests involve the block deletion F test applied to a single equation. For example, the test of whether a time-series x 'causes' a time-series y involves estimating a single equation of the form:

$$y_t = a + \sum_{s=1}^{T} a_{ys} y_{t-s} + \sum_{s=1}^{T} a_{xs} x_{t-s}$$

and testing the null hypothesis that all a_{xs}'s are zero.

However, unlike the standard practice, I conduct the causality tests within a VAR model. As Nelson and Schwert (1982) argue, this approach has more power than the single equation approach. Moreover, it does not impose stringent *a priori* assumptions regarding exogeneity or endogeneity (see Zellner and Palm (1974)).

A VAR process of order k, VAR(k), is defined as

$$\mathbf{x}_t = \mathbf{B}_0 + \mathbf{B}_1 \mathbf{x}_{t-1} + \ldots\ldots + \mathbf{B}_k \mathbf{x}_{t-k} + \mathbf{u}_t, \tag{10.1}$$

where $\mathbf{x} \equiv$ the vector of basic variables included, $k \equiv$ the lag length, $\mathbf{B}_j, j = 1,\ldots,$ $k \equiv$ coefficient matrix of $\mathbf{x}_{t-j}$ and $\mathbf{u} \equiv$ the vector of disturbance terms. Since there are four basic variables in our system, $\mathbf{x}$ is a 4×1 vector and $\mathbf{B}_j$ is a 4×4 matrix.

The system (10.1) was initially estimated by the Full Information Maximum Likelihood method of lag lengths $k = 1, 2, 3$. The chosen lag was based on Akaike's information criterion (AIC). AIC equals $\log|\Sigma| + 2 \cdot$ number of parameters/sample size, where Σ is the covariance matrix of $\mathbf{u}_t$ (see Judge *et al.*, 1988, p. 761). The causality test involves the statistical significance of deleting all lags of a variable in the right-hand side of an equation. This is based on the likelihood ratio test statistic $(N-q)ln(|\Sigma|^R/|\Sigma|^U)$, where N is the number of observations, q the number of parameters in the unrestricted model, and $|\Sigma|^R$ and $|\Sigma|^U$ are the determinants of error covariance matrices resulting from the restricted and unrestricted models respectively. Under the null, this statistic has a χ^2 distribution with r (the number of restrictions) degrees of freedom. For example, x_2 is interpreted as 'causing' x_1 if the null hypothesis that the coefficients of $x_{2t-1}, \ldots, x_{2t-k}$ in the equation for x_{1t} in (10.1) are all zero is rejected.

It is important to realize that the estimation of (10.1) is essentially an estimation of the internal mechanism of a dynamic system, and the causality tests address the statistical significance of a variable in the internal mechanism. Hence it is particularly relevant for testing the hypothesis that inequality may be important in the internal mechanism of business cycles.

Causality test results
The system (10.1) was estimated for four combinations of variables:

A. *CGINI, GY, GM* and *CRS*
B. *CGINI, GY, GM* and *CRL*
C. *CGINI, CUN, GM* and *CRS*
D. *CGINI, CUN, GM* and *CRL*.

Thus x = (*CGINI, GY/CUN, GM, CRS/CRL*). A and B contain the real GNP whereas C and D contain the rate of unemployment. A and C include the short-term interest rate whereas B and D include the long-term interest rate. The 'optimal' k was equal to one in each case. The results are reported in Table 10.1. Since the main issues are the explanation of real GNP and unemployment and their interactions with inequality, only those results that directly pertain to these issues are presented.

The results are quite supportive of the inequality hypothesis. Besides money supply and interest rate (short-run or long-run), inequality 'causes' real GNP at zero or 1 per cent level of significance. It may also be of interest that in terms of the magnitude of the χ^2 statistic, inequality is less strong than the interest rate but stronger than the money supply in explaining real GNP. Real GNP also causes inequality at the 2 or 3 per cent level of significance. Hence the evidence supports a feedback relationship between real GNP and inequality and hence the role of inequality in the internal mechanism of business cycles.

The results also support the notion that inequality may cause unemployment. In the presence of the short-term/long-term interest rate, inequality causes unemployment at zero/8 per cent level of significance. Thus this causal link is supported more strongly in the presence of a short-term interest rate than in the presence of a long-term interest rate. Incidentally, this happens to contradict the belief expressed in Blinder and Esaki (1978) – which is perhaps shared by the profession at large – that 'there is no reason to expect any important reverse causation from income distribution to unemployment'. Further, the evidence does not support the notion of causation from unemployment to income distribution. In other words, income inequality causes unemployment but unemployment does not cause inequality – exactly the opposite of the existing belief.

Table 10.1   Causality test results, 1947–90

Null Hypothesis	$\chi^2(1)$	Significance level in %
A. CGINI, GY, GM, CRS		
CGINI doesn't cause GY	13.058	0
GM doesn't cause GY	7.707	0
CRS doesn't cause GY	35.532	0
GY doesn't cause CGINI	5.693	2
B. CGINI, GY, GM, CRL		
CGINI doesn't cause GY	6.738	1
GM doesn't cause GY	3.327	7
CRL doesn't cause GY	11.961	0
GY doesn't cause CGINI	4.248	3
C. CGINI, CUN, GM, CRS		
CGINI doesn't cause CUN	8.924	0
GM doesn't cause CUN	0.056	82
CRS doesn't cause CUN	25.466	0
CUN doesn't cause CGINI	2.134	14
D. CGINI, CUN, GM, CRL		
CGINI doesn't cause CUN	3.020	8
GM doesn't cause CUN	0.034	85
CRL doesn't cause CUN	13.927	0
CUN doesn't cause CGINI	1.322	25

Impulse response functions and variance decompositions
Having tested for the internal mechanism linking inequality and real GNP/unemployment, we move on to estimate the impacts of unanticipated shocks or innovations within the VAR system. These are formalized in terms of impulse response functions and variance decompositions.

While causality tests deal with the statistical significance of interdependence in the internal mechanism, the dynamic impulse response functions and variance decompositions relate to the pattern and the quantitative significance of variations around the expected path due to innovations in individual variables. Dynamic impulse response functions are basically the moving average representations, whereas variance decompositions are an accounting of forecast variance due to innovations.

It is, however, well known that in general the dynamic impulse response functions and variance decompositions are sensitive to the specification of the simultaneous system of contemporaneous relationships. One begins with a system such as:

$$\mathbf{x}_t = \mathbf{A}_0 \mathbf{x}_t + \mathbf{A}_1 \mathbf{x}_{t-1} + \dots\dots + \mathbf{A}_k \mathbf{x}_{t-k} + \mathbf{e}_t,^4 \tag{10.2}$$

in which the diagonal elements of $\mathbf{A}_0$ are zero (and the constant term is disregarded for simplicity). Solving $\mathbf{x}_t$ in (10.2), the reduced form model is the same as (10.1), where $\mathbf{B}_j = (\mathbf{I} - \mathbf{A}_0)^{-1} \mathbf{A}_j, j = 1,\dots, k$, and

$$\mathbf{u}_t = \mathbf{A}_0 \mathbf{u}_t + \mathbf{e}_t. \tag{10.3}$$

The estimation of dynamic impulse response functions and variance decompositions requires prior estimation of the contemporaneous, simultaneous-equation, structural system (10.3). However, the problem is that all off-diagonal elements of $\mathbf{A}_0$ can be nonzero in principle, but it is not possible for all of them to be econometrically identified. Hence, the matrix $\mathbf{A}_0$ needs to be restricted.

Originally, Sims (1980a, 1980b) proposed an ordering of variables, or equivalently, a recursive class of models of (10.3), in which the choice of the ordering is entirely based on *a priori* beliefs. Later, Blanchard and Watson (1986) and Bernanke (1986) proposed more general structural modelling of $\mathbf{A}_0$.

Although the VAR technology is still evolving, Sims's original idea of ordering the variables remains appealing and a common practice – particularly when there is no guidance as to what may be considered a satisfactory structural model. As I have hinted before, it is too early to bank on any particular theoretical model or combination of models linking inequality and aggregate activities to use in an empirical analysis. Thus I elect to follow Sims's method of ordering the variables.

However, I go a bit further. There are four variables in our system: income inequality, real GNP (or the rate of unemployment), money supply and an interest rate. In total, there are 24 possible orderings. I suppose some rationalization can be made for each one of them. Which one then do we choose? The common practice would be to choose one purely on prior beliefs. This, I think, is extreme. Also, to analyse sensitivity we may want to select more than one specification. I do the following: allow prior beliefs as well as the data itself to select the ordering. Specifically, I assign money supply the number one in the ordering, with the belief that it is probably the most exogenous of the four.[5] This reduces the number of possible orderings of the remaining three variables to six. I let the data pick the 'best' two among the six alternative specifications, based on Akaike's information criterion applied to the system of equations (10.3).[6]

Estimation Results

Instead of estimating dynamic impulse response functions and variance decompositions for all four cases, A, B, C and D, I restrict myself to case A only, in order to avoid repetition and because these estimations, although interesting and important on their own, are not central to my original query into the internal mechanism.

First, equation (10.1) for system A was estimated by the Full Information Likelihood method for $k = 1$, 2 and 3. As mentioned earlier, the optimal k was equal to 1. The estimates of the coefficients of matrix $\mathbf{B}_1$ and their standard errors are reported in Table 10.2.

Table 10.2   *Estimates of the coefficients of $\mathbf{B}_1$ in system A*

Estimates			
−0.443	−0.089	0.033	0.0004
1.606	0.574	−0.194	−0.011
0.868	0.016	0.541	−0.001
14.312	20.121	5.731	0.076
Standard Errors			
0.169	0.041	0.028	0.0006
0.527	0.128	0.086	0.002
0.774	0.187	0.126	0.003
43.477	10.520	7.075	0.159

As described above, six alternative, recursive, simultaneous equation systems in the residuals of equation (10.1) were estimated (by OLS). The best two specifications turned out to be the models A1 and A2 specified in Table 10.3.[7]

From Table 10.3, it is interesting that in both models the data picked inequality as more exogenous than the real GNP, given that money supply is chosen *a priori* as the most exogenous of the four variables. In model A1, interest rate and inequality are ordered second and third, whereas in model A2, their ranks are switched. In both models, GNP is ranked the last and hence the GNP equation is the same in both models. Each coefficient in this equation is statistically significant at 5 per cent or less. The coefficient of the interest rate has a perverse sign, indicating that there may be some specification errors. But other coefficients have correct signs. In particular, the negative sign of the coefficient of inequality is consistent with the negative contemporaneous correlation between income inequality and real GNP noted in Chapter 9.

Table 10.3 Estimation of the contemporaneous-residuals models in system A

Model A1

$$u_{GM} = e_{GM}; \text{S.E.} = 0.0258 \tag{10.4a}$$

$$u_{CRS} = -20.451\, u_{GM} + e_{CRS}; \text{S.E.} = 1.368 \tag{10.4b}$$
$$\quad (8.267)$$

$$u_{CGINI} = 0.025u_{GM} - 0.001u_{CRS} + e_{CGINI}; \text{S.E.} = 0.005 \tag{10.4c}$$
$$\quad (0.035) \qquad (0.0006)$$

$$u_{GY} = 0.194u_{GM} + 0.006u_{CRS} - 0.990u_{CGINI} + e_{GY}; \text{S.E.} = 0.014, \tag{10.4d}$$
$$\quad (0.093) \qquad (0.002) \qquad (0.416)$$

Model A2

$$u_{GM} = e_{GM}; \text{S.E.} = 0.026 \tag{10.5a}$$

$$u_{CGINI} = 0.046u_{GM} + e_{CGINI}; \text{S.E.} = 0.005 \tag{10.5b}$$
$$\quad (0.034)$$

$$u_{CRS} = -17.505u_{GM} - 63.533u_{CGINI} + e_{CRS}; \text{S.E.} = 1.338 \tag{10.5c}$$
$$\quad (8.273) \qquad (37.817)$$

$$u_{GY} = 0.194u_{GM} + 0.006u_{CRS} - 0.990u_{CGINI} + e_{GY}; \text{S.E.} = 0.014 \tag{10.5d}$$
$$\quad (0.093) \qquad (0.002) \qquad (0.416)$$

Note: Terms in parentheses are standard errors.

As expected, the contemporaneous impact of money stock on the interest rate is negative and the coefficient is statistically significant in each model. The coefficient of inequality in the interest rate equation (10.5c) is significant at 10 per cent. The negative sign is consistent with the heterogenous time preference framework. Greater inequality would increase the total demand for interest-earning assets (bonds), leading to an increase in the bond price or a decrease in the interest rate. The impact of money supply on inequality is positive but statistically insignificant in each model.

Given the estimates of matrices $\mathbf{B}_1$ and $\mathbf{A}_0$ (from Tables 10.2 and 10.3), the dynamic impulse response functions are calculated as the moving average representations. Table 10.4 reports the impulse responses up to six periods forward due to standardized (1 standard deviation) innovations. (All entries are multiplied by 1000.)[8]

Table 10.4 Dynamic impulse response functions: models A1/A2 in system A

Period forward	Dynamic impulse response of income inequality due to (standardized) innovation in			
	Inequality	Real GNP	Money supply	Interest rate
0	0.55/0.56	0.00/0.00	0.12/0.12	–0.15/0.00
1	–0.19/–0.19	–0.13/–0.13	0.01/0.01	0.03/–0.02
2	0.05/0.02	0.00/0.00	0.03/0.03	0.09/0.10
3	–0.01/–0.02	0.01/0.01	0.05/0.05	0.02/0.02
4	0.02/0.02	0.01/0.01	0.04/0.04	–0.01/–0.01
5	0.00/0.01	0.00/0.00	0.02/0.02	–0.01/–0.01
6	0.00/0.00	0.00/0.00	0.01/0.01	0.00/0.00

Period forward	Dynamic impulse response of real GNP due to (standardized) innovation in			
	Inequality	Real GNP	Money supply	Interest rate
0	–0.54/–0.77	1.42/1.42	0.06/0.06	0.98/0.82
1	0.57/0.85	0.82/0.82	0.31/0.31	–1.18/–1.00
2	–0.04/0.19	–0.05/–0.05	–0.27/–0.27	–0.88/–0.88
3	–0.09/–0.06	–0.20/–0.20	–0.45/–0.45	–0.08/–0.10
4	–0.10/–0.14	–0.08/–0.08	–0.28/–0.28	0.20/0.17
5	–0.02/–0.05	0.03/0.03	–0.10/–0.10	0.12/0.11
6	0.00/0.00	0.04/0.04	–0.02/–0.02	0.00/0.00

Period forward	Dynamic impulse response of money supply due to (standardized) innovation in			
	Inequality	Real GNP	Money supply	Interest rate
0	0.00/0.00	0.00/0.00	2.58/2.58	0.00/0.00
1	0.47/0.51	0.02/0.02	1.55/1.55	–0.25/–0.12
2	0.10/0.13	–0.11/–0.11	0.84/0.84	–0.15/–0.12
3	0.08/0.08	–0.08/–0.08	0.46/0.46	0.01/0.03
4	0.03/0.02	–0.04/–0.04	0.28/0.28	0.04/0.05
5	0.03/0.02	–0.01/–0.01	0.18/0.18	0.02/0.03
6	0.02/0.02	0.00/0.00	0.12/0.12	0.00/0.00

Period forward	Dynamic impulse response of the interest rate due to (standardized) innovation in			
	Inequality	Real GNP	Money supply	Interest rate
0	0.00/–35.54	0.00/0.00	–52.76/–52.76	136.80/133.79
1	–3.07/–10.22	28.57/28.57	13.65/13.65	28.05/26.64
2	11.08/16.40	16.89/16.89	16.16/16.17	–22.47/–19.10
3	1.24/6.13	–0.51/–0.51	1.04/1.04	–19.03/–18.29
4	–1.30/–0.54	–4.43/–4.43	–5.71/–5.71	–2.69/–2.97
5	–1.61/–2.55	–1.99/–1.99	–4.06/–4.06	3.89/3.39
6	–0.36/–1.02	0.36/0.36	–1.00/–1.00	2.62/2.47

There are several interesting features in the estimated dynamic impulse response functions. Since the focus of this VAR model is on real GNP and income inequality, let me concentrate on these variables.

Consistent with the lead-lag correlations observed in Chapter 9, the initial lagged impact of innovations in real GNP on income inequality is negative (−0.19). An innovation in money supply has positive contemporaneous as well as lagged impacts on income inequality. Comparatively, the impact of innovations in money supply on income inequality is more persistent than the impact of innovations in real GNP on income inequality.

The contemporaneous negative impact of innovations in inequality on real GNP (−0.54/−0.77) is a consequence of the negative coefficient of inequality in the GNP equations (10.4d) and (10.5d) and consistent with the contemporaneous correlation between innovations in inequality and real GNP observed in Chapter 9. The initial lagged effects are positive, again consistent with the lead-lag correlations presented in Chapter 9. The dynamic response of GNP to innovations in inequality is significantly different in magnitude between the two models because the ranking of inequality is different. Finally, the dynamic response of real GNP to innovations in general is more persistent than that of income inequality.

I now turn to variance decompositions. For each variable, they were stable after the 2-period horizon. Table 10.5 reports them.

Table 10.5   Variance decompositions: models A1/A2 in system A

Variance decomposition (at 3-period horizon and beyond in %)	Due to innovations in			
	Inequality	Real GNP	Money supply	Interest rate
Income inequality	83/88	4/4	5/5	8/3
Real GNP	9/19	39/39	7/7	45/35
Money supply	2/3	0/0	97/97	1/0
Interest rate	1/7	4/4	13/13	82/76

As Table 10.5 shows, most of the variations in income inequality, money supply and interest rate are due to their own innovations. This is particularly interesting in the case of the interest rate and inequality since neither one is ranked first, and moreover, they are ranked third in one of the models (models A2 and A1 respectively).

The variance decomposition of the real GNP is most interesting. The impacts of own innovations and those in money stock are stable between models A1 and A2. But the impacts of innovations in the interest rate and inequality are sensitive to the specification of the contemporaneous-residuals model. In particular, innovations in income inequality explains 9 per cent or 19 per cent of total variations in real GNP around its expected path depending on whether inequality is ranked second or third. In both cases, however, it is less than the impact of innovations in the interest rate (45/37 per cent), but higher than that in the money supply, 7 per cent.

The main result on the impact of inequality on real GNP that seems to emerge is that a significant proportion of unanticipated variation in real GNP can be attributed to innovations in inequality. However, it must be noted that the numbers *do not* represent *total* variations. They represent only the unanticipated variations or variations around the expected path. The expected path may itself vary or oscillate.

This completes our VAR analysis linking income inequality to real activities such as real GNP and unemployment. In sum, the empirical evidence seems generally to support the inequality hypothesis of business cycles – at least for the US in the postwar period.

Next, I turn to examine the implications of inequality for the money and stock markets.

III   Income inequality and the demand for money
The standard argument for scale economies in the (real) demand for money implies that the more dispersed incomes are, the less will be aggregate demand for money. However, in Chapter 7 I explored the hypothesis which is the opposite: the more dispersed incomes are, the *greater* will be the aggregate demand for money. This was based on a model in which households have heterogeneous time preference. Here I present empirical evidence in support of this hypothesis.

As I mentioned in Chapter 7, a recent paper by Cover and Hooks (1991) has already examined empirically the impact of income inequality on the demand for M1 money for postwar US; incidentally, their results support my hypothesis. In what follows, I basically extend their analysis in two aspects. First, they consider the sample period 1949–88, whereas I consider a larger sample period, 1947–90. Second, they include a measure of the long-term interest rate as the opportunity cost of holding money. I include a short-term interest rate and a long-term interest rate separately as well as together.

As one would expect, the time-series of the real M1 is nonstationary, but its log-difference or the growth rate is stationary. Therefore, the money demand function is estimated in differences. The growth rate of real M1 is depicted in Figure 10.1.

As explanatory variables, the standard practice is to include (a) the lagged dependent variable, the coefficient of which is interpreted as one minus the rate of 'adjustment' to the desired money holding; (b) a scale variable: real GNP, real personal consumption expenditure or aggregate wealth; and (c) an opportunity cost variable: a short-term or a long-term interest rate. This is based on some model of a 'representative agent'. But when a household-level model is aggregated over households with heterogeneous time preference, the distribution of income and wealth would also matter.

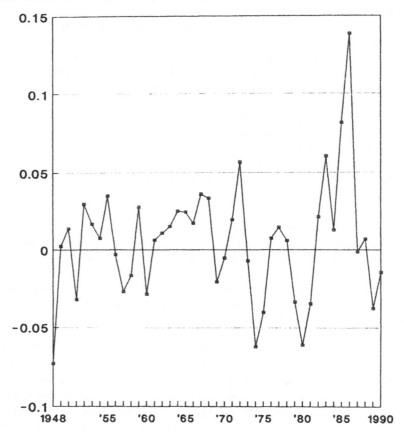

Source: See Appendix 10.1.

Figure 10.1   Growth rate of real M1 in the US, 1948–90

In the following regression analysis I include the lagged dependent variable, real GNP and total personal consumption expenditure as alternative scale variables, the six-month commercial paper rate and the AAA-rated corporate bond rate as representing respectively a short-term and a long-term interest rate, and the Gini ratio of income distribution. Wealth variables are ignored. (Recall that continuous time-series data on wealth distribution does not even exist.)

I include an additional variable, however, namely, a dummy for the year 1986. As Figure 10.1 shows, the real M1 increased from 1985 to 1986 by 14 per cent, which is clearly an outlier in comparison to the rest of the observations. This was a function of an unusually high growth rate of nominal M1 equal to 15 per cent and an inflation rate of 1 per cent from 1985 to 1986. Given that the data

Table 10.6   Regression results on demand for money, 1947–90

Regression of GRM_t on	A	B	C	D	E	F
Constant	–0.018	–0.030	–0.007	–0.027	–0.014	–0.030
GRM_{t-1}	0.271	0.116	0.179	0.059	0.239	0.114
S.E.	0.104	0.080	0.106	0.082	0.108	0.082
Sig. in %	1	15	10	47	3	17
Dummy–86	0.093	0.099	0.066	0.091	0.078	0.098
S.E.	0.026	0.019	0.030	0.023	0.030	0.022
Sig. in %	0	0	3	0	1	0
GY_t	0.676	—	0.415	—	0.578	—
S.E.	0.177		0.183		0.197	
Sig. in %	0		3		1	
GC_t	—	1.053	—	0.984	—	1.043
S.E.		0.134		0.158		0.154
Sig. in %		0		0		0
CRS_t	–0.011	–0.006	—	—	–0.008	–0.006
S.E.	0.003	0.002			0.004	0.003
Sig. in %	0	0			7	4
CRL_t	—	—	–0.021	–0.011	–0.009	–0.001
S.E.			0.006	0.005	0.008	0.006
Sig. in %			0	4	27	89
$CGINI_t$	1.802	1.152	1.514	1.271	1.616	1.145
S.E.	0.697	0.465	0.736	0.491	0.714	0.474
Sig. in %	1	2	5	1	3	1
$\bar{R}^2$	0.61	0.80	0.59	0.77	0.61	0.79
D.W.	2.03	1.67	1.84	1.57	1.97	1.66

used are of annual frequency – as income inequality data is available at this frequency only – the number of observations is rather limited (43 to be exact). Hence a single outlier observation may impose a significant burden on other variables and the absence of a dummy may entail a significant specification error. This is the rationale for the inclusion of the dummy. As will be seen, the coefficient of this dummy is highly significant in each regression.

Compared to the VAR analysis, the new variables are defined as follows:

GRM   growth rate of real M1
GC   growth rate of real personal consumption expenditure.

Altogether, six regressions were run, depending upon the inclusion of particular variables. In each regression, the diagnostics for serial correlation, heteroskedasticity, functional form of the equation and normality were fine. The results are reported in Table 10.6.

In discussing the results, I would not concentrate on basic explanatory variables other than inequality since they are not the focus. However, it must be noted from Table 10.6 that their signs are expected and they are generally statistically significant (including the dummy), except for the long-term interest rate when both interest rates are included in the regression (E and F).

The most interesting finding, from our viewpoint, is that *the estimated coefficient of inequality is consistently positive in sign and statistically significant at 5 per cent or less in each equation.* This supports the hypothesis that, other things remaining the same, an increase in income inequality would increase the aggregate demand for money. In terms of the magnitude, the coefficients of $CGINI_t$ in (A) to (F) imply that a unit increase at time t in the second decimal point in the Gini ratio, for example, from 0.35 to 0.36, is associated with an increase in money demand at time t in the range of 1.15 to 1.80 per cent.

Thus the hypothesis that greater inequality may lead to greater real demand for money finds empirical support in terms of the demand for M1 money in the postwar US.

IV   Income inequality and the stock price

In Chapter 7 I also formulated the hypothesis that an increase in inequality increases the aggregate demand for stocks. However, unlike demand for money, there is no established literature on the estimation of demand function for stocks in the aggregate. In particular, time-series data on aggregate quantity of stocks does not seem to be readily available. I concentrate instead on the stock price – the hypothesis being that an increase in inequality results in an increase in the real stock price. This is an interesting hypothesis on its own. For example, it has been remarked that the increasing wealth and income disparities in the US in recent years have had a positive impact on the average stock price.[9]

At the household level, the demand for stocks would be a function of return on stocks, return on competing assets, riskiness of asset returns and scale variables such as nonhuman wealth and income. Given heterogeneous rates of time preference across households, the demand for stocks in the aggregate will depend, besides the characteristics of returns, on aggregate wealth and income and their distribution. However, I continue to ignore wealth variables. For simplicity, I also ignore riskiness of assets.

From the viewpoint of estimation, we may then specify the 'desired' aggregate demand for stocks in real terms as

$$f_t^* = f^*(\rho_{st}, \rho_{ct}, Y_t, IN_t), \tag{10.5}$$

where $\rho_{st} \equiv$ the total return on stocks, $\rho_{ct} \equiv$ the vector of total returns on competing assets, $Y_t \equiv$ the aggregate income and $IN_t \equiv$ an index of distribution of income. The total returns ρ_{st} and ρ_{ct} would include income return as well as capital gains.

Similar to the derivation of the empirical money demand function, we may invoke 'adjustment costs' in holding the desired amount of stocks, and specify the dynamics of actual stockholding, f_t, as

$$f_t - f_{t-1} = \lambda(f_t^* - f_{t-1}), \tag{10.6}$$

where λ is the coefficient of adjustment. Substituting (10.5) into (10.6) and rearranging,

$$f_t = (1-\lambda)f_{t-1} + \lambda f_t^*. \tag{10.7}$$

The supply of stocks to the market is equal to existing stocks plus the new issues. The latter is an outcome of choice between equity and debt financing, which involves complex, intertemporal decision-making facing the firms. A satisfactory treatment of the supply side will involve specification of a dynamic structural model, the estimation of which together with the demand side would be intricate. I opt to avoid the supply side by postulating that the total supply of stocks is given, that is,

$$s_t = \bar{s}. \tag{10.8}$$

This means that the model being developed is essentially a demand-side model. In equilibrium, the demand for stock equals the supply of stocks in real terms, that is,

$$f_t = p_{zt}s_t,$$
(10.9)

where p_{zt} is the price of stocks in real terms. In view of (10.5), equations (10.7), (10.8) and (10.9) implicitly define

$$p_{zt} = \alpha\, p_{zt-1} + \beta f^*\left(\rho_{st}, \rho_{ct}, Y_t, IN_t\right),$$
(10.10)

where $\alpha = 1 - \lambda$ and $\beta = \lambda/\bar{s}$. Furthermore, by definition,

$$\rho_{st} = r_{st} + p_{zt} / p_{zt-1} - 1,$$

where r_{st} is the income return on stocks and $p_{zt}/p_{zt-1}-1$ equals the capital gain. Substituting this in (10.10), we obtain a reduced-form solution for p_{zt} of the form:

$$p_{zt} = p_z\left(p_{zt-1}, r_{st}, \rho_{ct}, Y_t, IN_t\right).$$
(10.11)

Equation (10.11) forms the basis of the estimated regression equations.

The *Standard and Poor 500* index in real terms and the income return on this index in real terms were chosen to represent p_{zt} and r_{st} respectively. There are several potential candidates for assets that compete with stocks and hence several choices for ρ_{ct}. Perhaps the closest are the long-term corporate bonds. I include the returns on Salomon Brothers long-term high-grade corporate bond Index. In some regressions, I also include the returns on US treasury bills and six-month commercial paper rate as representative of short-term bond markets. The real GNP and the Gini ratio were taken to represent Y_t and IN_t respectively. See Appendix 10.1 for data sources.

Two sets of regressions were run. One is directly based on (10.11), which is essentially derived from equilibrium in the stock market. However, in the general equilibrium, the stock and bond markets clear simultaneously. Empirically, there may be considerable simultaneity, especially between stock and long-term bond prices. In (10.11), bond prices appear in ρ_{ct} in the capital gains component. Hence a further reduced-form estimation was done on the basis of (10.11') (below) in which r_{bt}, the income return on long-term bonds, substitutes for the total return. ρ_{oct} stands for the return on other competing assets.

$$p_{zt} = p_z\left(p_{zt-1}, r_{st}, r_{bt}, \rho_{oct}, Y_t, IN_t\right).$$
(10.11')

It turns out that the time-series of the real stock price is nonstationary, while its first-difference (the growth rate) is stationary. Hence, equations (10.11) and (10.11') are estimated in differences.

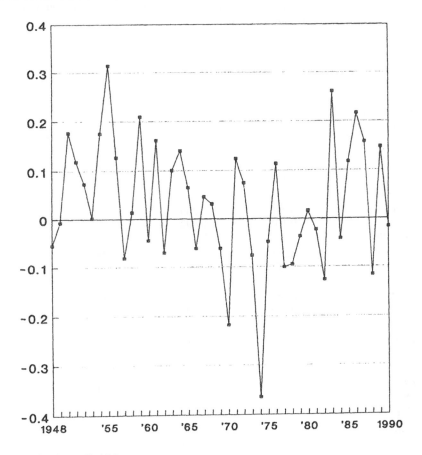

Source: See Appendix 10.1

Figure 10.2   Growth rate of real stock price in the US, 1948–90

Figure 10.2 plots the growth rate of the real stock price. As we see, there are two outliers: the observations at 1955 and 1974, approximately 31 per cent and –37 per cent respectively. The sharp increase in the real stock price in 1955 is a function of an unusually sharp increase in the nominal stock price of a magnitude of 31 per cent coupled with nearly 0 per cent inflation (actually a negligible deflation). The large decline in the real stock price in 1974 is a result of a 23 per cent decrease in stock price coupled with a high inflation rate of 11 per cent – both presumably due to the first oil price shock. In order to reduce the distortions imposed by these outliers, I include two dummies, dummy-55 and dummy-74, in addition to the explanatory variables in equations (10.11) and (10.11'). The coefficient of each of these dummies turns out to be highly significant.

Table 10.7A   Regression results on stock price based on equation (10.11), 1947–90

Regression of $GRSP_t$ on	A	B	C
Constant	−0.008	−0.018	−0.014
$GRSP_{t-1}$	−0.021	0.032	0.007
S.E.	0.127	0.117	0.128
Sig. in %	87	80	96
Dummy-55	0.295	0.289	0.308
S.E.	0.101	0.092	0.101
Sig. in %	1	0	0
Dummy-74	−0.366	−0.313	−0.361
S.E.	0.108	0.100	0.107
Sig. in %	0	0	0
$CRIK_t$	0.344	−0.002	1.475
S.E.	0.656	0.606	1.124
Sig. in %	60	100	19
$CRTB_t$	−0.384	−0.371	−0.396
S.E.	0.123	0.112	0.123
Sig. in %	0	0	0
$CRTT_t$	—	—	−1.269
S.E.			1.027
Sig. in %			22
$CRRS_t$	—	−0.030	—
S.E.		0.010	
Sig. in %		1	
GY_t	1.225	1.654	1.483
S.E.	0.741	0.686	0.758
Sig. in %	10	2	6
$CGINI_t$	6.220	6.000	5.779
S.E.	3.020	2.740	3.019
Sig. in %	5	3	6
$\bar{R}^2$	0.47	0.56	0.47
D.W.	1.85	2.13	1.99

Table 10.7B   Regression results on stock price based on equation (10.11'),
1947–90

Regression of $GRSP_t$ on	D	E	F
Constant	–0.020	–0.031	–0.018
$GRSP_{t-1}$	0.027	0.039	0.026
S.E.	0.140	0.135	0.142
Sig. in %	85	77	85
Dummy–55	0.335	0.316	0.334
S.E.	0.109	0.106	0.111
Sig. in %	0	0	0
Dummy–74	–0.347	–0.299	–0.349
S.E.	0.115	0.114	0.117
Sig. in %	0	1	0
$CRIK_t$	3.095	1.319	3.069
S.E.	1.760	1.921	1.790
Sig. in %	9	50	9
$CRIB_t$	–3.532	–1.953	–3.753
S.E.	1.713	1.834	2.044
Sig. in %	5	29	7
$CRTT_t$	—	—	0.269
S.E.			1.314
Sig. in %			84
$CRRS_t$	—	–0.025	—
S.E.		0.013	
Sig. in %		6	
GY_t 1.740	2.093	1.684	
S.E.	0.768	0.761	0.827
Sig. in %	3	1	5
$CGINI_t$	5.684	5.971	5.706
S.E.	3.261	3.140	3.308
Sig. in %	9	6	9
$\bar{R}^2$	0.39	0.44	0.37
D.W.	2.17	2.37	2.14

Tables 10.7A and 10.7B report regression results based on equations (10.11) and (10.11') respectively. The definitions of new variables are as follows:

GRSP   growth rate of *S&P 500* index in real terms as the real stock price

CRIK   first difference in the real income return on stocks

CRTB   first difference in the total income return on long-term bonds in real terms

CRIB   first difference in the income return on long-term bonds in real terms

CRRS   first difference in the six-month commercial paper rate in real terms

CRTT   first difference in the total return on US treasury bills in real terms.

The diagnostics for autocorrelation, heteroscedasticity, functional form and normality were good except for normality in regression B. Several features of these regressions are noteworthy.

(a) The signs of basic explanatory variables are correct except for *GRSP* in A and *CRIK* in B in Table 10.7A. In any case, these coefficients are statistically insignificant.

(b) The coefficient of *CRIK* is generally statistically insignificant. This means that the own-income-return effect on the stock price may not be important. But note that this is not the *total* return on stocks which would include capital gains.

(c) Total return as well as income return on long-term bonds are generally significant (except in regression E) in explaining the stock price.

(d) The coefficient of *CRTT* is statistically insignificant, indicating that US treasury bills and stocks may not be good substitutes.

(e) However, the coefficient of the six-month commercial paper rate is generally significant.

(f) The real GNP coefficient is statistically significant in all regressions, and moreover, its magnitude its fairly stable. In each case, it is greater than unity, suggesting that a 1 per cent increase in real GNP would be associated with a more than 1 per cent increase in the real stock price.

(g) From the perspective of our main pursuit, the most important finding is that *the coefficient of income inequality is positively signed and is statistically significant at 9 per cent or less in each regression.* This supports the hypothesis that greater inequality may lead to higher stock prices. Furthermore, the estimated coefficients are remarkably stable. It ranges from 5.68 in regression equation D to 6.22 in the regression equation A. According to these regressions, a unit increase in the second decimal point in the Gini ratio (for example, from 0.35 to 0.36) is associated with an increase in the real stock price in the range of 5.68–6.22 per cent.

The empirical exercises end here.

V Concluding remarks

Perhaps the most significant result of this chapter is that income inequality 'causes' real GNP and vice versa in the postwar US even when controlling for money supply and interest rates. Understandably, some scholars have reservations about the term 'causality'. But this is not at all critical. More objectively, the causality test checks the statistical significance of the information content of one time-series in predicting the one-period forecast of another – whether or not one may want to interpret this as 'causality'. Put differently, the test deals with the statistical significance of the interactive internal mechanism of dynamic systems – which is exactly suited to verifying if inequality is important in the internal mechanism of business cycles. The test results support the hypothesis that inequality is significant in the internal mechanism of business cycles, in terms of variation in output and the rate of unemployment.

While a VAR analysis is used to test the link between inequality on one hand and aggregate output or unemployment on the other, single-equation, contemporaneous regression is used to test if inequality has significant marginal power in explaining real money demand and the real stock price. The evidence is again supportive in terms of sign and statistical significance. The magnitude of the coefficient of inequality is remarkably stable – especially in the stock price equation – across different regressions based on which other variables are included. For example, the stock price regressions suggest that an increase in the Gini ratio by one-tenth of a decimal point is associated with a 5.68–6.22 per cent increase in the *S&P 500* index in real terms.

Clearly, these results are suggestive and should not be taken as anything close to being conclusive evidence in support of the hypotheses I have explored. The empirical analysis pertains only to the US economy in the postwar era. The unavailability of inequality data for other countries for a 'reasonable' number of years precludes similar empirical exercises for those countries. Even for the US, the available data is only at annual frequency. This means that the number of observations (in the postwar era) is rather limited and it puts a severe constraint on the number of relevant variables to be included simultaneously in the analysis.

There is also the risk of specification error such as 'isn't the inequality coefficient picking up the effect of something else which may affect inequality?'. The answer is 'maybe' – just as much as 'maybe not'. The question of 'what could have happened if we had more variables included or we had more frequent data' cuts both ways and is purely speculative. The fundamental problem is the scarcity of data. It is hoped that more resources will be devoted to gathering more frequent and better data on wealth and income inequality. Only then will more definitive empirical studies be possible. But until then I submit that the positive empirical support should enjoy the benefit of the doubt.

Appendix 10.1 Data sources

Gini ratio: Described in Chapter 9.

GNP: Described in Chapter 9.

Personal consumption expenditure: *Economic Report of the President.*

Civilian rate of unemployment: *Economic Report of the President.*

M1 money stock: *Historical Statistics for the US: Colonial Times to 1970,* Department of Commerce, 1975, and *Economic Report of the President.*

Six-month commercial paper rate: *Economic Report of the President.*

AAA-rated corporate bond rate: *Economic Report of the President.*

S&P 500 index: *Historical Statistics* (for the period 1947–70); and *Economic Report of the President* and *Survey of Current Business* (for later years).

Income return on *S&P 500*: *Stocks, Bonds, Bills and Inflation (SBBI)*, Chicago: Ibbotson Associates, 1992.

Total and income return on Salomon Brothers long-term high grade corporate bond index: *SBBI.*

Total return on US treasury bills: *SBBI.*

The quantities, prices and returns in real terms, wherever used, were obtained through deflating by the consumer price index or subtracting the rate of inflation based on the consumer price index.

Notes

1. See Laidler (1985) for a detailed discussion of theoretical and empirical issues pertaining to the demand for money.
2. Some studies, e.g., Feldstein (1980), Fama (1981) and Summers (1981), have examined the impact of inflation on the average stock return.
3. A possible reason for the nonstationarity of the unemployment rate may be an increase in the natural rate of unemployment over time. The first difference in the rate of unemployment is used, for example, in Schwert (1987).
4. More generally, one could specify $\mathbf{D}e_t$ in place of e_t, where $\mathbf{D}$ is a non-identity matrix.
5. This is counter to the spirit of the real business-cycle theory.
6. The criterion reduces to minimizing the product of standard errors of the four equations.
7. The model A1 was slightly preferred to the model A2 by Akaike's criterion.
8. The initial, period-0, impact of an innovation in the interest rate on the real GNP is perverse (positive and equal to 0.98/0.82). This is because of the positive sign of the interest rate coefficient in the GNP equation (10.4d) or (10.5d). The following lagged impacts (for the next three periods) are, however, negative, as expected.
9. A news piece by Associated Press, published in the 23 August 1990 issue of the daily *Herald Times* in Bloomington, Indiana, under the heading 'IRS Report: The Rich are Getting Richer', said that an IRS study showed that wealth inequality had dramatically increased in the US in the eighties (1986 being the latest year in this study). The study also noted that during 1982 and 1986 the Dow Jones Industrial Average more than doubled.

PART IV

CONCLUSION

11 Final words

Many things come to mind. The best I can do is to place a perspective on this work relative to the existing general approach to business cycles and suggest some directions for future research.

The currently dominant business-cycle theory emphasizes external shocks as the main factor in explaining business cyclical changes. Often, when I have mentioned to my colleagues that I have been working on business cycles, they have asked: Is it real or monetary? This is indicative of the considerable disagreement amongst business-cycle specialists today as to whether business cycles can be explained better by real or by monetary shocks. But there is no disagreement about the maintained hypothesis that it is some kind of an external shock, or a combination of shocks, that is mainly responsible for business fluctuations. This monograph is based on a different maintained hypothesis. It premises that internal mechanisms of a macro system can also produce significant business fluctuations. To avoid misunderstanding, however, it must be made clear that the external shocks and the internal mechanisms are mutually consistent. Indeed, the business-cycle models that stress some form of external shock do naturally contain their own internal mechanisms. However, the critical distinction lies in the degree of emphasis. The external-shock-based theories do not emphasize internal mechanisms as something which can generate significant oscillations or fluctuations consequent upon some shock that occurred in the past, whereas it is quite possible that some expansions or recessions of actual economies can mostly be explained by the internal dynamics and not by an external shock which may have simply triggered a process of adjustment in the beginning.

As I said in Chapter 1, it is seldom true that any particular theory is logically false. There is no single approach to business cycles that can ever hope to be the correct one, with anything else being incorrect. Theory A can be argued to be imbedded in the framework of theory B and vice versa. But it is the difference in emphasis, rigour and scope which essentially separates one theory from another. In this sense, this monograph may be viewed as proposing a 'new' theory of business cycles.

Specifically, the main theory is that inequality of wealth and income and heterogeneity among economic units in a capitalist economy are factors that can cause a fluctuating or oscillatory adjustment path of aggregate output. Thus, while inequality is often thought – or blamed – in the context of social ethics, it is shown that it has an important bearing on aggregate efficiency. In general, the existence of a nonmonotonic path of output hinges upon some combination of behavioural, technological and market distortions or imperfections, and the models developed in this monograph are no exception to this. But it is wrong to deduce that it is hence the distortions which cause fluctuations or oscillations – not inequality and heterogeneity. Because, by themselves, distortions cannot produce non-monotonicity or fluctuations. They form the background, in the presence of which different factors interact with one another to produce fluctuations. It must be noted that the amplitude of oscillations or fluctuations should, generally, increase with the number of distortions. For instance, all graphic illustrations of oscillations in the monograph are based on rational expectations and infinite lifetime, among other assumptions. Relaxation of either or both of these should enhance the scope of oscillations. Moreover, given the level of distortion, the scope of oscillations will increase with the degree and the number of sources of heterogeneity.

I have provided a list of qualifications to this theory in Chapter 1 for the sake of avoiding possible misunderstandings and wrong expectations. For example, it is not advocated that inequality and heterogeneity unidirectionally 'cause' changes in aggregate output but that they cause each other. Also, like any other theory, this theory is neither necessary nor sufficient to explain business cycles. The ultimate test lies in empirical evidence. It is important that, from whatever data are available, the empirical evidence presented in Chapter 10 supports this thesis – at least for the US in the postwar period. At present, however, there is a general scarcity of data on distributional changes, which does not permit very comprehensive empirical analysis, comparable to those in contemporary macroeconometrics. But it would be a serious mistake and logical falsity to deduce from this something such as 'hence it is not a relevant theory'. Such an attitude would contain not only the potential for considerable social costs but also a Catch-22. We would not trust the theory because the empirical evidence is not 'convincing enough' (whatever we mean by 'convincing enough'). At the same time, lack of a theory may be cited as the main reason for not devoting enough resources to collecting systematic and more frequent data on distributional changes. This monograph is meant to break this circuit.

In Part I, I develop a series of theoretical models, some of which are extensions of existing macro dynamic models and some relatively new. Through these models I have tried to explain (a) different interactive mechanisms between inequality or heterogeneity, on the one hand, and aggregate activities, on the other, that are capable of producing an oscillatory or fluctuating time path of aggregate output; and (b) the types of distortions that need to be present as parts of the necessary environment. This is not to say that the distortions identified are the most important ones in actual economies. But neither can their presence be denied. In Part II, I have shown that inequality and heterogeneity may have important implications for financial markets. In Part III, I have presented some empirical analysis to support some of the main hypotheses.

Although research into the role of inequality and heterogeneity in macro analysis has grown rapidly in recent years, the objective I have set in this monograph is more ambitious, in that it is argued that inequality and heterogeneity are not just important in understanding the impact of monetary and fiscal policies on macro variables but they may be central to business fluctuations, irrespective of whether the shocks are policy-induced or related to technology and tastes.

Given my objective, I have started at ground zero – nearly; more so on the empirical front than with the theory. For example, there is the underconsumption theory which alludes to distributional changes and downturns; but it is far from being precise or self-contained. (Recall that I am referring to personal distribution, not functional distribution.) On the empirical side however, there is virtually none in the sense that most of the existing work on macro activities and inequality examine the effect of the former on the latter. Simultaneity is disregarded by the maintained hypothesis.

Against this backdrop, applying conventional criteria to evaluate this work may not be appropriate. In theorizing, the current norm in the business-cycle literature is to come up with a model that can mimic some of the observed contemporaneous correlations. However, not much time-series data, let alone their quality, on wealth and income distribution measures are available. Also, we do not have estimates of the distribution of individual behavioural parameters across heterogeneous economic units. Therefore, there is not much point in attempting to match observed correlations. Actual correlations among aggregates can be artificially generated by an 'appropriate' choice of distribution of behavioural parameters that we do not know about in the first place.

Starting at ground zero also implies naturally that unity is not perhaps one of the strong suits of this monograph – unlike most monographs in economics I have seen that are more like a synthesis of existing literature on a specialized topic than original research. Of course, there is some unity across the individual chapters. Obviously, a lot more needs to be done before considerable unity results; but then, it will be more like a natural outcome than something to be striven for.

Here are some issues I have thought about and some suggested by various colleagues, which are not addressed in the monograph and which, I hope will be undertaken in future research.

(a) Besides difference in tastes, inequality in wealth and income arises and propagates in a capitalist society due to a number of factors, such as productivity differences, inheritance, bequest and marriage. Inequality itself may be perpetuated in so far as it implies differences in the acquisition of human capital. There is literature which addresses some of these issues, but, by and large, it does not examine their implications for business cycles (Scheinkman and Weiss, 1986, is an exception). A natural extension will be to investigate other sources of economic inequality.

(b)   In so far as inequality in the household sector is concerned, I have developed business-cycle models with asymmetric behaviour in terms of capital accumulation, lobbying for taxes or transfers and demand for assets. It is believed that inequality also affects aggregate demand for investment in risky projects, which, in turn, may have implications for the expected level and variation of aggregate output.

Furthermore, the overall level of business regulation in a market economy over time resulting from political lobbying could very well be a function of the concentration of wealth and income. Thus inequality may affect aggregate output as far as regulations play a role in determining aggregate output.

(c)   Not all types of inequality in a capitalist society may be considered 'bad'. Some are desirable. The ones that are particularly detrimental may have to do with envy. It will be interesting and quite challenging to model the notion of envy in general equilibrium and examine its consequences for the functioning of the macro economy.

(d)   Given that inequality and heterogeneity are factors for business fluctuations, it is implicit that a reduction of inequality through redistributive policies will have a positive impact on social welfare. But, naturally, this has to be weighed against efficiency losses in terms of the incentive to engage in productive activity. This would imply some sort of 'optimal' inequality or redistributive policies in the presence of heterogeneous agents. An important and ambitious task will be to characterize the optimal redistributive policy interventions.

(e)   More specifically, recall that the loan market is totally suppressed in all models in Part I. It will be worthwhile to relax it with a weaker form of imperfection, such as borrowing constraints.

(f)   On the empirical front, it is envisioned that some day it will be possible to build and structurally estimate macroeconometric models with heterogeneous households and firms, which can be used for regular forecasting. This will, I conjecture, be one of the most ambitious research agendas in macroeconometrics in the future.

Needless to say, the above is only a small and incomplete list.

In closing, let me reiterate the central message of this monograph, which is that distributional changes may be an important piece of the business-cycle puzzle. Given the enormous importance of the business-cycle phenomenon, the more we are able to understand the process as a whole, the better off we are. To continue to ignore distributional changes may be tantamount to committing a serious type 2 error. A prerequisite for reducing the risk of this error is more theoretical work as well as the collection of more and better-quality data on wealth and income inequality.

The theoretical and the empirical exercises presented in this monograph may not be nearly sufficient to 'establish' that distributional changes are one of the fundamental factors underlying business cycles. But they are indicative of this. More work is warranted, and it is hoped that this monograph provides impetus to this endeavour.

References

Alesina, A. (1989), 'Politics and Business Cycles in Industrial Democracies', *Economic Policy*, **4**(1), April.

Alesina, A. and D. Rodrik (1991), 'Distributive Politics and Economic Growth', Harvard University, March, mimeo.

Alesina, A. and J.D. Sachs (1988), 'Political Parties and the Business Cycle in the United States, 1948 – 84', *Journal of Money, Credit and Banking*, **20**(1), February.

Atkeson, A.G. and R.E. Lucas (1991), 'On Efficient Distribution with Private Information', University of Chicago, mimeo.

Atkinson, A.B. (1983), *The Economics of Inequality*, 2nd edn, Oxford: Oxford University Press.

Balke, N. and D.J. Slottje (1989), 'A Macroeconometric Model of Income Inequality in the US', Working Paper No. 8835, Southern Methodist University.

Ball, L. (1988), 'Is Equilibrium Indexation Efficient?', *Quarterly Journal of Economics*, **103**(2), May.

Banerjee, A.V. and A.F. Newman (1991), 'Risk-bearing and the Theory of Income distribution', *Review of Economic Studies*, **58**(2), April.

Barro, R.J. (1990), 'Government Spending in a Simple Model of Endogenous Growth', *Journal of Political Economy*, **98** (2, part 2), October.

Batra, R. (1987), *The Great Depression of 1990*, New York: Simon & Schuster.

Batra, R. (1988), *Surviving the Great Depression of 1990*, New York: Simon & Schuster.

Baumol, W.J. and J. Benhabib (1989), 'Chaos: Significance, Mechanism, and Economic Applications', *Journal of Economic Perspectives*, Winter.

Becker, R.A. (1980), 'On the Long-run Steady State in a Simple Dynamic Model of Equilibrium with Heterogeneous Households', *Quarterly Journal of Economics*, **95**(2), September.

Becker, R.A. and C. Foias (1987), 'A Characterization of Ramsey Equilibrium', *Journal of Economic Theory*, **41**(1), February.

Benhabib, J., S.S. Jafarey and K.G. Nishimura (1988), 'The Dynamics of Efficient Intertemporal Allocations with Many Agents, Recursive Preferences, and Production', *Journal of Economic Theory*, **44**(2), April.

Bernanke, B.S. (1986), 'Alternative Explanations of the Money–Income Correlation', in *Real Business Cycles, Real Exchange Rates and Actual Policies*, Carnegie–Rochester Conference Series on Public Policy, **23**, Autumn.

Bernanke, B.S. and M. Gertler (1987), 'Banking and Macroeconomic Equilibrium', in W.A. Barnett and K. Singleton (eds), *New Approaches to Monetary Economics*, New York: Cambridge University Press.

Bernanke, B.S. and M. Gertler (1989), 'Agency Costs, Net Worth and Business Fluctuations', *American Economic Review*, **79**(1), March.

Bhagwati, J.N. (1980), 'Lobbying and Welfare', *Journal of Public Economics*, **14**(3), December.

Bhagwati, J.N. (1982), 'Directly Unproductive, Profit-seeking DUP Activities', *Journal of Political Economy*, **90**(5), October.

Blair, K.D. and A.A. Heggestad (1978), 'Bank Portfolio Regulation and the Probability of Bank Failure', *Journal of Money, Credit and Banking*, **10**(1), February.

Blanchard, O.J. and S. Fisher (1989), *Lectures on Macroeconomics*, Cambridge, Mass.: MIT Press.

Blanchard, O.J. and D. Quah (1989), 'The Dynamic Effects of Aggregate Demand and Supply Disturbances', *American Economic Review*, **79**(4), September.

Blanchard, O.J. and M.W. Watson (1986), 'Are Business Cycles All Alike?', in R.J. Gordon (ed.), *The American Business Cycle: Continuity and Change*, Chicago: University of Chicago Press, for NBER.

Blinder, A.S. (1974), *Toward an Economic Theory of Income Distribution*, Cambridge, Mass.: MIT Press.

Blinder, A.S. (1987), 'Credit Rationing and Effective Supply Failures', *Economic Journal*, **97**, June.

Blinder, A.S. and H. Esaki (1978), 'Macroeconomic Activity and Income Distribution in the Postwar United States', *Review of Economics and Statistics*, **60**(4), November.

Bodkin, R.G., L.R. Klein and K. Marwah (1991), *A History of Macroeconometric Model-Building*, Aldershot, Hants.: Edward Elgar.

Braun, D. (1991), *The Rich Get Richer: The Rise of Income Inequality in the United States and the World*, Chicago: Nelson-Hall.

Brock, W.A. (1991), 'Causality, Chaos, Explanation and Prediction in Economics and Finance', in J. Casti and A. Karlqvist (eds), *Beyond Belief: Randomness, Prediction and Explanation in Science*, Boca Raton, Fla: CRC Press.

Brock, W.A. and S.P. Magee (1978), 'The Economics of Special-interest Politics: the Case of Tariff', *American Economic Review Papers and Proceedings*, **68**(2), May.

Brock, W.A. and S.J. Turnovsky (1981), 'The Analysis of Macroeconomic Policies in Perfect Foresight Equilibrium', *International Economic Review*, **22**(1), February.

Brock, W.A., D.A. Hsieh and B. LeBaron (1991), *Nonlinear Dynamics, Chaos and Instability*, Cambridge, Mass.: MIT Press.

Buse, A. (1982), 'The Cyclical Behaviour of the Size Distribution of Income in Canada, 1947–78', *Canadian Journal of Economics*, **15**(2), May.

Calomiris, C.W. and R.G. Hubbard (1991), 'Tax Policy, Internal Finance, and Investment: Evidence from the Undistributed Profits Tax of 1936–37', University of Pennsylvania and Columbia University, September, mimeo.

Campbell, J.Y. and N.G. Mankiw (1989), 'Consumption, Income and Interest rates: Reinterpreting the Time Series Evidence', in O. Blanchard and S. Fisher (eds), *NBER Macroeconomics Annual*, Cambridge, Mass.: MIT Press.

Campbell, J.Y. and N.G. Mankiw (1990), 'Permanent Income, Current Income and Consumption', *Journal of Business and Economic Statistics*, **8**(3), July.

Campbell, J.Y. and N.G. Mankiw (1991), 'The Response of Consumption to Income: a Cross-country Investigation', *European Economic Review*, **35**(4), May.

Cooper, R.L. (1972), 'The Predictive Performance of Quarterly Econometric Models of the United States', in B.G. Hickman (ed.), *Econometric Models of Cyclical Behaviour*, New York: Columbia University Press.

Cover, J.P. and D.L. Hooks (1991), 'Money Demand and Income Distribution: Evidence from Annual Data', University of Alabama, June, mimeo.

Cukierman, A. and A.H. Meltzer (1986), 'A Positive Theory of Discretionary Policy, the Cost of Democratic Government and the Benefits of a Constitution', *Economic Inquiry*, **24**(3), July.

Das, S. and S.P. Das (1991), 'On the Theory of Industry Evolution', Indiana University, mimeo.

Das, S.P. (1990), 'Foreign Lobbying and the Political Economy of Protection', *Japan and the World Economy*, **2**.

Das, S.P. (1991), 'Economic Inequality and Business Cycles: The Asymmetric Pecuniary Externality Effect', Indiana University, mimeo.

Davis, S.J. and J.C. Haltiwanger (1992), 'Gross Job Creation, Gross Job Destruction and Employment Reallocation', *Quarterly Journal of Economics*, **107**(3), August.

deMeza, D. and D.C. Webb (1987), 'Too Much Investment: a Problem of Asymmetric Information', *Quarterly Journal of Economics*, **102**(2), May.

Diamond, D.W. and P.H. Dybvig (1983), 'Bank Runs, Deposit Insurance, and Liquidity', *Journal of Political Economy*, **91**(3), June.

Di Cagno, D. (1990), *Regulation and Bank's Behaviour Toward Risk*, Aldershot, Hants.: Dartmouth.

Dixit, A. and J.E. Stiglitz (1977), 'Monopolistic Competition and the Optimal Product Diversity', *American Economic Review*, **67**(3) June.

Dominguez, K.M., R.C. Fair and M.D. Shapiro (1988), 'Forecasting the Depression: Harvard versus Yale', *American Economic Review*, **78**(4), September.

Dunne, T., M.J. Roberts and L. Samuelson (1988), 'Patterns of Firm Entry and Exit in U.S Manufacturing Industries', *Rand Journal of Economics*, **19**, Winter.

Eckstein, O. and A. Sinai (1986), 'The Mechanisms of the Business Cycle in the Postwar Era', in R. Gordon (ed)., *The American Business Cycle: Continuity and Change*, Chicago: University of Chicago Press, for NBER.

Epstein, L.G. and J.A. Hynes (1983), 'The Rate of Time Preference and Dynamic Economic Analysis', *Journal of Political Economy*, **91**(4), August.

Ericson, R.E. and A. Pakes (1989), 'An Alternative Theory of Firm and Industry Dynamics', Columbia University and Yale University, September, mimeo.

Fama, E.F. (1981), 'Stock Returns, Real Activity, Inflation and Money', *American Economic Review*, **71**(4), September.

Farmer, R.E.A. (1984), 'A New Theory of Aggregate Supply', *American Economic Review*, **74**(5), December.

Feldstein, M.S. (1980), 'Inflation and the Stock Market', *American Economic Review*, **70**(5), December.

Fields, G.S. (1989), 'A Compendium of Data on Inequality and Poverty for the Developing World', Cornell University, mimeo.

Friedman, B.M. (1983), 'The Role of Money and Credit in Macroeconomic Analysis', in J. Tobin (ed.), *Macroeconomics, Prices and Quantities*, Washington, D.C.: Brookings Institution.

Friedman, B.M. (1986), 'Money, Credit and Interest Rates in the Business Cycle', in R.J. Gordon (ed.), *The American Business Cycle: Continuity and Change*, Chicago: University of Chicago Press, for NBER.

Friedman, M. and A.J. Schwartz (1963), *A Monetary History of the United States: 1867–1960*, Princeton: Princeton University Press.

Frisch, R.A.K. (1933), 'Propagation Problems and Impulse Problems in Dynamic Economics', in *Economic Essays in Honor of Gustav Cassel*, London: Frank Cass.

Gabisch, G. and H.-W. Lorenz (1987), *Business Cycle Theory: A Survey of Methods and Concepts*, Berlin and Heidelberg: Springer-Verlag.

Gale, D. and M. Hellwig (1985), 'Incentive-compatible Debt Contracts, I: The One-period Problem', *Review of Economic Studies*, **52**, October.

Gertler, M. (1988), 'Financial Structure and Aggregate Economic Activity: An Overview', *Journal of Money, Credit and Banking*, **20**(3, part 2), August.

Gertler, M. and S. Gilchrist (1991), 'Monetary Policy, Business Cycles, and the Behaviour of Small Manufacturing Firms', New York University, mimeo.

Geweke, J. (1985), 'Macroeconometric Modeling and the Theory of the Representative Agents', *American Economic Association Papers and Proceedings*, **75**(2), May.

Goodwin, R.M. (1951), 'The Non-linear Accelerator and the Persistence of Business Cycles', *Econometrica*, **19**, January.

Gordon, R.J. (ed.) (1986), *The American Business Cycle: Continuity and Change*, Chicago: University of Chicago Press, for NBER.

Grandmont, J.-M. (1986), *Nonlinear Economic Dynamics*, New York: Academic Press.

Grandmont, J.-M. (1987), 'Distributions of Preferences and the Law of Demand', *Econometrica*, **55**(1), January.

Granger, C.W.J. and P. Newbold (1986), *Forecasting Economic Time Series*, 2nd edn, New York: Academic Press.

Greenwald, R. and J.E. Stiglitz (1986), 'Information, Finance Constraints, and Business Fluctuations', June, mimeo.

Gurley, J.G. and E.S. Shaw (1955), 'Financial Aspects of Economic Development', *American Economic Review*, **45**(4), September.

Hall, R.E. and J.B. Taylor (1986), *Macroeconomics: Theory, Performance and Policy*, New York: W.W. Norton.

Hartog, J. and J.G. Veenbergen (1978), ' Long-run Changes in Personal Income Distribution', *De Economist*, **126**(4).

Haslag, J.H., W.R. Russell and D.J. Slottje (1989), *Macroeconomic Activity and Income Inequality in the United States*, Greenwich, Conn.: Jai Press.

Hibbs, D.A. (1977), 'Political Parties and Macroeconomic Policy', *American Political Science Review*, **71**(4), December.

Hildenbrand, W. (1983), 'On the "Law of Demand"', *Econometrica*, **51**(4), July.

Hubbard, R.G. (1991), *Financial Markets and Financial Crises*, Chicago: University of Chicago Press, for NBER.

Jaffee, D.M. and T. Russell (1976), 'Imperfect Information, Uncertainty and Credit Rationing', *Quarterly Journal of Economics*, **90**(4), November.

Joint Economic Committee to the US Congress (1990), 'Falling Behind: the Growing Income Gap in America', Washington, D.C.: JEC.

Jovanovic, B. (1982), 'Selection and the Evolution of Industry', *Econometrica*, **50**(3), May.

Judge, G.J., R.C. Hill, W.E. Griffiths, H. Lutkepohl and T.C. Lee (1988), *Introduction to the Theory and Practice of Econometrics*, New York: John Wiley.

Kaldor, N. (1940), 'A Model of the Trade Cycle', *Economic Journal*, **50**, March.

Kaldor, N. (1956), 'Alternative Theories of Distribution', *Review of Economic Studies*, **23**(2).

Kalecki, M. (1935), 'A Macrodynamic Theory of Business Cycle', *Econometrica*.

King, R.G., C.I. Plosser and S.T. Rebelo (1988), 'Production, Growth and Business Cycles, I: The Basic Neoclassical Model', *Journal of Monetary Economics*, **21**(2/3), March/May.

Kirman, A.P. (1992), 'Whom or What Does the Representative Individual Represent?', *Journal of Economic Perspectives*, **6**(2), Spring.

Krueger, A.O. (1974), 'The Political Economy of Rent-Seeking Society', *American Economic Review*, **64**(4), September.

Laidler, D.E.W. (1985), *The Demand for Money: Theories, Evidence and Problems*, 3rd edn, New York: Harper & Row.

Laitner, J. (1989), 'Dynamic Determinacy and the Existence of Sunspot Equilibria', *Journal of Economic Theory*, **47**(1), February.

Laitner, J. (1990), 'Tax Changes and Phase Diagrams for an Overlapping Generation Model', *Journal of Political Economy*, **98**(1), February.

Lambson, V.E. (1991), 'Industry Evolution with Sunk Costs and Uncertain Market Conditions', *International Journal of Industrial Organization*, **9**(2), June.

Lindbeck, A. (1976), ' Stabilization Policy in Open Economies with Endogenous Politicians', *American Economic Review Papers and Proceedings*, **66**(2), May.

Lippi, M. (1988), 'On the Dynamic Shape of Aggregated Error Correction Models', *Journal of Economic Dynamics and Control*, **12**(2/3), June–September.

Litterman, R.B. (1986), 'Forecasting with Bayesian Vector Autoregressions – Five Years of Experience', *Journal of Business and Economic Statistics*, **4**(1), January.

Long, J.B. and C.I. Plosser (1983), 'Real Business Cycles', *Journal of Political Economy*, **91**(1), February.

Lucas, R.E. (1975), 'An Equilibrium Model of the Business Cycle', *Journal of Political Economy*, **83**(6), December.

Lucas, R.E. (1978), 'Asset Prices in an Exchange Economy', *Econometrica*, **46**(6), December.

Lucas, R.E. and N.L. Stokey (1984), 'Optimal Growth with Many Consumers', *Journal of Economic Theory*, **32**(1), February.

Magee, S.P. (1987), 'Endogenous Protection in the United States, 1900–1984', in R.M. Stern (ed.), *U.S. Trade Policies in a Changing World Economy*, Cambridge, Mass.: MIT Press.

Magee, S.P., W.A. Brock and L. Young (1989), *Black Hole Tariffs and Endogenous Policy Theory: Political Economy in General Equilibrium*, Cambridge: Cambridge University Press.

Mankiw, N.G. (1986), 'The Allocation of Credit and Financial Collapse', *Quarterly Journal of Economics*, **101**(3), August.

Mankiw, N.G. (1991), 'Macroeconomics in Disarray', *NBER Reporter*, Summer.

Mankiw, N.G. and S.P. Zeldas (1991), 'The Consumption of Stockholders and Nonstockholders', *Journal of Financial Economics*, **29**(1), March.

McCallum, B.T. (1989), *Monetary Economics: Theory and Policy*, London: Macmillan.

McRae, C.D. (1977), 'A Political Model of the Business Cycle', *Journal of Political Economy*, **85**(2), April.

Meade, J.E. (1964), *Efficiency, Equality and the Ownership of Property*, London: Allen & Unwin.

Metzler, L.A. (1941), 'The Nature and Stability of Inventory Cycles', *Review of Economic Studies*, **23**.

Minford, P. and D. Peel (1982), 'The Political Theory of the Business Cycle', *European Economic Review*, **17**(2), February.

Minsky, H.P. (1975), *John Maynard Keynes*, New York: Columbia University Press.

Minsky, H.P. (1982), *Can 'It' Happen Again?: Essays on Instability and Finance*, Armonk, N.Y: M.E. Sharpe.

Minsky, H.P. (1986), *Stabilizing an Unstable Economy*, New Haven, Conn.: Yale University Press.

Mitchell, D.W. (1982), 'The Effects of Interest-bearing Required Reserves on Bank Portfolio Riskness', *Journal of Financial and Quantitative Analysis*, **17**(2), June.

Mizoguchi, T. and N. Takayama (1984), *Equity and Poverty under Rapid Economic Growth*, Tokyo: Kinokuniya.

Nelson, C.R. and G.W. Schwert (1982), 'Tests for Predictive Relationship between Time Series Variables: A Monte Carlo Investigation', *Journal of the American Statistical Association*, **77**(377), March.

Nolan, B. (1987), *Income Distribution and the Macroeconomy*, Cambridge: Cambridge University Press.

Nordhaus, W.D. (1975), 'The Political Business Cycle', *Review of Economic Studies*, **42**(2), April.

Obstfeld, M. (1982), 'Aggregate Spending, and the Terms of Trade: Is There a Laursen–Metzler Effect?', *Quarterly Journal of Economics*, **97**(2), May.

Ohkawa, K. and M. Shinohara (eds)(1979), *Patterns of Japanese Economic Development: A Quantitative Appraisal*, New Haven, Conn.: Yale University Press.

Pakes, A. and R.E. Ericson (1990), 'Empirical Implications of Alternative Models of Firm Dynamics', Yale University and Columbia University, mimeo.

Persson, T. and G.E. Tabellini (1991), 'Is Inequality Harmful for Growth? Theory and Evidence', Cambridge, Mass.: NBER Working Paper no. 3599.

Phelan, C. (1991), 'Incentives, Inequality, and the Business Cycle', University of Wisconsin, November, mimeo, preliminary draft.

Phillips, K. (1990), *The Politics of Rich and Poor: Wealth and the American Electorate in the Reagan Aftermath*, New York: Random House.

Rao, C.R. (1973), *Linear Statistical Inference and Its Applications*, New York: John Wiley.

Rogoff, K. (1990), 'Equilibrium Political Business Cycles', *American Economic Review*, **80**(1), March.

Rogoff, K. and A. Sibert (1988), 'Elections and Macroeconomic Policy Cycles', *Review of Economic Studies*, **55**(1), January.

Roll, R. (1988), 'R^2', *Journal of Finance*, **43**(2), July.

Romer, C.D. (1989), 'The Prewar Business Cycle Reconsidered: New Estimates of Gross National Product', *Journal of Political Economy*, **97**(1), February.

Rotemberg, J.J. (1982), 'Monopolistic Price Adjustment and Output', *Review of Economic Studies*, **49**(4), October.

Rotemberg, J.J. (1987), 'The New Keynesian Microeconomic Foundations', in *Macroeconomics Annual*, Cambridge, Mass.: MIT Press, for NBER.

Runkle, D.E. (1987), 'Vector Autoregression and Reality', *Journal of Business and Economic Statistics*, **5**(4), October.

Samuelson, P.A. (1939), 'Interaction Between the Multiplier Analysis and Principle of Acceleration', *Review of Economic Studies*, May.

Sargent, T.J.(1978), 'Estimation of Dynamic Labour Demand Schedules under Rational Expectations', *Journal of Political Economy*, **86**(6), December.

Sargent, T.J. (1979), *Macroeconomic Theory*, New York: Academic Press.

Sargent, T.J. (1987), *Dynamic Macroeconomic Theory*, Cambridge, Mass.: Harvard University Press.

Sargent, T.J. and N. Wallace (1981), 'Some Unpleasant Monetarist Arithmetic', *Federal Reserve Bank of Minneapolis Quarterly Review*, **5**.

Scheinkman, J.A. and L. Weiss (1986), 'Borrowing Constraints and the Aggregate Economic Activity', *Econometrica*, **54**(1), January.

Schwert, G.W. (1987), 'Effects of Model Specification on Tests for Unit Roots in Macroeconomic Data', *Journal of Monetary Economics*, **20**(1), July.

Semmler, W. (ed.)(1989), *Financial Dynamics and Business Cycles: New Perspectives*, Armonk, N.Y.: M.E. Sharpe.

Sen, A.K. (1973), *On Economic Inequality*, Oxford: Oxford University Press.

Sherman, H.J. and G.R. Evans (1984), *Macroeconomics: Keynesian, Monetarist and Marxist Views*, New York: Harper & Row.

Shiller, R.J. (1990), 'The Term Structure of Interest Rates', in B.M. Friedman and F.K. Hahn (eds), *The Handbook of Monetary Economics*, Amsterdam: North-Holland.

Sims, C.A. (1980a), 'Comparison of Interwar and Postwar Business Cycles: Monetarism Reconsidered', *American Economic Review Papers and Proceedings*, **70**(2), May.

Sims, C.A. (1980b), 'Macroeconometrics and Reality', *Econometrica*, **48**(1), January.

Sims, C.A. (1987), 'Comment', *Journal of Business and Economic Statistics*, **5**(4), October.

Slutsky, E. (1937), 'The Summation of Random Causes as the Source of Cyclic Causes', *Econometrica*, **5**.

Smeeding, T.M., M.O'Higgins and L. Rainwater (1990), *Poverty, Inequality and Income Distribution in Comparative Perspective: The Luxembourg Income Study (LIS)*, Washington, D.C.: Urban Institute Press.

Smith, J.D. and S.D. Franklin (1974), ' The Concentration of Personal Wealth, 1922–1969', *American Economic Review Papers and Proceedings*, **64**(2), May.

Solow, R.M. (1956), 'A Contribution to the Theory of Economic Growth', *Quarterly Journal of Economics*, **70**(1), February.

Soltow, L. (1975), *Men and Wealth in the United States, 1850–1870*, New Haven, Conn.: Yale University Press.

Spence, A.M. (1976), 'Product Selection, Fixed Costs, and Monopolistic Competition', *Review of Economic Studies*, **43**(2), June.

Stadler, G.W. (1990), 'Business Cycle Models with Endogenous Technology', *American Economic Review*, **80**(4), September.

Stiglitz, J.E. (1969), 'Distribution of Income and Wealth among Individuals', *Econometrica*, **37**(3), July.

Stiglitz, J.E. and A. Weiss (1981), 'Credit Rationing in Markets with Imperfect Information', *American Economic Review*, **71**(3), June.

Stoker, T.M. (1986), 'Simple Tests of Distributional Effects on Macroeconomic Equations', *Journal of Political Economy*, **94**(4), August.

Summers, L.H. (1981), 'Inflation, the Stock Market, and Owner-occupied Housing', *American Economic Review Papers and Proceedings*, **71**, May.

Svensson, L.E.O. (1986), 'Sticky Goods Prices, Flexible Asset Prices, Monopolistic Competition, and Monetary Policy', *Review of Economic Studies*, **53**(3), July.

Takahashi, C. (1959), *Dynamic Changes of Income and its Distribution in Japan*, Tokyo: Kinokuniya Bookstore Co.

Taylor, J.B. (1980), 'Aggregate Dynamics and Staggered Contracts', *Journal of Political Economy*, **88**(1), February.

Taylor, L. and S.A. O'Connell (1985), 'A Minsky Crisis', *Quarterly Journal of Economics*, **100**, Supplement.

Terrones, M. (1990), 'Influence Activities and Economic Growth', University of Western Ontario, mimeo.

Thurow, L.C. (1976), *Generating Inequality*, London: Macmillan.

Townsend, R. (1983), 'Financial Structure and Economic Activity', *American Economic Review*, **73**(5), December.

Tufte, E.R. (1978), *Political Control of the Economy*, Princeton: Princeton University Press.

United States Department of Commerce (1975), *Historical Statistics of the U.S.: Colonial Times to 1970*.

United States Department of Commerce (annual), *U.S. Census Population Studies, P-60*, various issues.

Uzawa, H. (1968), 'Time Preference, the Consumption Function, and Optimum Asset Holdings', in J.N. Wolfe (ed.), *Value, Capital and Growth: Papers in Honor of Sir John Hicks*, Chicago: Aldine.

Valentine, L.M. (1987), *Business Cycles and Forecasting*, 7th edn, Cincinnati, Ohio: South-Western University Press.

Waldo, D.G. (1985), 'Bank Runs, the Deposit–Currency Ratio and the Interest Rate', *Journal of Monetary Economics*, 15(3), May.

Wallace, N. (1980), 'The Overlapping-Generations Model of Fiat Money', in J.H. Kareken and N. Wallace, *Models of Monetary Economics*, Minneapolis, Minn.: Federal Reserve Bank of Minneapolis.

Waller, C.J. and D.D. VanHoose (1991), 'Discretionary Monetary Policy and Socially Efficient Wage Indexation', mimeo, forthcoming in *Quarterly Journal of Economics*.

White, H.L. (1980), 'A Heteroskedasticity-consistent Covariance Matrix Estimator and Direct Test for Heteroskedasticity', *Econometrica*, 48(4), May.

Willet, R.D. (ed.) (1989), *Political Business Cycles: The Political Economy of Money, Unemployment and Inflation*, Durham: Duke University Press.

Williamson, J.G. (1991), *Inequality, Poverty and History*, Cambridge, Mass.: Basil Blackwell.

Williamson, J.G. and P.H. Lindert (1980), *American Inequality: A Macroeconomic History*, New York: Academic Press.

Winnick, A.J. (1989), *Toward Two Societies: The Changing Distributions of Income and Wealth in the U.S. since 1960*, New York: Praeger.

Woodford, M. (1989), 'Imperfect Financial Intermediation and Complex Dynamics', in W. Barnett, J. Geweke and K. Shell (eds), *Economic Complexity: Chaos, Sunspots, Bubbles and Nonlinearity*, New York: Cambridge University Press.

Young, L. and S.P. Magee (1986), 'Endogenous Protection, Factor Returns and Resource Allocation', *Review of Economic Studies*, 53(3), July.

Zarnowitz, V. (1992), *Business Cycles: Theory, History, Indicators and Forecasting*, Chicago: University of Chicago Press, for NBER.

Zellner, A. and F. Palm (1974), 'Time Series Analysis and Simultaneous Equation Econometric Models', *Journal of Econometrics*, 2(1), May.

Uselton, G.C. (1982) 'The Value of the Consumer Surplus ... and Changes in
  Asset Holdings', in D. ... eds, *Value Changes and Choices Programs in
  the Public and Private Choice Problems*.

Vickrey, W.M. (1961) *Bureaucracy Process ... and ...*, Ann Arbor: University
  School Survey, University of Chicago Press.

Wachter, D.G. (1978) 'Votes, Bonds, the Deposit Clearance Bank and the Internal
  Stabilization of ... ', *Economy History*, 18(1), May.

Wallace, N.J. (1981) ... 'On Stamping Government Money to Flat Money', in
  J.H. Kareken and N. Wallace, *Models of Monetary Economics*, Minneapolis,
  Minn.: Federal Reserve Bank of Minneapolis.

Walters, A. and D.G. VanHouse (1991) 'Deflationary Monetary Policy and
  Steady Inflation Wage Indexation', *... International ...*, Quarterly
  Journal of ... 56(4), 613.

Winer, S. (to be added), 'A Free ... of ... Choice using ...', *Economics
  and Choice Theory*, Cambridge University Press, *Economametrica*, 48(4), May.

Wilson, R.D. ed. (1989) *Political Business Cycles: The Political Economy of
  Money, Unemployment and Inflation*, Durham, Duke University Press.

Williamson, O. (1961) *Internships, Powers and Privacy*, Cambridge, Mass.:
  Joan Blackwell.

Williamson, J.G. and P.H. Lindert (1980) *American Inequality: A Macroeconomic History*, New York: Academic Press.

Wooten, John ... 'A Varied Time Societies: The Changing Distribution of
  Income and Wealth in the U.S.', ..., 1920, New York: Hunger.

Woodford, D. (1990) ... 'Imperfect Financial Intermediation and Complete
  Markets', in M. Alchian, J. Gleave and K. Sheu eds, *Economic
  Disequilibrium: Chaos, Sunspots, Bubbles and Nonlinearity*, New York:
  Cambridge University Press.

Young, J. and J.P. Neises (1986), 'Working under Pressure', *Labor Reforms and
  Business Activities', Review of Economic Studies*, 53(3), July.

Zaskowitz, W. (1992), *Between Capital Essays: Money, Economics and Institutions*, Chicago: University of Chicago Press, for NBER.

Zeldes, W. and P. Pesia (1981), 'Time Series Analysis and Distributions in
  Aggregate Economic Markets', *Journal of Econometrics*, 1(1), May.

Index